Classic Intangible Cultural Heritage of Textile in Three Northeastern Provinces

Zhao Hong and Ma Tao

Translated by Li Yingtao, Zhang Meng & Wang Tong

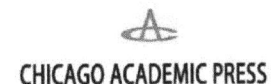

CHICAGO ACADEMIC PRESS

Classic Intangible Cultural Heritage of Textile in Three Northeastern Provinces
Author: Zhao Hong and Ma Tao
Translator: Li Yingtao, Zhang Meng & Wang Tong
Language: English
Word Count (for Space of All Pages): Approximately 310,000 words
Publisher: Chicago Academic Press
Number of Pages: 300
ISBN: 978-1-965890-74-5

Publishing   Chicago Academic Press

5923 N Artesian Ave

Chicago IL 60659

Email   contact@chicagoacademicpress.com

Website   http://chicagoacademicpress.com/

Book Size   6X9 inches

First Edition September, 2025

Translators' Profile

Li Yingtao is a professor at Jilin International Studies University, Dean of the School of English, and a master's degree supervisor. His research focuses on English-Chinese language contrast and translation. He has served as the chief editor or co-editor of 7 teaching materials, 4 academic works, and 11 translated works, and has also participated in compiling 1 dictionary.

Zhang Meng is a lecturer at the College English Teaching Department of Jilin International Studies University. Her research directions are second language acquisition and translation. She has participated in the compilation of 1 translated work and has published 9 articles in provincial journals and 3 articles in international conference journals.

Wang Tong, a postgraduate student majoring in English translation, is currently studying at Jilin International Studies University. Her research focuses on literary translation and medical translation. During her postgraduate studies, she has independently translated and proofread over 120,000 words of documents in the fields of literature, medicine, and law.

Summary

Textile intangible cultural heritage, as the essence of traditional Chinese culture, is not only the inheritance of skills, but also the continuation of the cultural connotations it carries. This book selects seven representative textile intangible cultural heritage projects in the three northeastern provinces, and introduces them from the aspects of origin and development, customs and interesting anecdotes, production materials and tools, production technology and techniques, craft characteristics and patterns, work appreciation, interviews with the inheritors, and the current situation and countermeasures of inheritance.

This book can be used by student majoring in textile and apparel as well as students of economics and management in textile colleges and universities, and can be used as a reference for textile intangible heritage enthusiasts. It can also be used as a reference for practitioners in the field of textile intangible cultural heritage protection, relevant government departments and theoretical researchers.

Preface

In the report of the 19th National Congress of the Communist Party of China, the leaders of the Party and the state pointed out that it is necessary to deeply explore the ideological concepts, humanistic spirit and moral norms contained in excellent traditional Chinese culture, and inherit and innovate in combination with the requirements of the times. As the essence of traditional Chinese culture, textile intangible cultural heritage (referred to as textile ICH) is not only the inheritance of skills, but more importantly, the continuation of the cultural connotation it carries. Its inheritance and development are of great significance for deeply excavating excellent traditional Chinese culture, cultivating national self-confidence, enhancing the historical, cultural, social and economic values of the textile industry and building a strong textile country.

The Modern Textile Industry Innovation Research Center of Tianjin Polytechnic University, with the mission of researching and popularizing textile ICH, has accumulated a large amount of text, pictures, videos and other materials, and has successively released a series of books on the appreciation of textile and clothing ICH in Beijing, Tianjin and Hebei regions, Henan Province, Shandong Province and Shaanxi Province.

This book selects seven representative textile ICH projects in the three northeastern provinces, and obtains first-hand information through face-to-face consultation and communication with the inheritors. Through the introduction of the origin and development of each representative project, production materials and tools, production technology and techniques, craft features and patterns, work appreciation, customs and interesting anecdotes, interviews with the inheritors, and the current situation and countermeasures of inheritance, it provides the readers with systematic and comprehensive understanding of the textile and clothing ICH projects in the three northeastern provinces.

In the process of writing this book, we have read and referred to the relevant information written by scholars and inheritors at home and abroad. Most of the pictures and other materials in this article come from our field shooting and research, some materials come from online resources such as Intangible Cultural Heritage Network and Baidu Encyclopedia, and some pictures come from local museums, such as the first chapter of the work of the picture by the Bohai Mohe Embroidery Museum. The pictures in Chapters 2 to 5 were all taken in the homes of the inheritors or provided by the inheritors. Here, we would like to express our sincere thanks to the inheritors interviewed and the authors of the materials read and referred to.

Zhao Hong, Ma Tao, Liu Yu, Xu Juan, Dai Wenya, Cao Xiuxi, She Zhaoting, Gao Shang and others undertook the writing of this book, which was drafted and finalized by Zhao Hong and Ma Tao.

As the protection of intangible cultural heritage of textile and clothing is being deepened, coupled with the limitations of the level of the editors, it is inevitable that there are imperfections in the book, and we sincerely invite readers to criticize and correct them.

Editor

October 2020

Contents

Chapter I Bohai Mohe Embroidery

Bohai Mohe Embroidery originated from the embroidery stitches of the Mohe people in the Bohai State and has a history of more than 1,300 years. This time honored embroidery is a general term for the Manchu embroidery in the Northeast region centered around Mudanjiang. It is a folk art form of the Mohe, Jurchen, and Manchu embroidery and is one of the outstanding traditional ethnic handicrafts in China. In July 2011, Bohai Mohe Embroidery was selected as a provincial-level intangible cultural heritage by the Department of Culture of Heilongjiang Province (Figure 1-1). On February 10, 2015, the ancient Manchu embroidery, "Bohai Mohe Embroidery", was included in the fourth batch of the national intangible cultural heritage protection list, falling into the category of traditional fine arts (Table 1-1). In May 2018, Sun Yanling, the fourth-generation inheritor, was recognized by the Ministry of Culture and Tourism of the People's Republic of China as a representative inheritor of the Manchu embroidery, a national-level intangible cultural heritage project (Figure 1-2). In October 2016, the Department of Culture of Heilongjiang Province awarded the title of the fifth-batch provincial-level representative inheritor of intangible cultural heritage in Heilongjiang Province to Jiang Lina, the fifth-generation inheritor (Figure 1-3).

Table 1-1 Introduction to Bohai Mohe Embroidery

Directory Name	Folk Embroidery · Bohai Mohe Embroidery
Directory Category	Traditional Fine Art
Directory Level	National
Declaration Unit or Region	Mudanjiang City, Heilongjiang Province
Inheritance Representative	Sun Yanling

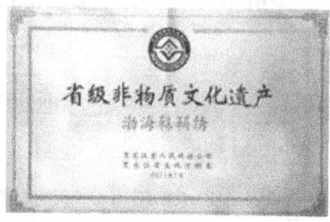

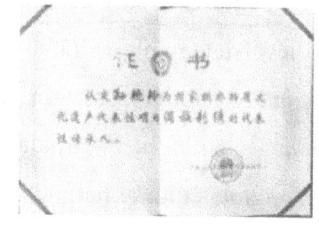

Figure 1-1 Bohai Wohe Embroidery has been selected as a Provincial Intangible Cultural Heritage

Figure 1-2 Certificate of Representative Inheritor of National Intangible Cultural Heritage Project

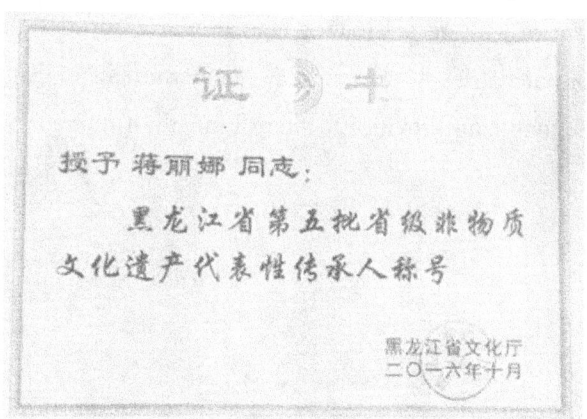

Figure 1-3 Certificate of Representative Inheritor of Provincial Intangible Cultural Heritage Project

Section I Origin and Development

I. The Origin of Bohai Mohe Embroidery

In 698 AD, Da Zurong, the leader of the Sumo tribe, led his people to cross eastward. They established a minority-led regime mainly composed of the Mohe people on Dongmu Mountain in the upper reaches of the Mudanjiang river, known as the Zhen State. In 705 AD, Empress Wu Zetian of the Tang Dynasty abdicated, and Emperor Zhongzong Li Xian ascended the throne. Then, he sent envoys to the Zhen State for appeasement. In 713 AD, Emperor Xuanzong of the Tang Dynasty conferred the title of "Prince of Bohai" on Da Zurong, and the state began to use the name "Bohai". In 755 AD, the capital was moved to Shangjing Longquan Prefecture (now Bohai Town, Ning'an City), and a series of extensive reforms were carried out following the model of the Tang Dynasty. In 762 AD, the Tang Dynasty issued an imperial edict to upgrade Bohai to a kingdom, known as the Bohai State. The main place of origin of Bohai Mohe Embroidery was Shangjing Longquan Prefecture, the capital of the Bohai State.

During the reign of King Da Renxiu, the economy of the Bohai State and the material and spiritual lives of the people improved significantly, and the country became increasingly prosperous, forming the well-known "Prosperous State across the Sea" in history. Since the Tang Dynasty and the Bohai State had close relations, the kings of the Bohai State paid tribute to the Tang Dynasty many times, and the Tang Dynasty rewarded its vassal states. Thus, a "tribute-reward trade" route from the Bohai State to the Tang Dynasty and its surrounding areas was formed, also known as the Northeast Asian Silk Road. This Silk Road not only enhanced the friendly relations between the Bohai State and the Tang Dynasty but also promoted the economic, political, and cultural exchanges and integration among the regions along the route and its surroundings.

During the period of the Bohai State, it officially initiated the practice of using Chinese characters from the official to the civilian level. At that time, the technologies in the court, architecture, metallurgy, sericulture, silk reeling, weaving, and embroidery in the Bohai State all emulated those of the Tang Dynasty. The handicraft industry developed unprecedentedly, creating the glorious Shangjing Culture and the Eastern-Sea Civilization. From the murals unearthed from the Tomb of Princess Zhenxiao in Helong County, Jilin Province in 1980, we can see eight maidens depicted in the murals wearing exquisite costumes with delicate patterns, which also proves from the side that the skills of sericulture, silk reeling, weaving, and embroidery in the Bohai State were already quite mature at that time. During the Sui and Tang Dynasties, the main textiles produced in Shangjing of Bohai were wool, hemp, and silk. Among them, the silk was the unique tussah silk in the Northeast, which was not only the raw material for silk but also for embroidery.

In the textiles found in the "Sarira Box" unearthed from the Shangjing Site in 1975, there were brocade, satin, gauze, silk, and embroidery. The main textiles at that time, such as "the cloth from Xianzhou, the brocade from Wozhou, and the silk from Longzhou (i.e., Shangjing Longquan Prefecture, now Longzhou County, Guangxi Zhuang Autonomous Region)" were well-known far and wide. This was greatly related to the local residents learning advanced sericulture, silk reeling, weaving, and embroidery skills from the Central Plains. The Mohe people in the Bohai State, the ancestors of the Manchu people, left extremely valuable cultural heritage for future generations. After the Bohai State was destroyed by the Khitan, a northern minority, the embroidery technique did not disappear with the change of dynasties. It had already been integrated into the national memory and the blood of old women and young girls, and was passed down from generation to generation. This shows the close inheritance relationship between Manchu embroidery at that time and the embroidery of the Manchu ancestors. At that time, the Ming and Qing imperial courts embroidered different patterns on the clothes according to the ranks of officials. Civil officials had birds embroidered on their clothes, while military officials had beasts. Since the Manchus entered the Central Plains, embroidery became popular from the imperial palace to the civilian population, becoming a national art and practical item that the Manchu people were proud of.

II. The Development of the Mohe Embroidery of the Bohai Kingdom

The inheritance pedigree of Bohai Mohe Embroidery is shown in Table 1-2. Sun Yanling, the fourth-generation national-level inheritor of Bohai Mohe Embroidery, is a descendant of the Zhenghuang Banner of the Manchu people. She learned embroidery from her mother and grandmother since childhood. As she grew older, her embroidery skills became more mature, and she gradually understood the history and culture of her own nation. She read books and consulted experts, and finally found out that the embroidery she learned since childhood was the Mohe Embroidery created by the Manchu ancestors. She has well inherited this ancient folk art.

Table 1-2 Inheritance Pedigree of Bohai Mohe Embroidery

Generation	Name	Gender	Date of birth	Inheritance method	Residence address
First generation	Mrs. Zhang (Li is her original family name)	Female	1902	Inherited through family	Yangfanggou, Bohai Town, Ning'an City, Mudanjiang City, Heilongjiang Province
Second generation	Mrs. Yu (Zhang is her original family name))	Female	1927	Inherited through family	Bohai Town, Ning'an City, Mudanjiang City, Heilongjiang Province
Third Generation	Yu Xiuying	Female	1951	Inherited through family	Bei'an Township, Mudanjiang City,

					Heilongjiang Province
Fourth Generation	Sun Yanling	Female	1978	Inherited through family	Mudanjiang City, Heilongjiang Province
Fifth Generation	Jiang Lina	Female	1988	Learned from a master	Mudanjiang City, Heilongjiang Province
	Wang Yanxia	Female	1981	Learned from a master	Mudanjiang City, Heilongjiang Province

In 2001, Sun Yanling and her husband Qu Kehao founded Duoduo Vocational Skills Training School, which is dedicated to the research and inheritance of Bohai Mohe embroidery. In 2009, they established Mudanjiang Bohai Ethnic Arts and Crafts Co., Ltd., which mainly deals in local ethnic arts and crafts, integrating the inheritance, research and development, production, processing, and sales of Bohai Mohe embroidery and cocoon silk. The company has 1,372 cooperative production-type embroiderers in China, 56 design, R & D, and marketing staff. It also runs the Bohai Mohe Embroidery Vocational Skills Training School under its banner, with 35 teaching and administrative staff. In ten years, more than 17,000 students have graduated from the school (Figure 1-4 to Figure 1-7). After just a few years of development, the company's sales outlets are spread across more than a dozen provinces in the country, and the Mohe embroidery products it produces are sold to overseas markets including South Korea, Japan, Europe, and the United States. From 2008 to the present, 7 re-employment training bases for laid-off workers have been established, training nearly 20,000 laid-off female workers. In 2009, a manual embroidery factory with 830 workers was set up in Rason City, North Korea, and in 2012, a high-end manual embroidery factory with 300 workers was established in Pyongyang, North Korea. Due to the reduction in production costs, the company has signed long-term order processing contracts with two major embroidery distributors in China.

Jiang Lina is from Mudanjiang City, Heilongjiang Province. She used to work as an embroiderer and learned from Sun Yanling. Later, she was selected by Sun Yanling as the fifth-generation inheritor of Mohe embroidery. While inheriting the exquisite production techniques of ancient Bohai Mohe embroidery, she has also promoted the traditional folk art of Mudanjiang on CCTV programs, bringing Bohai Mohe embroidery into the public view. She is mainly good at embroidering figures and flowers, with a unique personal style. She teaches more than a thousand embroiderers every year and has participated in more than ten international and domestic exhibitions. Her works are full of creativity and have unique style characteristics, and have won many international and provincial awards (Table 1-3). For example, on September 30, 2015, she was awarded the title of "Master of Arts and Crafts in Mudanjiang City" by the Mudanjiang Arts and Crafts Master Appraisal Committee; in December 2015, she made positive contributions to the success of the China Pavilion at the Milan Expo in Italy and was awarded an honorary certificate by the Organizing Committee of the China Pavilion at the Milan Expo; in 2018, her work "Harmonious Sound" was rated as the Gold Award in the High-quality Exhibition of the Harbin Folk and Folk-Custom Art Expo by the appraisal committee.

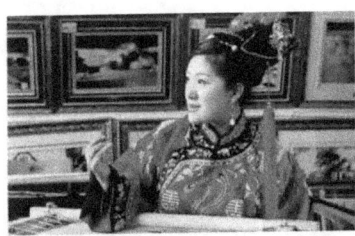

Figure 1-4 Sun Yanling, the Fourth-generation Inheritor of the Bohai Mohe Embroidery

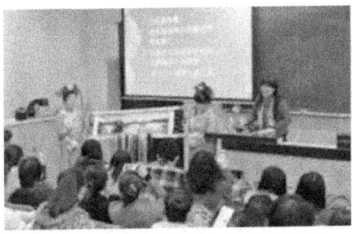

Figure 1-5 Ms. Sun Yanling Teaching in School

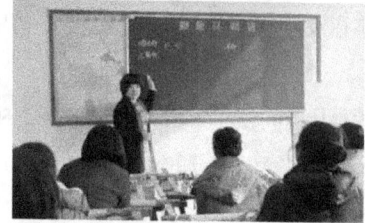

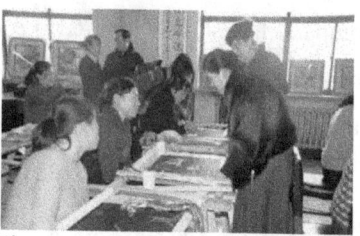

Figure 1-6 Ms. Sun Yanling Teaching Embroidery Skills (I)　Figure 1-7. Ms. Sun Yanling Teaching Embroidery Skills (II)

Since this research focuses on Ms. Jiang Lina, the fifth-generation inheritor, the honors obtained by Ms. Sun Yanling are not presented here.

Table 1-3 List of Some Honors Won by Ms. Jiang Lina

Date	Awarding Institution	Award Description	Certificate Display
October 2013	The People's Government of Mudanjiang City	The work "Unique Flower" won the Gold Award in the Arts and Crafts Exhibition of the Visual Arts Exhibition at the Intangible Cultural Heritage Expo of Heilongjiang Province (Mudanjiang City).	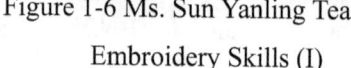
September 2015	The Women's Federation of Mudanjiang City and the Tourism Bureau of Mudanjiang City	Won the third-prize in the First Creative Competition of Hand-woven Cultural and Tourism Souvenirs	
September 30, 2015	The Mudanjiang Arts and Crafts Master Appraisal Committee	Awarded the title of "Master of Arts and Crafts in Mudanjiang City"	

May 2016	China (Shenzhen) International Cultural Industries Fair, Appraisal Committee of China Arts and Crafts Cultural Creativity Award, Shenzhen International Cultural Industries Fair Co., Ltd., Organizing Committee of China (Shenzhen) International Cultural Industries Fair	The work "Dawn in Snowy Village" won the Bronze Award of the "China Arts and Crafts Cultural Creativity Award" at the 2016 China (Shenzhen) International Cultural Industries Fair.	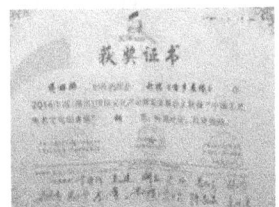
October 2017	China National Arts and Crafts Association, The 18th Exhibition of Works by Masters of Chinese Arts and Crafts and Fine Handicrafts	The work "Harmonious Sound" won the Excellence Award of the 2017 "Hundred Flowers Cup" China Arts and Crafts Fine Works Award at the 18th Exhibition of Works by Masters of Chinese Arts and Crafts and Fine Handicrafts.	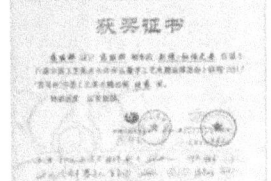
September 2018	Department of Culture of Heilongjiang Province	Won the First Prize in the "Beautiful Embroidery" category at the First Intangible Cultural Heritage Craft Competition in Heilongjiang Province.	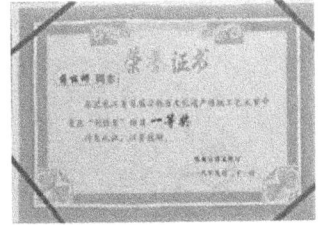

| December 2018 | Heilongjiang Artists Association, Harbin Folk Artists Association, Heilongjiang Intangible Cultural Heritage Society | The work "Harmonious Sound" (Bohai Mohe Embroidery) won the Gold Award in the High - quality Exhibition of the Harbin Folk and Folk - Custom Art Expo. | 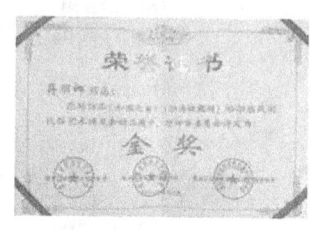 |
| December 2018 | Heilongjiang Folk Artists Association, Harbin Folk Artists Association, and Heilongjiang Intangible Cultural Heritage Protection Society | The work "Cedar in the Snow" (Bohai Mohe Embroidery) won the Gold Award at the High - end Works Exhibition of the Harbin Folk and Folk - Custom Art Expo. | 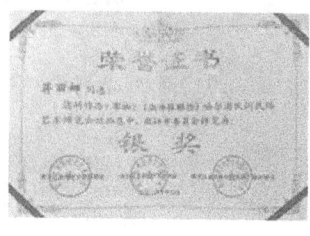 |

Section II Customs and Interesting Anecdotes

I. Mohe Embroidery-The "Pearl" of the Prosperous State East of the Sea

During the Tang Dynasty, after the silk-making technique from the Central Plains was introduced to the Bohai State via the Northeast Asian Silk Road, the local people, taking advantage of the natural geographical conditions, began to raise silkworms and produce silk. They passed down the embroidery technique from generation to generation. From a young age, they emphasized cultivating their children's embroidery skills. It's no exaggeration to say that the embroidery skills of seven-or eight-year-old children at that time were quite proficient. They could even complete exquisite embroidery works independently without the help of adults. As the Bohai State was located in the north with a cold climate, the local people often embroidered ear protectors and hats to keep warm. Also, due to the damp and cold climate that easily attracted mosquitoes, they embroidered many sachets, such as zodiac-themed sachets and tiger-head sachets. They would crush the locally-grown tobacco and put it into the sachets to repel mosquitoes. During festivals or when a child came of age, elders would give sachets to their descendants as a symbol of warding off evil and praying for good fortune. Since every household embroidered a large number of sachets, ear protectors, hats, etc., there were many idle embroidery products. So the local residents proposed to sell the surplus embroidery products to other regions to earn income. Subsequently, they gathered their embroidery products together and exchanged or sold them with people from other places. These exquisitely-made and meaning-laden embroideries were well-loved by the masses. They also provided a new source of income for the residents of the Bohai State and promoted the development of the surrounding areas. Therefore, Mohe embroidery was called the "pearl" of the "Prosperous State East of the Sea" by the people at that time.

II. Traditional Techniques Bear Fruit in the Modern Market

As time went by, Sun Yanling, the fourth-generation inheritor of Bohai Mohe embroidery, encountered great difficulties in the process of inheriting this art. Her embroidered works were ignored, and most people knew nothing about Bohai Mohe embroidery. However, these difficulties didn't dampen her love for Mohe embroidery. Her grandmother once told her, "We don't have to worry about food and clothing now, but Mohe embroidery is a technique left by our ancestors. We must continue to pass it on." Sun Yanling remembered her grandmother's advice and was determined to promote Bohai Mohe embroidery. So she founded a vocational skills training school and set up a manual embroidery training course. In the past few years of teaching embroidery skills, Sun Yanling found that embroidery works with special meanings were more popular. She told the embroiderers that when choosing themes, the works should not only be aesthetically pleasing and novel but also carry good meanings. For example, by putting a dou (a traditional Chinese measuring tool), an abacus, and an oil lamp together and naming it "Earning a Fortune Every Day", the embroidery works with such stories were indeed well-received by the public. Mohe embroidery gradually became known to more local people. With the help of the local government, Sun Yanling and the embroiderers participated in numerous domestic and international exhibitions. At the exhibitions, Sun Yanling found that although foreign people often praised the decorative embroidery works for their beauty, few were willing to buy them. Instead, some daily necessities and clothing items were snapped up. So, Sun Yanling changed the production direction of the products, integrating traditional techniques with modern market demands. She launched a series of Mohe embroidery derivative products, such as home textile clothing, tourist souvenirs, and daily necessities. Meanwhile, she established a special R & D team in Shenzhen to design and develop original products based on market research.

III. Shining on the International Stage

Mohe embroidery works have participated in nearly a hundred domestic and international exhibitions and have been reported by Chinese and foreign media over a thousand times. They have a certain influence on the international stage. At the International Exhibition and Fair of Traditional Handicrafts held in Perm, the sixth-largest city in Russia in 2019, hundreds of Mohe embroidery products were sold out within a few days. The Russian people also said, "From a distance, Mohe embroidery works are almost indistinguishable from oil paintings. They have a strong sense of three-dimensionality, bright colors, and vivid scenery, as if they were right in front of one's eyes." It can be seen that Mohe embroidery is not only popular in the domestic market. Combining both Eastern and Western styles, it also meets the aesthetic tastes of foreign friends and is well-loved by them. Through these overseas exhibitions and sales, more foreigners have come to know Mohe embroidery from Mudanjiang, and more Chinese ethnic elements have emerged in the international market.

Section III Production Materials and Tools

I. Production Materials

Bohai Mohe embroidery, a time-honored folk traditional art, requires materials such as base fabric and colored silk threads. It's worth mentioning that the main difference between the tussah silk home textile series of Bohai Mohe embroidery and southern embroidery lies in the silk threads. The silk thread raw material of Bohai Mohe embroidery comes from the fibers processed from the silk threads spat out by tussah silkworms raised by local people when they spin cocoons, namely tussah silk. In contrast, southern embroidery generally selects mulberry silk as the production material.

Tussah silkworms are a type of wild silkworms mainly living in the north. They are artificially raised in the wild oak forests in the mountains and feed on oak leaves. The protein and amino acid content of tussah silkworms is more than ten times that of mulberry silkworms. Mudanjiang City has a unique natural geographical environment for tussah silkworm production. The local tussah silkworm resources are rich and of excellent quality. The history of tussah silkworm rearing and embroidery is long (Figure 1-8 and Figure 1-9).

Tussah silk (Figure 1-10 to Figure 1-12) is composed of two parallel flat single filaments. Its main components are fibroin and sericin. Tussah silk is thick, fluffy, and stiff. The internal structure of the fiber has many pores. Since it is produced in the cold northern regions, it has good warmth-retention and elasticity, making it the preferred raw material for making embroidery products. Bohai Mohe embroidery inherits the ancestral craftsmanship and uses the raw materials made by ancient techniques, which gives today's embroidery works the characteristic of not rotting for a hundred years. Therefore, it is recognized by the embroidery collection circle, and socks made of tussah silk are also very popular among the public (Figure 1-13).

There are certain requirements for the selection of the base fabric. Different fabrics have different requirements for needles, threads, and patterns. The raw material of the base fabric for Bohai Mohe embroidery is mainly tussah silk. The fabric produced from this raw material has stronger breathability and more vivid colors.

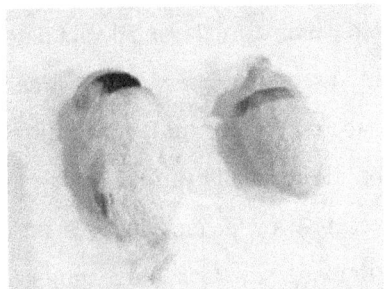

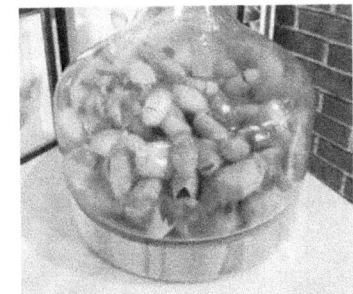

Figure 1-8 Tussah Silkworm Pupae (I)   Figure 1-9 Tussah Silkworm Pupae (II)

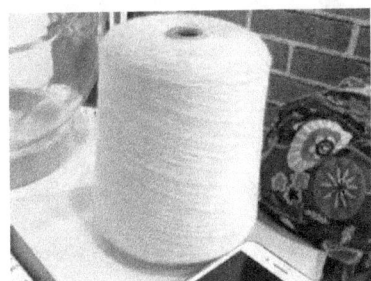

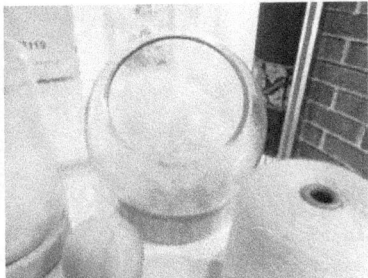

Figure 1-10 Tussah Silk (I)   Figure 1-11 Tussah Silk (II)

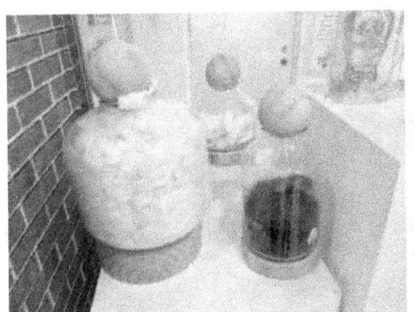

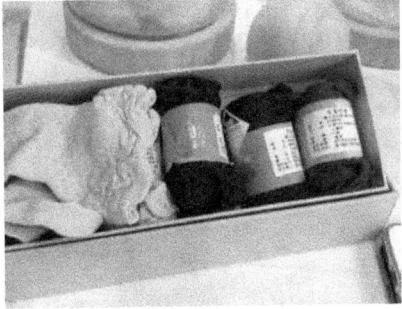

Figure 1-12 Dyed Tussah Silk   Figure 1-13 Socks Made of Tussah Silk

II. Production Tools

The main production tools for Bohai Mohe embroidery include embroidery hoops, embroidery needles, and scissors. Embroidery hoops can be divided into square hoops (Figure 1-14) and round hoops (Figure 1-15) according to their shapes. Most of them are made of wood or bamboo, and their function is to fix the base fabric to ensure that the embroidered patterns are flat and do not deform. Embroidery needles are the most commonly used tools in embroidery, mainly including pointed needles and round-headed needles. In the selection of embroidery needles for Bohai Mohe embroidery, small-eyed tail needles are more commonly used (Figure 1-16). Scissors have a wide range of uses, mainly for cutting thread ends, base fabrics, and drawing silk. Generally, appropriate scissors are selected according to the specific uses during the production process of Mohe embroidery (Figure 1-17).

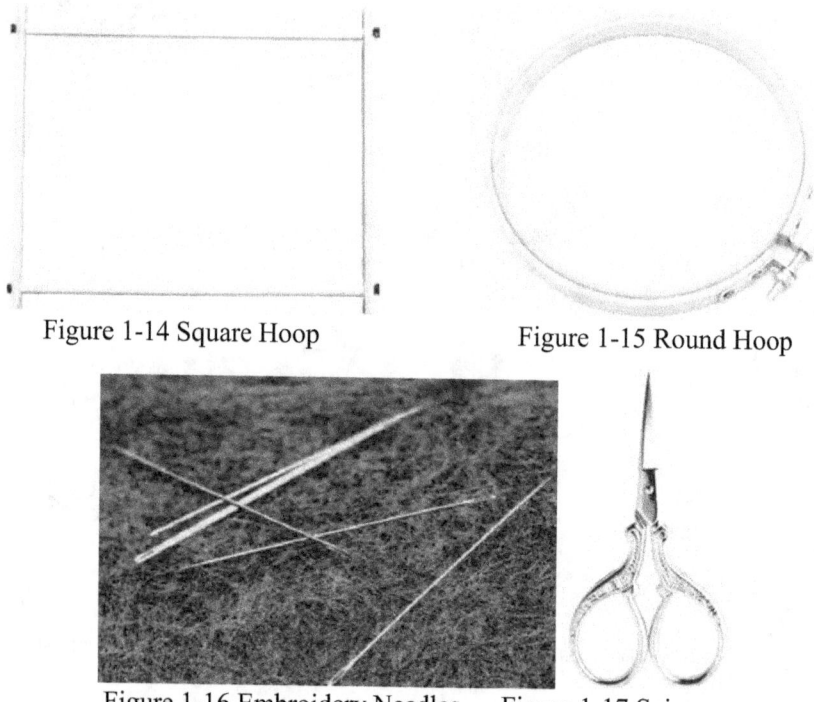

Figure 1-14 Square Hoop　　　　　Figure 1-15 Round Hoop

Figure 1-16 Embroidery Needles　　Figure 1-17 Scissors

Section IV Production Process and Techniques

The traditional technological process of Bohai Mohe embroidery mainly includes multiple procedures such as conceiving and drawing patterns, selecting materials, pasting the base fabric, choosing threads, stretching the embroidery frame, embroidering, making picture frames, and mounting. With the continuous progress of technology and the popularization of the Internet, the technological process of Mohe embroidery has gradually evolved into eight procedures: photography and scene-taking, material selection, computer-aided design, thread selection, stretching the embroidery frame, embroidering, picture frame making, and mounting.

I. Photography and Scene-taking

Photography and scene-taking is the first step of Bohai Mohe embroidery. The pattern style of a Mohe embroidery work is an important criterion for determining the quality of the work. In the past, the embroidery patterns were mostly based on the designer's own drawings. The drawing of patterns required combining the implied meaning, form, and folk customs with the content to be expressed, which placed high demands on the designer's embroidery experience. Experienced designers are often older and may not be able to incorporate modern and popular elements, failing to keep up with the development of the times. Therefore, using modern photography technology to conceive the patterns of Mohe embroidery works is an important node in the combination of contemporary Bohai Mohe embroidery and modern technology. "China's Snowy Village" and "Setting Sail" are representative works of photography and scene-taking for Bohai Mohe embroidery (Figure 1-18 and Figure 1-19).

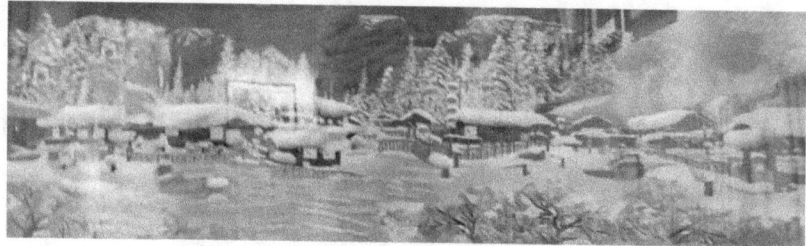

Figure 1-18 "China's Snowy Village" (I)

II. Material Selection

After the scene-taking is completed, the selection of the base fabric and matching threads is carried out. The choice of the base fabric directly affects the overall style of the work. Therefore, the base fabric should be selected according to the purpose and style of the embroidery work. The color selection of the base fabric for Bohai Mohe embroidery conforms to the cultural characteristics of the north, with bold color choices and vivid colors (Figure 1-20 and Figure 1-21).

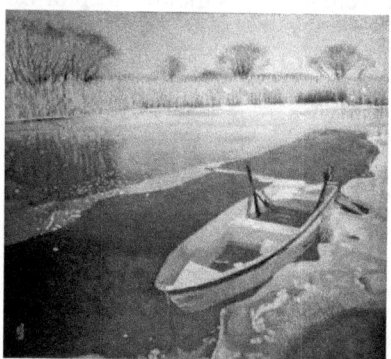

Figure 1-19 "Setting Sail"

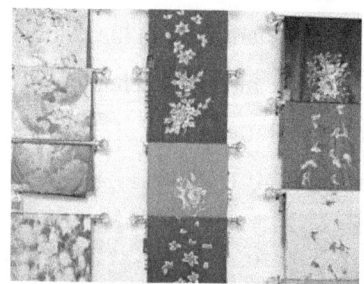

Figure 1-20 Selection of the Base Fabric Colors

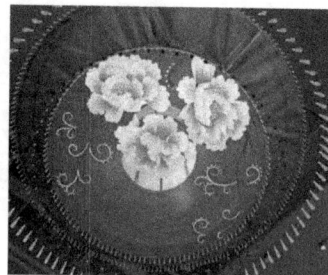

Figure 1-21 Black Base Fabric

III. Computer - aided Design

After selecting the base fabric, different from the previous practice of drawing, this technique innovatively uses modern technology to print the selected photos through a digital printer.

IV. Thread Selection

Thread selection refers to matching the thickness and color of the embroidery threads according to the needs of the embroidery pattern and the fabric. The main principle of thread selection is to make the work look as beautiful as possible. After printing the base fabric according to the photo, when selecting the matching threads based on the color and material of the base fabric, the northern characteristics are retained. The color matching has a sharp contrast, and new color systems are boldly tried. Sometimes, adjustments are also made according to the specific pattern to make the work more distinctive.

V. Stretching the Embroidery Frame

Stretching the embroidery frame mainly means placing the base fabric on the embroidery frame to stretch it, facilitating subsequent embroidery. Generally, the tightness of the base fabric should be moderate. Too loose or too tight will affect the final effect of the embroidery.

VI. Embroidery

Embroidery is the most crucial and time-consuming step in the whole process. Sometimes, it takes several months for an embroiderer to complete an excellent Mohe embroidery work. The embroidery stitches used also vary in different regions. Originally, the residents of the Bohai State used the "chicken-claw stitch" to complete the embroidery. Later, Sun Yanling transformed the "chicken-claw stitch" into the "triangle stitch". This stitch is also a unique technique of Mohe embroidery. After 4-8 layers of superposition and staggered embroidery, it is very suitable for embroidering works on the theme of Northeast ice and snow. The embroidered ice and snow scenes have a crystal-clear feeling, with very good visual effects.

VII. Picture Frame Making

After the Mohe embroidery is completed, the works for ornamental purposes need to be put into picture frames. The picture frame should be selected according to the colors of the base fabric and the matching threads, and sometimes the specific pattern of the work is also taken into consideration.

VIII. Mounting

Mounting means ironing the embroidery work smoothly and then mounting it into a picture frame to make the work more beautiful and conducive to preservation and collection. Generally, the work should be ironed flat before mounting to prevent wrinkles during the mounting process. The ironed work looks smoother and more lustrous (Figure 1-22 and Figure 1-23).

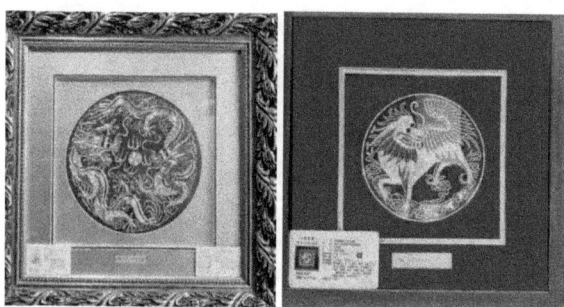

Figure 1-22 Mounted Work (I)   Figure 1-23 Mounted Work (II)

Section V Process Characteristics and Patterns

I. Realistic Perspective

The Bohai Mohe embroidery technique has integrated the unique mountain culture of Northeast China from inheritance to development. It ingeniously combines modern photography technology with the Northeast triangular stitch technique. The embroidered artworks are colorful and have a realistic perspective. Different from other embroidery methods, Mohe embroidery does not use the designer's drawing method to prepare the base cloth before embroidery. Instead, it directly integrates the intended meanings and contents into the photos through modern photography. The embroidered works not only have diverse styles and themes and are colorful, but most importantly, they can achieve a realistic effect similar to an oil painting when viewed from afar. In addition, Mohe embroidery inherits the traditional "chicken-claw stitch". In the past in Northeast China, this stitch was mainly used to sew animal leather clothes for keeping warm. If ordinary parallel stitches were used, the leather clothes would be easily damaged. Therefore, the ancestors have passed down this "chicken-claw stitch" to the present. Later, the fourth-generation inheritor, Sun Yanling, improved the "chicken-claw stitch" and named it the "triangular stitch". This stitch has relatively large stitches, and the stitch size gradually decreases layer by layer. The final embroidery is delicate and exquisite, combining the tenderness of southern embroidery and the grandeur of northern embroidery.

II. North-South Differences

Different from the mulberry silk used in the South, Bohai Mohe embroidery uses the cocoon silk of tussah silkworms raised by local people in the wild, that is, tussah silk. This tussah silk is relatively rough and has high brightness, so it has strong coloring power during the dyeing process. Due to the use of the "triangular stitch" modified by Sun Yanling in the embroidery process, the stitches are layered on top of each other, making the final embroidery similar to Western oil paintings. The themes of Su embroidery in the South are mostly flowers, plants and trees, while the works of Bohai Mohe embroidery mainly focus on the ice and snow in Northeast China, more expressing the rough and unrestrained local customs of Northeast China. Over the years, with the improvement of living conditions and the influence and integration of Han culture, the Manchu Mohe embroidery technique has retained its simple craftsmanship style and the shaman culture content such as Manchu mythological legends. It has also learned from the embroidery techniques of Shandong embroidery in the Central Plains and Su embroidery in the South of the Yangtze River, forming a unique artistic style with a wide range of themes, rich cultural connotations, exaggerated shapes, and delicate techniques hidden in the rough composition.

III. Integration into People's Daily Lives

The handmade embroidered products of Bohai Mohe embroidery naturally rely on professional embroiderers, and these embroiderers must undergo specialized centralized training. After training, the embroiderers can do hand-embroidery at home and increase their income by completing the embroidery. The Bohai Mohe Embroidery Museum also receives visitors in daily life, explaining the origin and development of Mohe embroidery to the public and displaying the charm of the embroidered products. In particular, on weekends, many primary, middle and high school students often come to the Mohe Embroidery Museum to learn about this ancient technique. In recent years, the museum has tens of thousands of exhibits and has become an important place to promote Bohai Mohe embroidery and spread local historical culture.

IV. Close Relevance to the Trend of the Times

Although Bohai Mohe embroidery is an ancient technique, some modern and fashionable elements have been integrated into many of its embroidered products, closely following modern life. In the later color-adjusting process of some Mohe embroidery works, in order to make the embroidery more modern, the color of tussah silk is usually brightened on the basis of the original picture. The embroidered works not only meet the contemporary people's aesthetic standards but also retain the charm of the original painting. Mohe embroidery has also launched a series of derivatives according to the modern market demand, including tourist souvenirs, business gifts, home textile products, etc. These derivatives have been put on the market and have achieved good sales results. In addition, the fourth-generation inheritor, Sun Yanling, has established a research and development base for Bohai Mohe embroidery in Shenzhen. Leading a specialized R & D team, she conducts a series of market research to develop characteristic products. Mudanjiang City, as the birthplace of Mohe embroidery and also the production base, provides product sources for domestic and foreign markets.

Section VI Appreciation of Works

The embroidery products of Bohai Mohe embroidery mainly include clothes, shoes, hats, etc. The content of the embroidery works mostly draws inspiration from the flowers, plants, fish, and insects, mountains, rivers, forests, flying birds and beasts, the sun, moon, and stars, good fortune, wealth, and happiness, auspiciousness and prosperity, weddings, funerals, child-birth, and longevity that the common people love. There are four main representative series of Bohai Mohe embroidery works. Various decorative painting embroidery series, such as embroidery paintings of ice and snow scenery, embroidery paintings of pets, etc.; modern home textile series, such as silk quilts, lamps, glazed yarn bottles, table chess, etc.; modern clothing, shoes and hats series, such as embroidered shoes, embroidered clothing, bags, etc.; souvenirs for tourism and business gifts with Mohe embroidery elements series.

I. Decorative Painting Embroidery Series

The "Three Oddities in Northern Guan" are presented in the form of embroidery (Figure 1-24). There was a folk saying at that time, which went "Paste the window paper on the outside, hang up two children, and unmarried girls smoke tobacco pipes". Since there were many wild beasts in the Manchu area, children were hung up to ensure their safety. The tobacco leaves in the tobacco pipes smoked by unmarried girls were used to drive away mosquitoes. This work has an inner diameter of 60cm × 70cm and an outer frame of 100cm × 100cm. It is hand-embroidered using stitches such as triangular stitches, random stitches, overlapping stitches, joining stitches, and rolling stitches. It is a work by the famous painter Zhang Shuangfeng, which recreates the childhood memories and rural life.

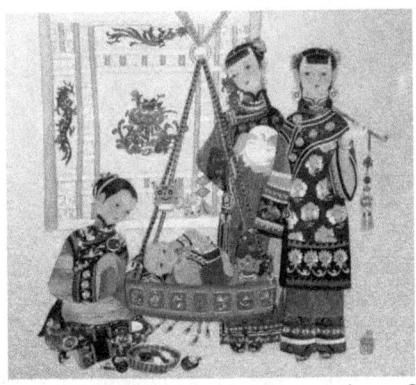

Figure 1-24 "Three Oddities in Northern Guan"

Many works of Bohai Mohe embroidery are themed on natural scenery (Figure 1-19, Figure 1-25, Figure 1-26). The work "Setting Sail" (Figure 1-19) has an inner diameter of 70cm×85cm and an outer frame of 100cm×100cm. The scenery is spectacular, giving a magnificent feeling. The sailing boats in the embroidery represent setting sail against the wind, fighting the waves, and never stopping. It implies setting sail smoothly and having a satisfactory life. Among the Mohe embroidery of landscapes, the embroidery works themed on ice and snow are very popular. "Chinese Snow Town" (Figure 1-25) has an inner diameter of 29cm×98cm and an outer frame of 64cm×133cm. It is hand-embroidered using stitches such as triangular stitches, laying stitches, applying stitches, and random stitches. When seeing this embroidery, we feel as if we are on the scene. The highest peaks, the densest forests, the clean sunlight, the thick snow, and the simple life all come into view. See Figure 1-14, Figure 1-25, and Figure 1-26 for other works in the same series.

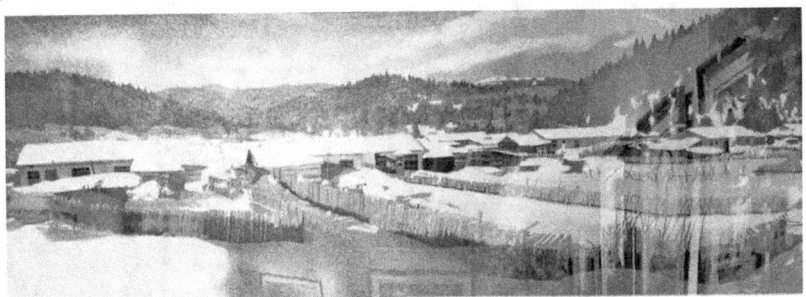

Figure 1-25 "China's Snowy Village" (II)

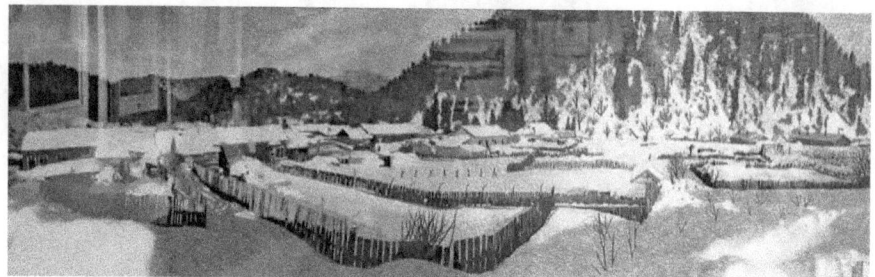

Figure 1-26 "China's Snowy Village" (III)

The work "Frontier Girl" (Figure 1-27) has an inner picture size of 55cm × 65cm and an outer frame of 88cm × 100cm. It is a work by Kong Xi, a member of the Chinese Realistic Painting School, based on "Memories of Youth". The action of the girl in the work holding her hands tightly makes the work vivid, presenting a calm and amiable style. See Figure 1-28 for a similar figure embroidery.

The double-sided animal embroidery "Cat" (Figure 1-29) uses 25 color combinations and is embroidered with stitches such as triangular stitches, virtual-real stitches, flat stitches, and joining stitches. It took 440 hours to complete. There is a folk saying: A cat raising its right paw symbolizes attracting wealth, with money flowing in continuously; raising its left paw symbolizes attracting customers and having a prosperous business.

In Mohe embroidery, flowers, plants, trees, and various animals are also the main sources of inspiration (Figure 1-30 to Figure 1-35).

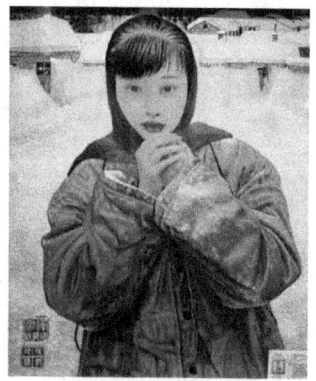

Figure 1-27 "Frontier Girl"

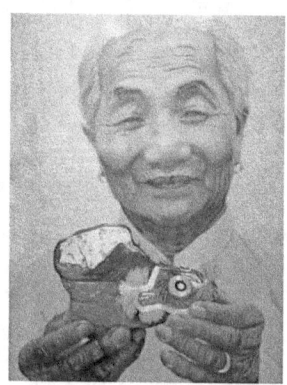

Figure 1-28 "Kindness"

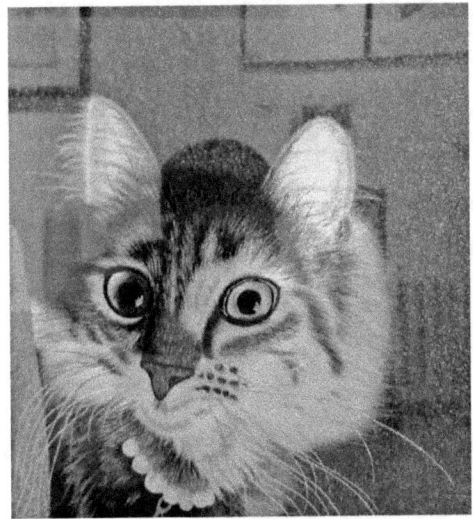

Figure 1-29 "Cat"

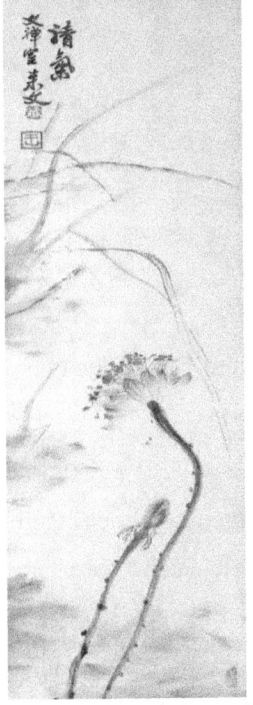
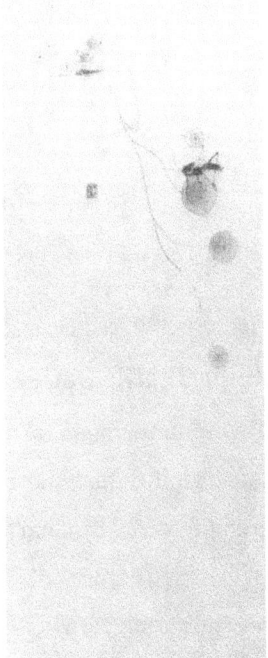

Figure 1-30 "Ink Lotus"　Figure 1-31 "Summer Joy"

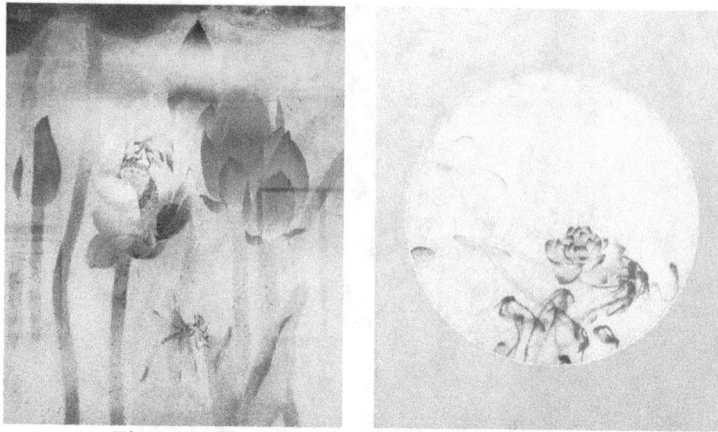

Figure 1-32 "Red Lotus" Figure 1-33 "Lotus"

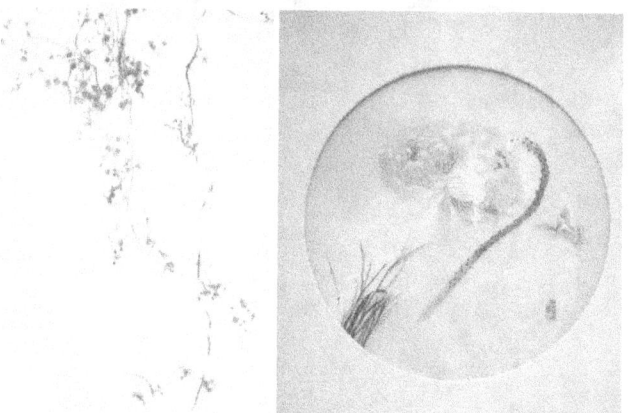

Figure 1-34 "Red Beans" Figure 1-35 "Blue Lotus"

V. Modern Home Textile Series

Compared with quilts made of mulberry silk, quilts made of tussah silk have stronger breathability and more gorgeous luster (Figure 1-36). Home-related products embroidered by hand (double-sided embroidery), such as lamps and glazed yarn bottles (Figure 1-37 and Figure 1-38), are mainly made of glazed yarn nets. The glazed yarn nets are more wear-resistant than the window screens we use in daily life, with stronger luster and no fading. They are a specially processed material with high tightness. These lamps and yarn bottles are easy to clean and can be directly wiped with a wet cloth. Table chess supplies are also very popular products in the modern home textile series (Figure 1 - 39).

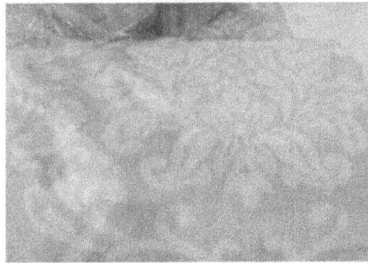 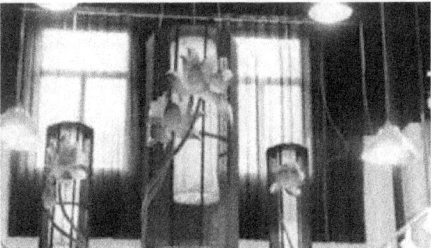

Figure 1-36 Tussah Silk Quilt　　Figure 1-37 Mohe - embroidered Lamp

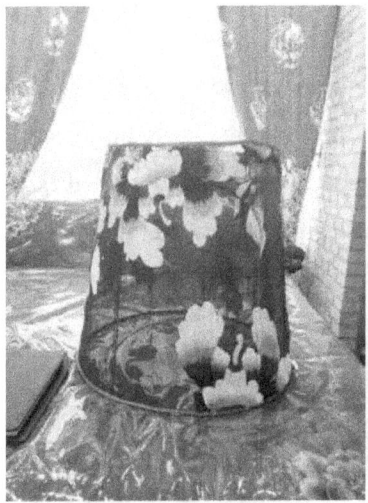 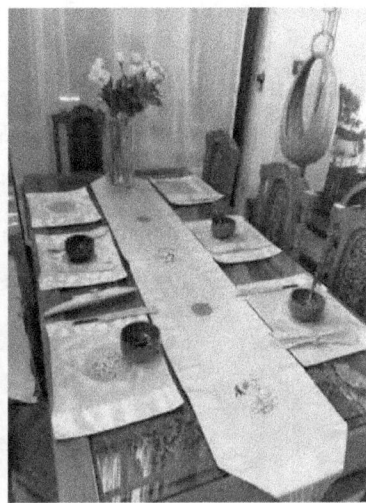

Figure 1-38 Glazed Yarn Bottle　　Figure 1-39 Table Chess Supplies

VI. Modern Clothing, Shoes and Hats Series

The application of Mohe embroidery in clothing, shoes and hats is more extensive, such as hats, silk scarves, shawls, cheongsams, shirts, throw pillows, handbags, etc. in people's daily lives. Among them, silk scarves are especially popular (Figure 1-40 and Figure 1-41). These silk scarves are mainly made of tussah silk, with a smooth and delicate fabric, which is deeply loved by ladies.

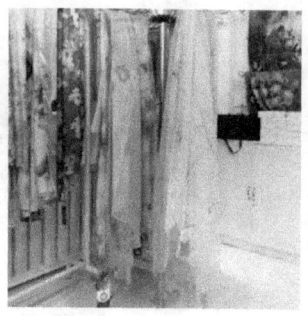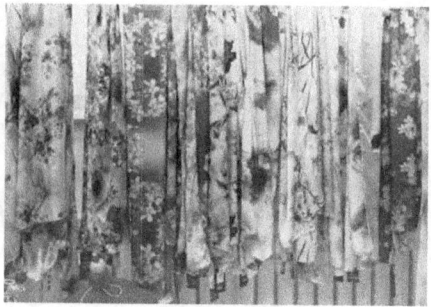

Figure 1-40 Silk Scarf Made of Tussah Figure 1-41 Silk Scarf Made of Tussah

Silk (I)   Silk (II)

Tussah silk bags specially designed for ladies are also very popular among the public (Figure 1-42). The patterns on the bags are mainly of flowers, plants, trees, with relatively bright colors, suitable for contemporary ladies to carry when going out daily. These bags have been put on the market and have achieved good sales. They are also presented as national gifts to international friends (Figure 1-43).

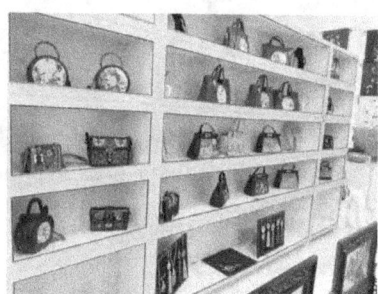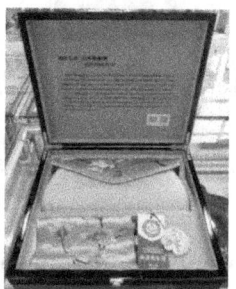

Figure 1-42 Ladies' Bags with Various   Figure 1-43 Mohe Embroidery as a

Patterns   National Gift

The application of Mohe embroidery in shirts and Manchu cheongsams is very extensive, as shown in Figure 1-44 to Figure 1-47.

There are many ancient Manchu costumes still circulated in the Northeast region, including hairbands, hats, earmuffs, shoes, wallets, aprons, bellybands, etc. The patterns on these costumes are mainly of flowers, plants, fish, insects, mountains, rivers, forests, symbolizing good fortune, wealth, and prosperity.

Manchus often use hairbands, hats, and earmuffs in their daily wear (Figure 1-48 to Figure 1-49). In cold winter, they usually wear earmuffs and hats to keep warm. The shoes worn by Han women who bound their feet in the past (Figure 1-50) were about three-inch long, similar in size to children's tiger-head shoes. The wallet hand-embroidered by the second-generation inheritor of Mohe embroidery (Figure 1-51). Manchu women often wear aprons when doing housework. The apron shown in Figure 1-52 is embroidered with tiger heads and flowers, symbolizing good luck and prosperity.

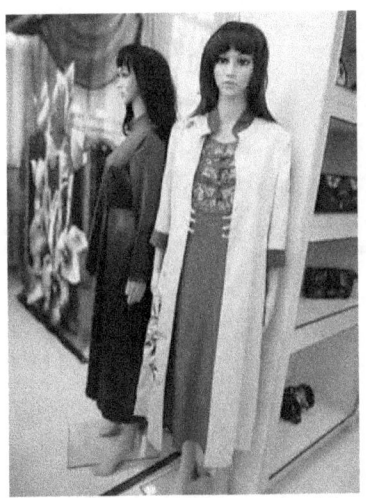
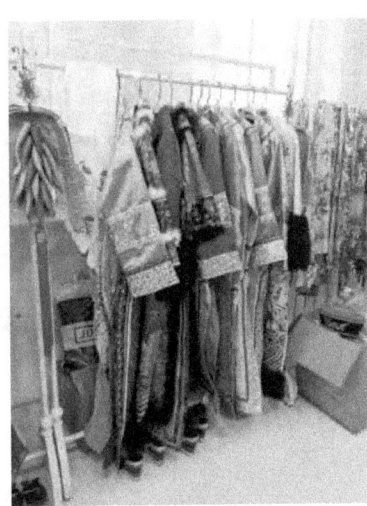

Figure 1-44 Modern Clothing   Figure 1-45 Cheongsam (I)

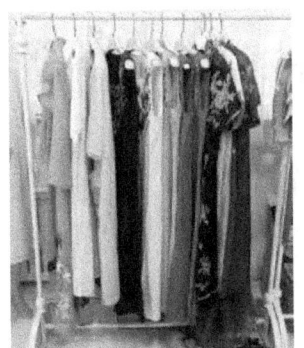
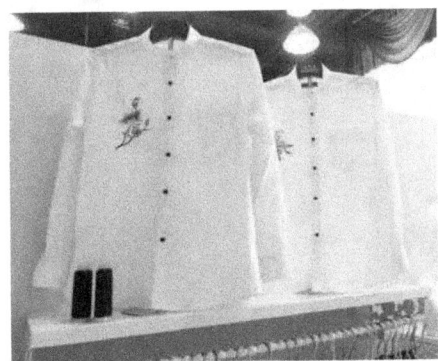

Figure 1-46 Cheongsam (II)   Figure 1-47 Shirt

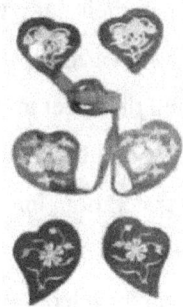

Figure 1-48 Manchu Hair Band

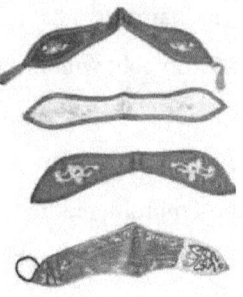

Figure 1-49 Ear Muffs Worn by

Manchu People in Winter

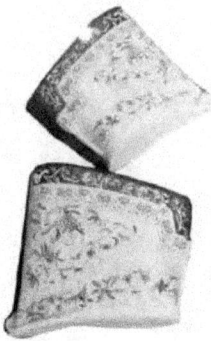

Figure 1-50 "Three-inch Golden

Lotus" Shoes

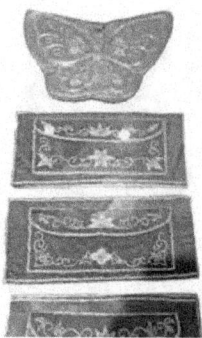

Figure 1-51 Wallet Made by the

Second-generation Inheritor

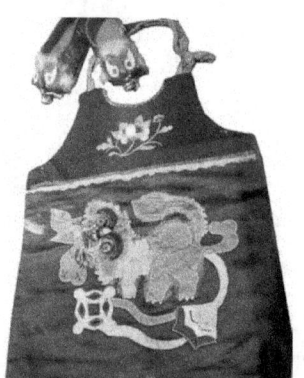

Figure 1-52 Apron

IV. Tourist Souvenirs and Business Gift Series

Tourist souvenirs and business gifts are the primary choices for souvenirs and collectibles in international exchanges, art communications, business negotiations, and conference commemorations. The inheritor has developed small gifts by combining embroidery with modern technological elements (Figure 1-53). From a distance, it looks like a notebook, but in fact, it is a power bank with a USB flash drive attached. It is suitable for various mobile phone models. After opening it, you can see data cables of various models on one side (Figure 1-54).

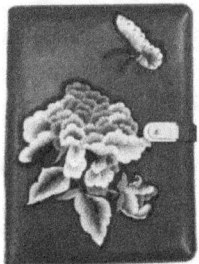 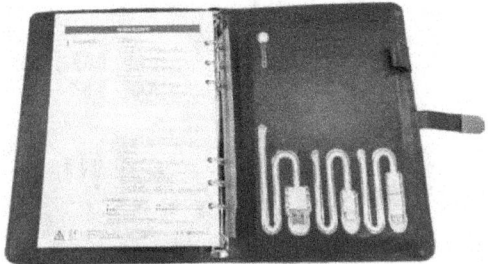

Figure 1-53 Appearance of the Power Bank

Figure 1-54 Inside of the Power Bank

Tourist souvenirs and business gifts also include many mini-sized ladies' handbags (Figure 1-55). The patterns on the handbags are mainly peonies, with red and yellow as the main colors. Some typical cultural and creative products have also been put on the market, such as mouse pads (Figure 1-56).

The inheritor has specially designed tourist souvenir notebooks (Figure 1-57) and souvenir card holders (Figure 1-58) for tourists. They are convenient to carry, exquisitely made, and pleasing to the eye. Among them, purses, pendants, toothpick holders, bracelets, rings, earrings, wallets, LED lights, etc. are all common souvenirs and gifts, as shown in Figure 1-59 to Figure 1-68.

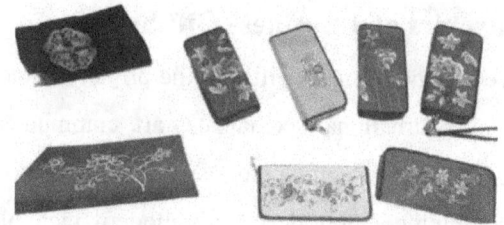

Figure 1-55 Ladies' Handbag

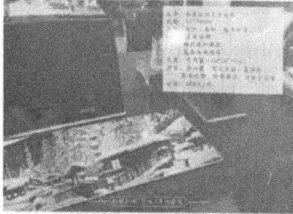
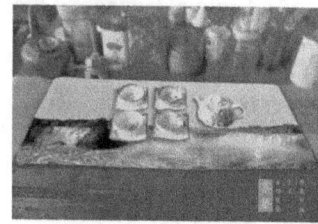

Figure 1-56 Mouse Pad

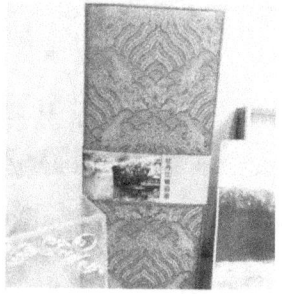

Figure 1-57 Travel Souvenir

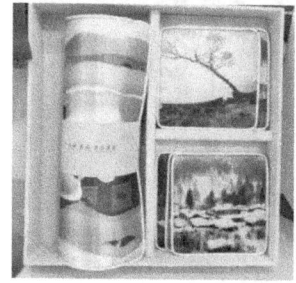

Figure 1-58 A Set of Souvenir Card

Holders

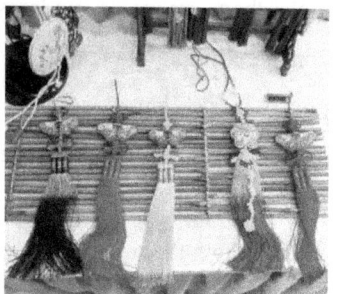

Figure 1-59 Purse Pendant (I)

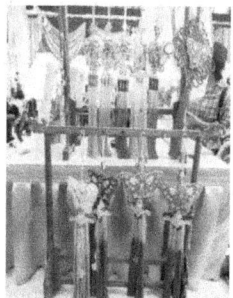

Figure 1-60 Purse Pendant (II)

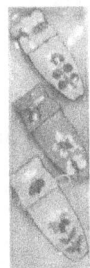 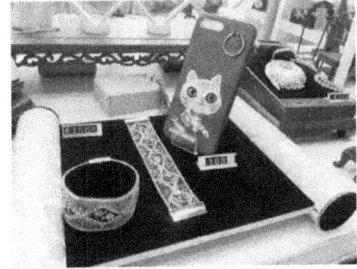 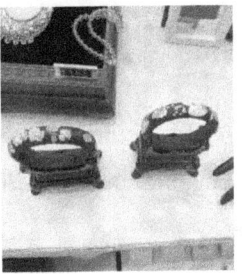

Figure 1-61 Toothpick Holder

Figure 1-62 Bracelet (I)

Figure 1-63 Bracelet (II)

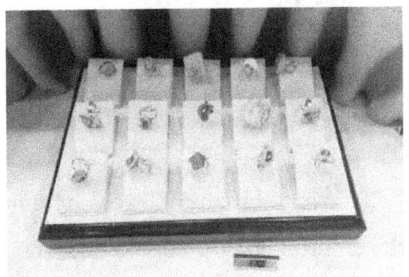 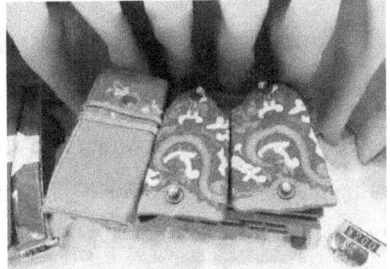

Figure 1-64 Ring

Figure 1-65 Mohe Embroidery Wallet (I)

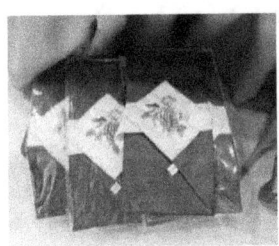 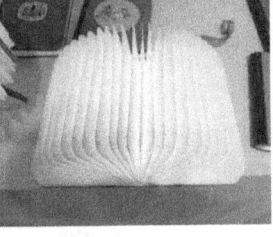 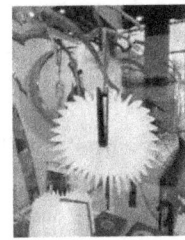

Figure 1-66 Mohe Embroidery Wallet (II)

Figure 1-67 LED Light (I)

Figure 1-68 LED Light (II)

Section VII Interviews with Inheritors

To further conduct in-depth research on and inherit and innovate the intangible cultural heritage of Bohai Mohe embroidery, the author organized this research. Since Ms. Sun Yanling, the fourth-generation inheritor, was on a business trip in Shenzhen during the research period, the author interviewed Ms. Jiang Lina, the fifth-generation inheritor of Bohai Mohe embroidery.

I. May I ask: Could you briefly introduce the current development status of the Bohai Mohe Embroidery?

Ms. Jiang Lina: Currently, we mainly promote and develop Mohe embroidery products through two channels: online and offline. Online, we have a dedicated sales platform. Offline, we have exhibition halls, a training department in the city center, and the Manchu embroidery museum in Shenzhen. Some long-term cooperative old customers, enterprises, and public institutions will specially customize some products from us. Some embroidery works are also sold through auctions, and many high-quality products are sold at auctions. Most of our household textile products are customized by old customers.

II. May I ask: What difficulties have you encountered in promoting the Mohe Embroidery?

Ms. Jiang Lina: In fact, while promoting Bohai Mohe embroidery, we have also driven the development of the entire embroidery industry in Heilongjiang. Various types of embroidery in different regions have also developed. In Harbin, we launch a new series every year. Our chairperson, Sun Yanling, has many creative ideas. One year, our company created "ice and snow embroidery", which involves pasting cotton on the frame of the work to give it a snowy texture, and that's how it got its name. Later, a studio in Harbin also created ice and snow embroidery. Now, many peers are doing this kind of embroidery, and imitation among each other is very common. For example, as soon as we launch a new product, someone will quickly follow and imitate it. This should be considered a major difficulty.

III. Has the local government created any conditions to encourage the development of Bohai Mohe embroidery?

Ms. Jiang Lina: Most of our embroiderers are laid-off workers and surplus rural labor. The local government's labor department has a special training fund policy to support these people. They can participate in embroidery training for free. This not only solves the employment problem for some people but also provides labor for the development of Mohe embroidery. In addition, there are protection funds for national-level intangible cultural heritage projects. We can understand the government's support policies according to our own needs and actively apply for relevant funds if they are suitable for our intangible cultural heritage project.

IV. May I ask: Who provides the information about the large-scale exhibitions you usually attend?

Ms. Jiang Lina: The municipal or provincial government will provide information about the exhibitions and cover the booth fees for free. We only need to bear our own expenses for accommodation, food, and transportation. There are two main purposes for attending these exhibitions. One is to promote our Bohai Mohe embroidery, and the other is to sell tourist souvenirs. These products are very popular among local people.

V. May I ask: Does the Mohe Embroidery cooperate with schools?

Ms. Jiang Lina: Yes, we are currently working on a project called "Intangible Cultural Heritage Enters Schools". This project is being carried out in Mudanjiang and Shenzhen, mainly targeting primary schools, such as Mudanjiang Experimental Primary School and Mudanjiang Guanghua Primary School. In this project, we distribute material kits to the students and teach them embroidery techniques. We have also carried out similar projects in universities, such as Heilongjiang Preschool Teachers College, Mudanjiang Normal University, and Mudanjiang University, where we have provided similar training courses.

VI. May I ask: What do you think of "Intangible Cultural Heritage Entering the Campus"?

Ms. Jiang Lina: I think traditional culture should start from children. We should let them understand China's traditional intangible cultural heritage. On the one hand, we bring this intangible cultural heritage into schools. On the other hand, many students also come to our exhibition hall. Some kindergarten children, after learning about the Intangible Cultural Heritage Museum, will come to our exhibition hall during their social practice classes. In addition, Korean middle schools often bring some Korean international students to our exhibition hall. The normal college also cooperates with us frequently to promote the exchange and integration between international students and Chinese traditional culture.

VII. May I ask: What are your expectations for the future development of the Bohai Mohe Embroidery?

Ms. Jiang Lina: First, we hope it can enter thousands of households. Mohe embroidery is not only an art hanging on the wall but can also be integrated into people's daily lives. It must not only be beautiful and appreciable but also practical, which is the path we need to continue to explore in our cultural and creative products in the future. Second, we hope that our intangible cultural heritage project will not only be introduced into primary schools but also have more development in junior high and high schools, so that more children can learn about this culture. From the mouths of children to their parents, and then to the whole family, more people will get to know this intangible cultural heritage.

VIII. May I ask: How do you select the inheritors?

Ms. Jiang Lina: I'm currently preparing to find the sixth-generation inheritors. Generally, we select several young trainees as inheritors. Our trainees are mainly divided into three age groups. The first group is from 30 to 40 years old, mostly housewives who regard being an embroiderer as their second job. The second group is from 50 to 70 years old. The oldest embroiderer we cooperate with is 70 years old. The third group is from 40 to 50 years old. Most of them are intermediate-level embroiderers. They have enough physical strength and good eyesight and mainly rely on embroidery to earn a living.

IX. May I ask: How do you think we can encourage young people to join in?

Ms. Jiang Lina: I think we need to cultivate their interest. Only when they truly like this culture from the bottom of their hearts can they persevere.

Section VIII Current Situation and Countermeasures of Inheritance

I. Inheritors' Contributions to the Development of Embroidery Skills

In recent years, Ms. Sun Yanling and Ms. Jiang Lina have led the Mohe embroidery works to participate in numerous exhibitions both at home and abroad, receiving unanimous praise from people from all walks of life. They have also been invited to participate in embroidery courses and pass on the embroidery skills to primary school students, middle school students, and college students, making significant contributions to the promotion of Bohai Mohe embroidery.

In April 2017, Ms. Jiang Lina participated in the 958 Intangible Cultural Heritage Art Exhibition in Heilongjiang Province. In May, Ms. Sun Yanling and Ms. Jiang Lina participated in the Mudanjiang Intangible Cultural Heritage Protection Day event. Also in May, with the initiative of intangible cultural heritage entering schools, Ms. Jiang Lina promoted Mohe embroidery at Chang'an Primary School. In October, Ms. Sun Yanling and Ms. Jiang Lina participated in the First Mudanjiang Creative Fine Arts Exhibition, as shown in Figures 1-69 to -72.

In January 2018, Ms. Jiang Lina participated in the Harbin Fashion Week, showcasing Bohai Mohe embroidery works. In March, with the intangible cultural heritage entering schools, Ms. Jiang Lina went to the Vocational Education Center. In May, Ms. Jiang Lina participated in the Cultural Exchange Conference in Hamburg, Germany. In June, Ms. Sun Yanling and Ms. Jiang Lina were invited to shoot the program "Travel with the Anchor". In July, Ms. Jiang Lina participated in the 2017-2018 Cultural Consumption Achievement Exhibition. Also in July, female students from Dong Girls' High School in Busan, South Korea came to the Bohai Mohe Embroidery Exhibition Hall for cultural exchanges. In September, Ms. Jiang Lina received 90 primary and secondary school teachers from Heilongjiang Province. Also in September, Ms. Jiang Lina participated in the Heilongjiang National Learning Activity Week. In October, Ms. Jiang Lina participated in the "Heilongjiang Global Promotion Event by the Ministry of Foreign Affairs". In November, Ms. Jiang Lina participated in the "2018 China International Travel Mart". In December, Ms. Jiang Lina participated in the Heilongjiang Winter Cultural Tourism Promotion Event, as shown in Figures 1-73 to 1-84.

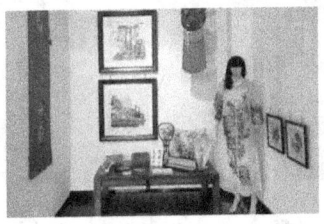

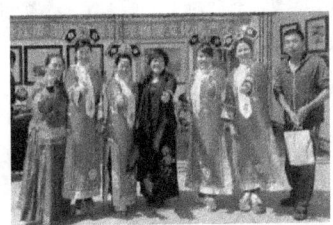

Figure 1-70 Sun Yanling (4th from the left) and Jiang Lina (3rd from the right) Participating in the Mudanjiang Intangible Cultural Heritage Protection Day Event

Figure 1-69 Exhibits of the 958 Intangible Cultural Heritage Art Exhibition in Heilongjiang Province

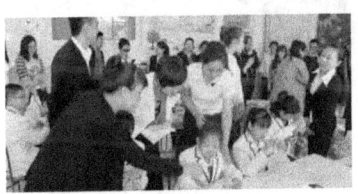

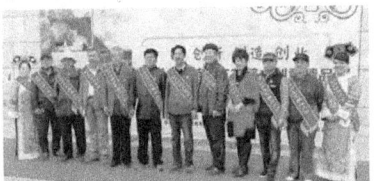

Figure 1-72 Jiang Lina (1st from the right) Participating in the First Mudanjiang Creative Fine Arts Exhibition

Figure 1-71 Ms. Jiang Lina Promoting the Mohe Embroidery at Chang'an Primary School

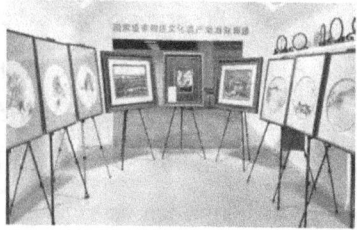

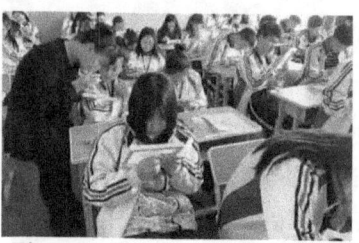

Figure 1-73 The Mohe Embroidery Exhibition Area Fashion Week

Figure 1-74 Ms. of the Harbin Jiang Lina Promoting the Mohe Embroidery at the Vocational Education Center

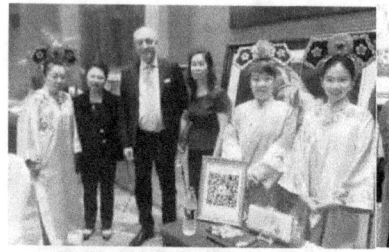

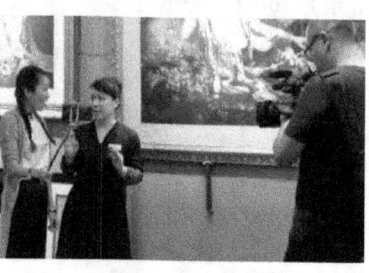

Figure 1-75 Ms. Jiang Lina (2nd from the right) Participating in the Cultural Exchange Conference in Hamburg, Germany

Figure 1-76 Ms. Jiang Lina (2nd from the left) Shooting "Travel with the Anchor"

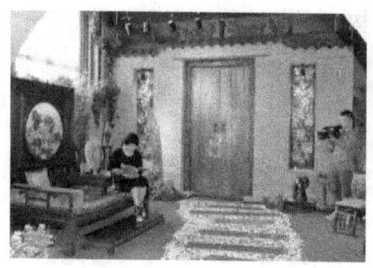

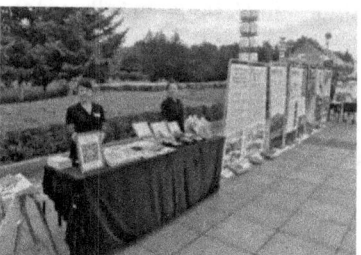

Figure 1-77 Ms. Sun Yanling Shooting "Travel with the Anchor"

Figure 1-78 Ms. Jiang Lina Participating in the 2017-2018 Cultural Consumption Achievements Exhibition

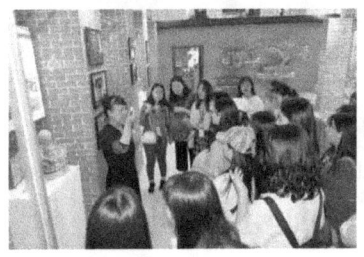

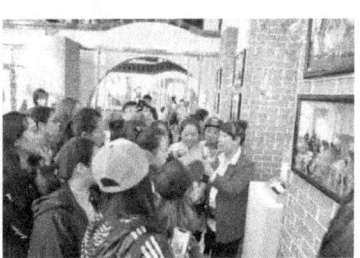

Figure 1-79 Ms. Jiang Lina Receiving South Korean International Students

Figure 1-80 Ms. Jiang Lina Receiving Primary and Secondary School Teachers

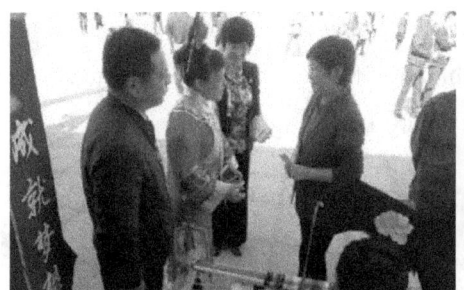

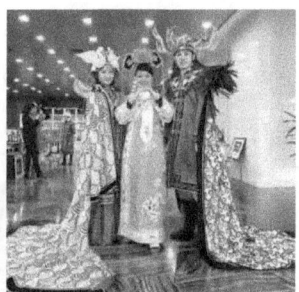

Figure 1-81 Ms. Jiang Lina Participating in the Heilongjiang National Learning Activity Week

Figure 1-82 Ms. Jiang Lina Participating in the "Heilongjiang Global Promotion Event" by the Ministry of Foreign Affairs

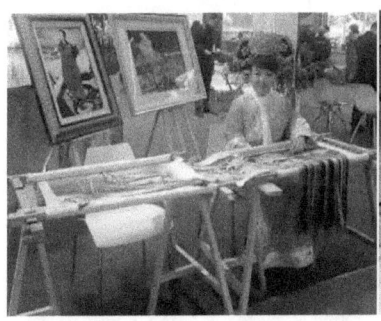

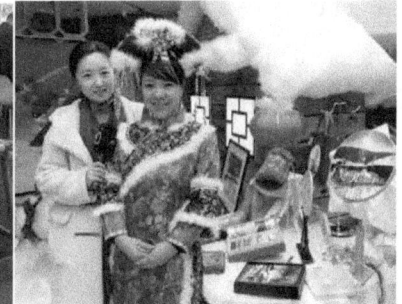

Figure 1-83 Ms. Jiang Lina Participating in the 2018 China International Travel Mart

Figure 1-84 Ms. Jiang Lina Participating in the Heilongjiang Winter Cultural Tourism Promotion Event

In January 2019, Ms. Jiang Lina participated in the 2019 Well-off Longjiang Poverty-Alleviation New Year Goods Fair and was interviewed on-site and live-broadcast by the "Legal Channel" of Heilongjiang Radio Station. In April, she participated in the 4th China Folk Art Expo. In May, she took part in the 12th China Arts Festival Performing Arts and Cultural and Creative Products Expo. From June 26th to 29th, she participated in the 10th China-Russia Cultural Fair and was interviewed by the radio station of Amur Oblast. In October, she joined the "Belt and Road" China-Russia Mudanjiang International Cultural and Tourism Photography Exhibition. At the grand event, she presented three excellent works to celebrate the 70th anniversary of the founding of the Communist Party of China were launched and widely praised. In November, an individual exhibition of National Intangible Cultural Heritage was held in Beijing, as shown in Figure 1-85 - Figure 1-90.

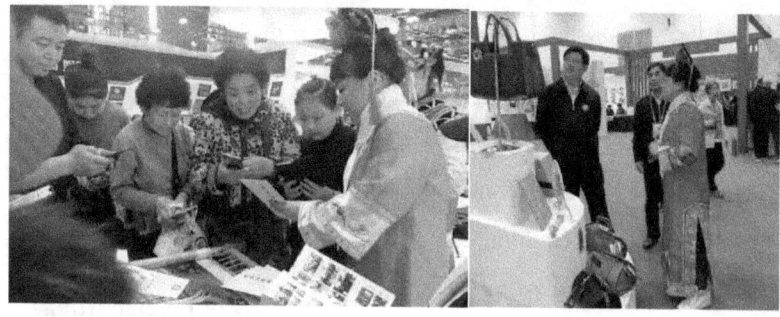

Figure 1-85 Ms. Jiang Lina Participating in the 2019 Well-off Longjiang Poverty Alleviation New Year Goods Fair

Figure 1-86 Ms. Jiang Lina Participating in the 4th China Folk Art Expo

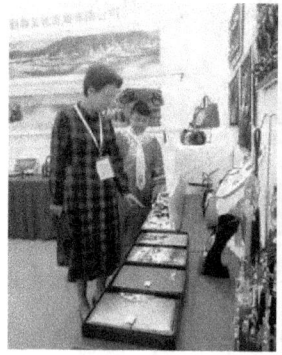
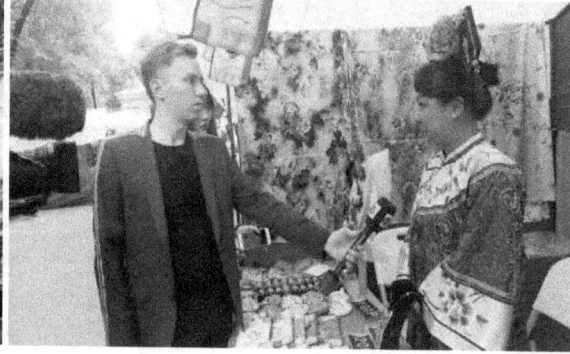

Figure 1-87 Ms. Jiang Lina
Participating in the 12th China Art
Festival Performing Arts and Cultural
and Creative Products Expo

Figure 1-88 Ms. Jiang Lina
Participating in the 10th China-Russia
Cultural Fair

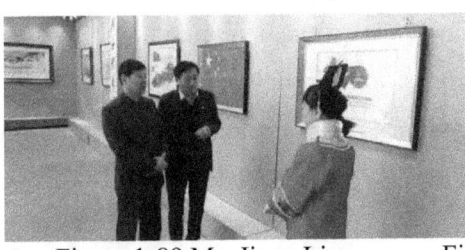

Figure 1-89 Ms. Jiang Lina
Participating in the "Belt and the
Road" China-Russia Mudanjiang
International Cultural and Tourist
Photography Exhibition

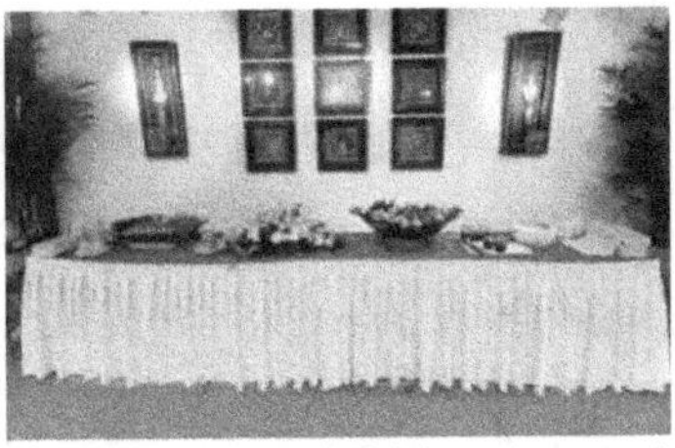

Figure 1-90 The Exhibition Area of
Individual Exhibition of National
Intangible Cultural Heritage in
Beijing

II. Current Situation of Inheritance

Although the Bohai Mohe Embroidery has been included in the National Intangible Cultural Heritage List, its future development still faces many challenges. From the present situation, the factors restricting the inheritance and development of the Mohe Embroidery are as follows:

1. Insufficient promotion and limited coverage of Mohe embroidery

Although the inheritors have participated in dozens of domestic and international exhibitions with the support of the government, this ancient craft still seems very distant to ordinary people. The public's understanding and knowledge of Mohe embroidery need to be improved.

2. The inheritors are aging and unstable, and there is a large gap in the age-structure distribution of embroidery women

Young embroidery women are relatively scarce. Most of them are laid-off workers or surplus rural laborers, who regard embroidery as their second job or a way to supplement their family income in their spare time. Since the main labor force in embroidery is mostly older, their physical strength and eyesight are not as good as those of young embroidery women, resulting in a decline in the speed and quality of embroidery. Most young people are not willing to really learn, research, innovate and develop Bohai Mohe embroidery. The sustainable development of Bohai Mohe embroidery is struggling, and its future is worrying.

3. Imperfect sales channels

Currently, the sales of Bohai Mohe embroidery lack a fixed channel. It mainly relies on old customers and customization by enterprises and institutions, supplemented by auctions and sales at exhibitions. In addition, with the increase in tariffs in recent years, the overseas export sales channel of Mohe embroidery has been cut off. This sales model is often highly uncertain and unstable. Therefore, how to build a perfect sales channel is the main problem faced by the inheritance and development of Bohai Mohe embroidery at present.

III. Countermeasures of Inheritance

With the continuous development of the times, the ancient craft of Bohai Mohe embroidery has also been greatly impacted. To address the above problems encountered in the process of inheriting and developing Bohai Mohe embroidery, it cannot rely solely on the government, universities, and inheritors to solve them. It requires the joint efforts of the whole society. The author believes that we can start from the following aspects to deal with the problems in the current development process of the Mohe embroidery.

1. Strengthening the Promotion and Popularization of Bohai Mohe Embroidery

While collecting and displaying Bohai Mohe embroidery handicrafts, museums should conduct research on Bohai Mohe embroidery through high-tech means. Utilize modern network communication methods, such as filming the embroidery process of Mohe embroidery, explaining its origin and development, and publicizing its customs and traditions. This can enhance people's spiritual enjoyment and strengthen their awareness of the cognition and protection of Bohai Mohe embroidery. Museums can also hold some public-welfare exhibitions. At these exhibitions, they can display their original and characteristic works or creative tourism products, and abandon the production of low-end and featureless products. They should develop and produce delicate handicrafts with local characteristics to arouse people's interest, gradually increase the popularity of Bohai Mohe embroidery, and establish a brand effect. The government can promote the cooperation between Mohe embroidery and the local tourism industry, integrate embroidery skills into the local tourism culture, and launch original tourism souvenirs in the tourism market.

2. Changing the Training Mode of Inheritors and Expanding the Talent Team

It is necessary to transform from the traditional static inheritance model to the dynamic inheritance model. The traditional training methods of inheritors, such as family inheritance and master-apprentice inheritance, are no longer applicable in modern society. Only by breaking through the inheritance model based on the family unit or the master-apprentice system and commercializing traditional handicrafts can we avoid the situation of difficulty in finding apprentices and weak inheritance. Although the inheritors of Bohai Mohe embroidery have proficient craftsmanship, they are generally older and their cultural levels need to be improved. Therefore, the government needs to increase support for inheritors. With the help of the government, inheritors should conduct embroidery craft training for laid-off workers or unemployed women, and conduct secondary training for individual inheriting artisans after a certain period. In addition, cooperation can be carried out with institutions of higher learning, enterprises and public institutions. Offer elective courses in universities, train employees of enterprises and public institutions, and conduct regular assessments to expand the embroidery talent team. At the same time, a large number of college students should be attracted to pay attention to embroidery skills, stimulate their interest in this craft, and achieve the goal of inheriting and protecting Bohai Mohe embroidery.

3. Improving the Sales Channels of Embroidery Products

The development of Bohai Mohe embroidery cannot rely solely on national policies or traditional self-sales methods. Instead, it should actively integrate into the modern creative marketing model and keep up with the trend. Organize the professional and large-scale production of Mohe embroidery to reduce production costs; carry out market-oriented operations and commercial management to reduce intermediate transaction costs. Establish a dedicated R & D and marketing team to conduct market research according to market demand and produce creative products that meet the needs of the public in a targeted manner. Strive to retain traditional skills while maximizing profits and better inherit the intangible cultural heritage of Bohai Mohe embroidery.

References

[1] China Intangible Cultural Heritage Network-China Intangible Cultural Heritage Digital Museum. http://www.ihchina.cn/.

[2] Sun Yanling. By turning ancient techniques into fashionable products, Mohe embroidery was put on the world booth.

https:/heilongjiang.dbw.cn/system/2017/07/31/057729444.shtml.

[3] https://baike.baidu.com/item/% E6% 9F% 9E% E8% 9A% 95% E4% B8%9D/9450541?fr = aladdin.

[4] Bohai Mohe embroidery: fashion industry at your fingertips.

http://www.sohu.com/a/78637531 _ 119718.

[5] Sun Yanling. Bohai Mohe Embroidery: "Needle Tip Ballet" jumps out of the world . Manchu skills continue the national soul. http://www.sohu.com /a/192779924 _ 99995046.

[6] Visiting the experimental area |Like a painting but not a painting, Mohe embroidery has been handed down for thousands of years. http://www. ruili.gov.cn/.

[7] Bohai Mohe embroidery made its debut at the 4th China (Weifang) Folk Art Expo. http://www.wfnews.com.cn/news/2019-04/18/content_ 2106132. htm.

Chapter II Ningguta Manchu Embroidery

Ningguta Manchu embroidery gets its name because it originated in Ningguta, the birthplace of the Manchu ethnic group. Ningguta Manchu embroidery has distinct Manchu characteristics. In 2012, it was included in the intangible cultural heritage list by the Mudanjiang People's Government; in 2013, it was included in the fourth batch of intangible cultural heritage lists of Heilongjiang Province, classified as traditional art (Table 2-1 and Figure 2-1). In April 2014, Ms. Jia Xiulan was recognized as the provincial representative inheritor of Ningguta Manchu embroidery (Figure 2-2). In July 2008, Ms. Jia Xiulan founded the Ningguta Manchu Embroidery Workshop. After being explored, sorted out, and innovated by the Ningguta Manchu Embroidery Workshop, this ancient traditional folk embroidery technique has now achieved large-scale production. Its products are not only popular among domestic customers but also exported to countries and regions such as Russia, the United States, Canada, Togo, Kazakhstan, Japan, and Southeast Asia.

Table 2-1 Introduction to Ningguta Manchu Embroidery

Name of the List	Ningguta Manchu Embroidery
Category of the List	Traditional Arts
Level of the List	Provincial
Declaration Unit or Region	Ning'an City, Heilongjiang Province
Provincial Inheritance Representative	Jia Xiulan

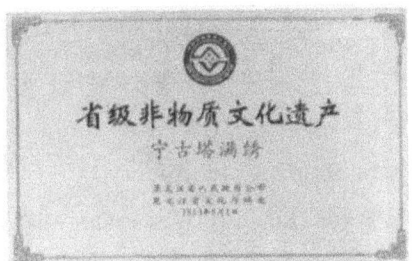

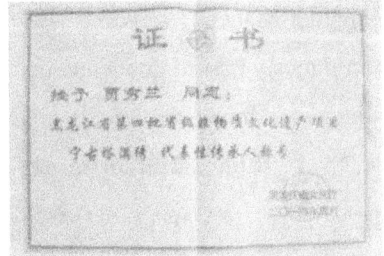

Figure 2-1 Certificate of Provincial Intangible Cultural Heritage Project in Heilongjiang Province

Figure 2-2 Certificate of Representative Inheritor of Provincial Intangible Cultural Heritage Project in Heilongjiang Province

Section I Origin and Development

I. The Origin of Ningguta Manchu Embroidery

Ningguta Manchu embroidery originated in the birthplace of the Sushen ethnic group, the ancestors of the Manchu people. According to archaeological research on cultural relics, it has a history of more than 5,000 years. In ancient times, the Manchu ancestors believed in Shamanism and advocated shaman dance culture and various primitive arts. The record in *New Book of Tang: Biography of Bohai* that "There were cloth from Xianzhou, brocade from Wozhou, and silk from Longzhou…" shows that the people in the Ningguta area started embroidery around the Bohai State period of the Tang Dynasty. Judging from the silk cloth wrapped around the Sarira unearthed locally and the costumes of the figures in the murals of Princess Zhenxiao's tomb, the Manchu people at that time had mastered the techniques of Ningguta Manchu embroidery. During the Jin Dynasty of the Jurchen ethnic group, the integration of Central Plains embroidery culture and Khitan embroidery culture brought new development to Ningguta embroidery. In the Qing Dynasty, Ningguta Manchu embroidery became widely popular among the people. Generation after generation of inheritors have been committed to promoting the inheritance of Ningguta Manchu embroidery, enabling this precious cultural heritage to be continuously passed down and developed. The inheritors of each generation of Ningguta Manchu embroidery are shown in Table 2-2.

Table 2-2 Inheritors of Ningguta Manchu Embroidery

Generation	Name	Gender	Date of Birth	Ethnicity	Inheritance Mode
1st	Li Shuqin	Female	1932	Manchu	Family
2nd	Zhang Xueqin	Female	1903	Manchu	Master-apprentice
3rd	Chen Yuhua	Female	1930	Manchu	Master-apprentice
4th	Jia Xiulan	Female	1954	Manchu	Family
5th	Zhang Bowen	Female	1980	Manchu	Family
5th	Tan Jiali	Female	1984	Manchu	Master-apprentice

II. The Development of Ningguta Manchu Embroidery

Ms. Jia Xiulan, the fourth-generation inheritor of Ningguta Manchu Embroidery (Figure 2-3), is 65 years old. She started learning Manchu embroidery from her mother at the age of 10. At 16, she took Zhang Xueqin as her master to study Manchu embroidery. During her college years, she studied at Mudanjiang Normal University. After graduation, she further studied music and aesthetics at the Central Conservatory of Music. The literary and artistic theories as well as auditory arts have enabled her to have deeper understanding and sublimation of painting and embroidery.

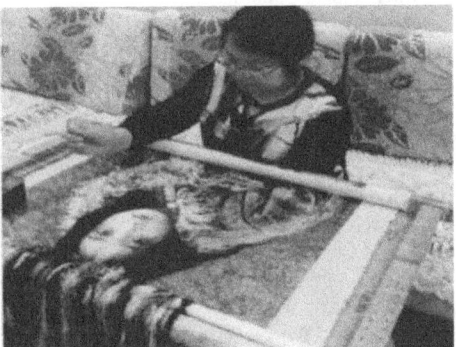

Figure 2-3 Ms. Jia Xiulan doing Ningguta Manchu Embroidery

As an inheritor of Manchu culture, in order to rescue and inherit the techniques of Manchu court embroidery, Ms. Jia Xiulan has always adhered to the development concept of "inheriting Manchu culture and promoting the spirit of the Northeast". With Manchu culture as the core and local culture as the characteristic, she further inherits and explores the cultural essence of Manchu embroidery in the Northeast. On July 7, 2008, Ms. Jia Xiulan founded the "Manembro Workshop". Her embroidery works have been recognized by experts and all sectors of society and are deeply loved by people from all walks of life. The honors won by the inheritor Jia Xiulan are shown in Table 2-3.

Table 2-3 Honors Obtained by Inheritor Jia Xiulan

Date	Awarding Institution	Award Description	Certificate Display
August 2012	China Arts and Crafts Association	The Manchu embroidery work "Flowers in Full Bloom, Bringing Prosperity" won the silver award in the 2012 "Golden Phoenix · Longjiang Division" Innovative Product Design Grand Prix at the 7th China · Longjiang International Cultural and Art Industry Expo.	
October 2014	China Arts and Crafts Association	The Manchu embroidery work "Thousand-Handed and Thousand - Eyed Avalokitesvara" won the bronze award in the "China Original · Hundred Flowers Cup" China Arts and Crafts Excellent Works Award at the 15th China Arts and Crafts Masters' Works and International Artistic Fine Products Expo.	
June 2015	Intangible Cultural Heritage Protection Center of Heilongjiang Province	Awarded the First-Session Inheritance and Transmission Award for Inheritors of Heilongjiang Intangible Cultural Heritage.	
October 2017	China Arts and Crafts Association	The embroidery work "Meditation" won the silver award in the 2017 "Hundred Flowers Cup" China Arts and Crafts Excellent Works Award at the 18th China Arts and Crafts Masters' Works and Handicraft Fine Products Expo.	

From August 16th to 18th, 2013, Ms. Jia Xiulan led more than 10 embroiderers to participate in the 6th China (Mudanjiang)-Russia (Far East) International Wood Industry Expo, which was grandly held at the Mudanjiang International Convention and Exhibition Center. Ms. Jia Xiulan's exhibited works received guidance and comments from veteran artists and were highly praised by leaders at all levels (Figure 2-4).

From August 22nd to 26th, 2013, Ms. Jia Xiulan led the embroiderers of Manembro Workshop to participate in the 8th China Heilongjiang International Cultural and Art Expo held at the Harbin International Convention and Exhibition Center. At the expo, the excellent performances of the skillful embroiderers from Manembro Workshop and the exquisite embroidery works they created won high praise and recognition from people from all walks of life (Figure 2-5).

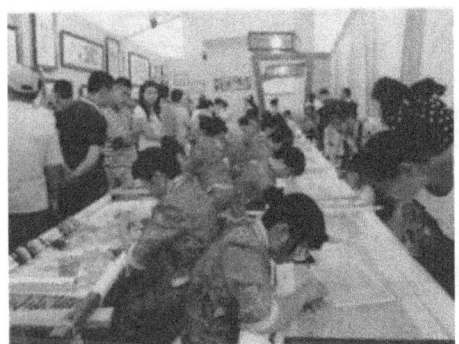

Figure 2-4 Participation in the 6th China (Mudanjiang)-Russia (Far East) International Wood Industry Expo

From October 18th to 20th, 2014, the World Crafts Culture Festival hosted by Dongyang City was held. The event was themed "Revitalize World Arts and Crafts, Inherit Minor Handicraft Skills, Develop Cultural and Creative Industries, and Jointly Create the Glory of Handicraft Labor". Through exhibitions, conferences, forums and other activities, it presented a prosperous, diverse, harmonious, lively and unrestrained atmosphere. Representatives from nearly 60 countries participated in the performances to showcase the cultural customs of their respective countries. As a folk handicraft organization in

Heilongjiang Province, Manembro Workshop was invited to participate and exhibited the distinctive Ningguta Manchu embroidery works at the expo, which attracted the attention of domestic and foreign peers and friends from all circles (Figure 2-6).

On July 11th, 2016, the Taiwan Affairs Office of the State Council invited a group of a thousand Taiwanese college students to participate in a summer camp on the Chinese mainland. The Taiwan Affairs Office of Heilongjiang Province arranged for 47 of them to visit and exchange ideas at the Ningguta Manchu Embroidery Museum (Figure 2-7).

On July 12th, 2017, Ningguta Manchu embroidery, as a representative of Heilongjiang Province in China, participated in the Astana Expo in Kazakhstan. As a business card of Heilongjiang Province, Ningguta Manchu embroidery displayed still-life and portrait works to countries around the world, presenting the beautiful scenery of Heilongjiang Province and expressing the hope to build a happy future together with people all over the world (Figure 2-8).

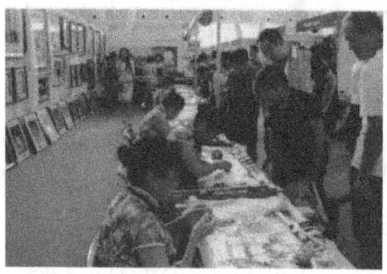

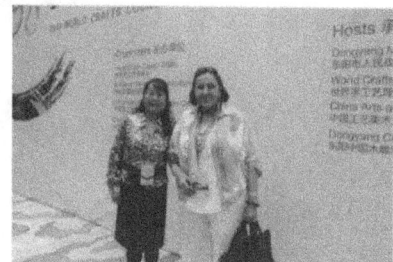

Figure 2-6 A Photo of Ms. Jia Xiulan (left) and Gada Sijiawei (right), the President of the Asia-Pacific Region of the World Crafts Council

Figure 2-5 Participation in the 8th Cultural and Art Expo

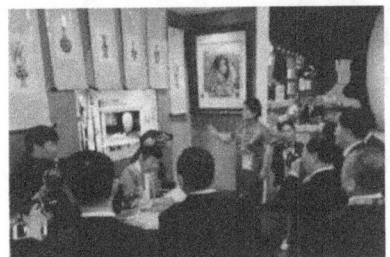

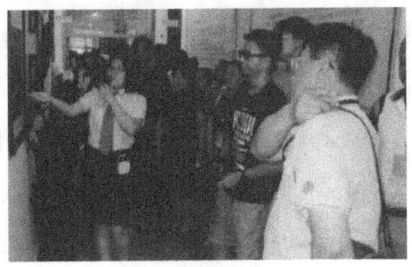

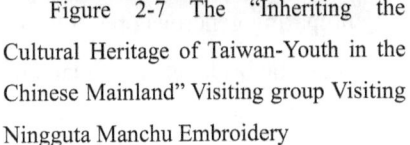

Figure 2-7 The "Inheriting the Cultural Heritage of Taiwan-Youth in the Chinese Mainland" Visiting group Visiting Ningguta Manchu Embroidery

Figure 2-8 Ms. Jia Xiulan Giving an Explanation at the Kazakhstan Expo

Section II Customs and Interesting Anecdotes

I. The Sedan Chair Hangers of "Daxiashu"

After a Manchu young man and woman fall in love, before marriage, the groom's family needs to send betrothal gifts (commonly known as "presenting betrothal gifts") to the bride's family, usually preparing generous ones. One day before the wedding, accompanied by bridesmaids, the bride takes a sedan chair to a pre-borrowed place near the groom's family to stay. There are two embroidered sedan chair hangers on both sides of the sedan chair (Figure 2-9). They are used to exorcise ghosts and evil spirits when the bride gets married, commonly known as "Daxiashu". The next day, the groom comes to the place where the bride is staying to fetch her. This custom is due to specific historical reasons. During the Qing Dynasty, soldiers were engaged in continuous battles and could not return home for years. Manchu women had to borrow a house near the military camp to wait for marriage. Over time, it became a custom.

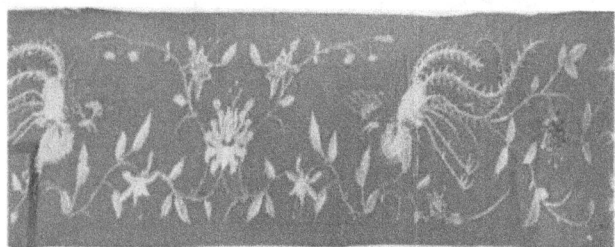

Figure 2-9 Sedan-Chair Hangers

II. The Indispensable Cloud-shaped Collar in Weddings

The cloud-shaped collar (Figure 2-10) originated and developed in the Sui Dynasty and became popular in the Qing Dynasty. During the Qing Dynasty, people from all social strata would wear cloud-shaped collars, which were especially a must-have for brides. There are mainly two shapes of cloud-shaped collars. One is in the shape of "sihe ruyi" (a kind of auspicious pattern), and the other is strip-shaped. Generally, it consists of eight hanging clouds in two layers, with patterns embroidered on each hanging cloud, either flowers, birds, insects or scenes from operas. There are many stitching methods for embroidering cloud-shaped collars, such as rolling stitch, looping stitch, pine-needle stitch, parallel stitch, joining stitch, satin stitch, French knot stitch, couching stitch, and gold-coiling stitch. The embroidered patterns include figures, animals, plants, bridges, etc. The curves are smooth, the stitches are fine, and the colors are elegant. It is a folk art. The "cloud - shaped collars" worn by women during the sacrifice to gods in the Qing Dynasty were very precious and were not shown to outsiders on ordinary days. They were only worn during the sacrifice to gods.

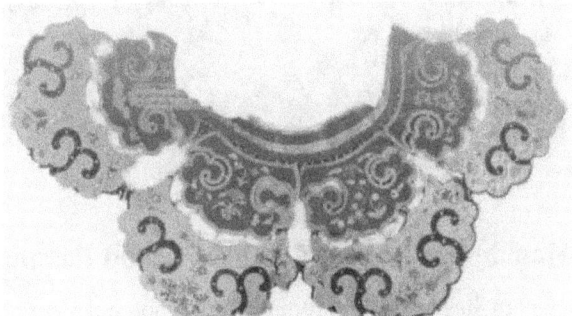

Figure 2-10 The Cloud-shaped Collar

III. The "Family Heirloom" Pillow Tops

Pillow tops (Figure 2-11) are typical Manchu "women's chamber" embroidery and one of the intarsia arts. Every Manchu pillow top is a precious Manchu heirloom and a magnificent flower in China's ethnic embroidery art. Traditionally, Manchu pillow tops mostly use the four colors representing the eight banners of the Manchu as the basic tones. The composition is elegant, and the colors are bright, fully showing the Manchu beliefs, folk customs, and mythological legends of different periods. Pillow tops record the joys and sorrows of generations of Manchus. Even one pillow top may tell a story and is a form of historical record of the Manchu people. For example, pillow tops embroidered with patterns like "Snow in June", "Peony and Phoenix", "Sweet-scented Osmanthus Filling the Hall", "Lotus Bearing Seeds", "Liu Hai Playing with the Golden Toad" have a history of more than a hundred years, reflecting the Manchu ancestors' ideas that all things have spirits, the unity of heaven and man, and the harmony between man and nature.

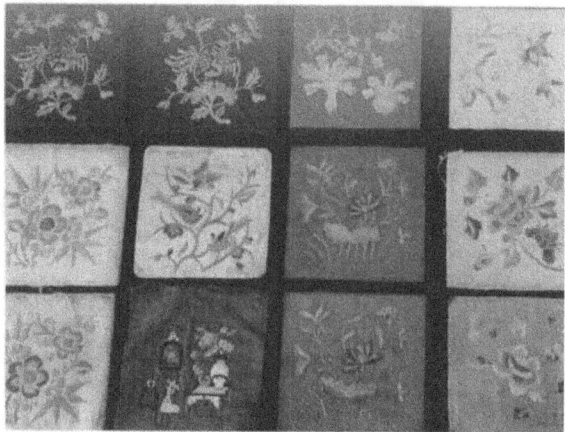

Figure 2-11 Pillow Tops

IV. Filling Manchu Embroidery with Love and Passing It on

Ms. Jia Xiulan has many apprentices. She not only devotes herself to teaching Ningguta Manchu embroidery but also cares about them in daily life. Whenever her students encounter difficulties, she tries her best to help them. Among her apprentices, there are several prominent figures who are deaf-mutes. Ms. Jia started teaching them embroidery when they were in their teens, leading them to support themselves and improve their living conditions. Moreover, she let them live in her home and subsidized them every month. When the students got married, she provided them with all the help she could, and even took the initiative to act as a matchmaker to help them achieve a happy marriage. The apprentices are sincerely grateful to her.

Section III Production Materials and Tools

The materials and tools required for Ningguta Manchu embroidery are quite common, mainly including embroidery cloth, embroidery needles, embroidery threads, embroidery frames, scissors, pens, etc.

I. Embroidery Cloth

For Ningguta Manchu embroidery, the embroidery cloth (Figure 2-12) mostly uses solid-colored fabrics, with white and black being the most commonly used. Embroiderers will select the appropriate fabric material and color according to the style and purpose of the works.

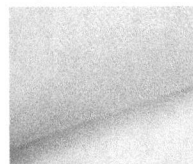

Figure 2-12 Embroidery Cloth

II. Embroidery Needles

Embroidery needles (Figure 2-13) are the most commonly used tools in embroidery. Generally, there are two types: one is the pointed-tip needle, and the other is the round-tip needle. The pointed-tip needle is the most commonly used in Ningguta embroidery. If the embroidery cloth is a fabric with fine holes, the round-tip needle should be selected.

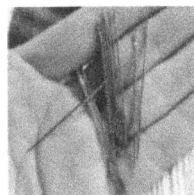

Figure 2-13 Embroidery Needles

III. Embroidery Threads

The commonly used embroidery threads (Figure 2-14) in Ningguta Manchu embroidery are generally two types: pure-cotton embroidery threads and ply yarns. The pure-cotton fine embroidery thread is composed of a single strand of yarn and can also be plied. There are about 40 color systems, and each color system is divided into 6-9 color gradations. The ply yarn is composed of six strands of yarn, which has a natural luster and elegant colors, and each color system of the embroidery thread contains a gray component. Both silk threads and tussah silk threads are suitable for embroidery on soft base fabrics such as soft satin, and can also be used for double-sided embroidery on glass silk gauze (a very thin and transparent gauze specifically used for double-sided embroidery).

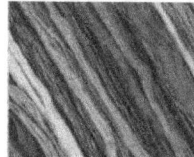

Figure 2-14 Embroidery Threads

IV. Embroidery Frames

Nowadays, Ningguta Manchu embroidery is often used to create large-scale paintings, so embroidery frames are very commonly used. The upper part of the embroidery frame is an embroidery hoop, which is used to fix the embroidery cloth. Only when the embroidery cloth is fixed can a flat and non-deformed embroidery be created. One side of the embroidery hoop usually holds the required embroidery threads. The embroidery frame is shown in Figure 2-15.

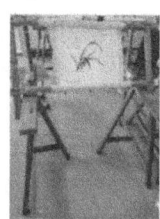

Figure 2-15 Embroidery Frame

V. Pen

Pens (Figure 2-16) are used for tracing the pattern. Generally, before starting to embroider, embroiderers will draw the design on the selected embroidery cloth.

VI. Scissors

Scissors (Figure 2-17) are the most basic and common tools in embroidery, which are used for cutting.

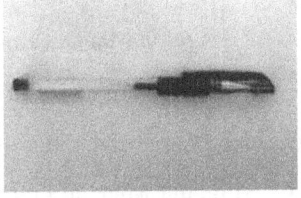 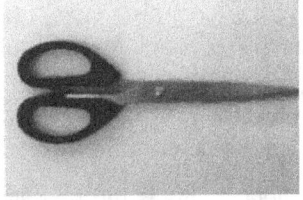

Figure 2-16 A Pen   Figure 2-17 Scissors

Section IV Production Process and Techniques

The procedures of Ningguta Manchu embroidery are complex and mainly rely on manual work. The main technological process is shown in Figure 2-18.

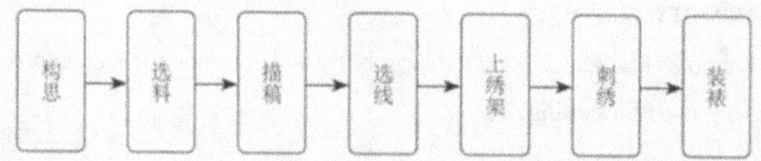

Figure 2-18 Technological Process of Ningguta Manchu Embroidery

I. Conception

The embroiderer needs to first conceive the pattern, color and purpose of the embroidery. This is the first step of Ningguta Manchu embroidery. If the embroiderer doesn't have a general idea of the pattern in mind, she won't be able to create a good work.

II. Material Selection

Material selection (Figure 2-19) means that after the conception, the embroiderer will choose the appropriate embroidery cloth according to the conceived pattern. Different embroidery cloths have different requirements for needles, threads and patterns. Only when the embroidery cloth is paired with the corresponding needles, threads and patterns can a good work be embroidered.

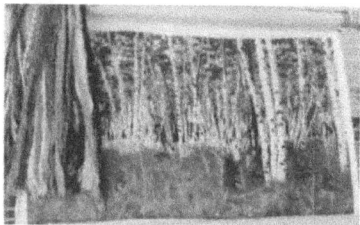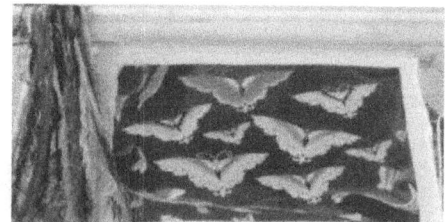

Figure 2-19 Material Selection

III. Pattern Tracing

Pattern tracing (Figure 2-20) refers to the process of the embroiderer lightly tracing the conceived pattern on the embroidery cloth before embroidery. The structure of the drawn pattern should be reasonable so that the embroidered work will be natural and vivid.

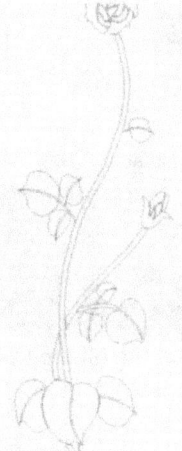

Figure 2-20 Pattern Tracing

IV. Thread Selection

Thread selection (Figure 2-21) means choosing appropriate embroidery threads according to the pattern and purpose conceived by the embroiderer to prepare for the next step. For each color system of embroidery threads, two more color gradations should be selected so that the embroidered work will look natural and beautiful with a uniform transition, and the work will be as delicate as a photo.

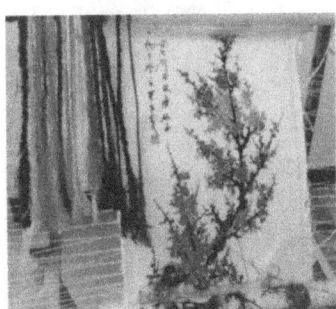

Figure 2-21 Thread Selection

V. Mounting on the Embroidery Frame

Mounting on the embroidery frame (Figure 2-22) is to place the embroidery cloth on the embroidery frame after the embroidery cloth and threads are selected. In this way, the embroidered work will be flat and even.

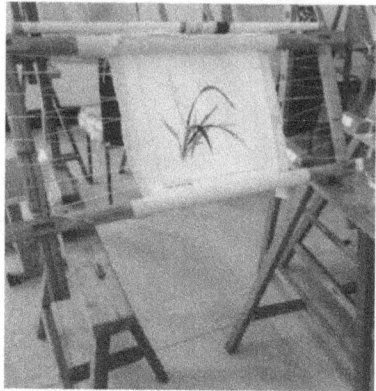

Figure 2-22 Mounting on the Embroidery Frame

VI. Embroidery

Embroidery (Figure 2-23) is the next process after the embroiderer finishes tracing the pattern. During embroidery, one should keep calm so that the stitches of the embroidered work will be delicate.

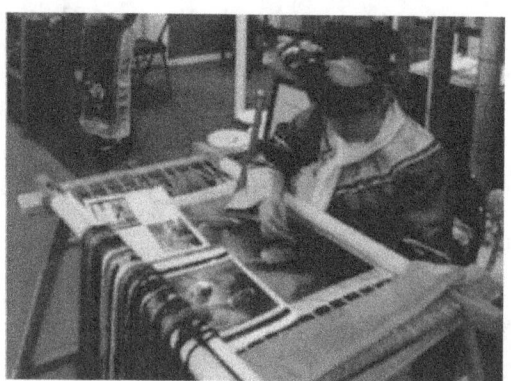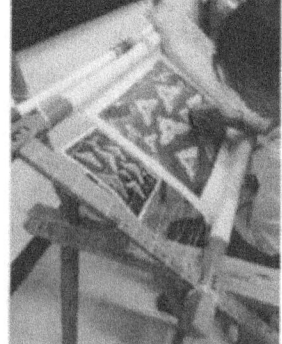

Figure 2-23 Embroidery

VII. Mounting

Mounting involves selecting an appropriate mounting method according to the different uses of the work. This helps to better preserve the work. The mounted work is shown in Figure 2-24.

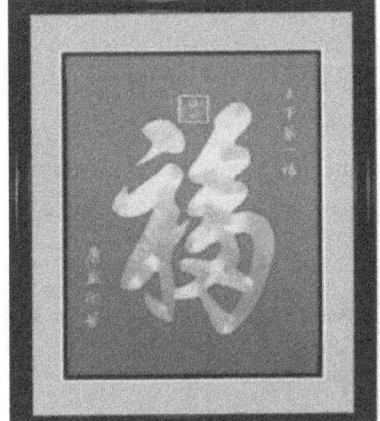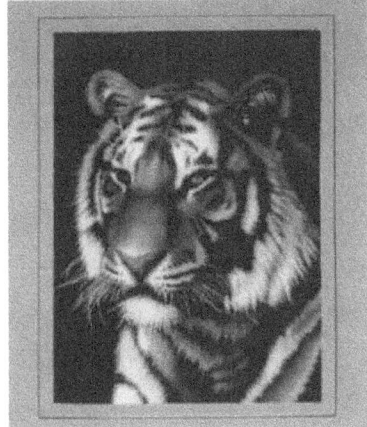

Figure 2-24 Mounting

Section V Process Characteristics and Patterns

Since ancient times, hand embroidery has always been deeply loved by people, and it was especially popular in the Qing Dynasty. In people's lives, from emperors and concubines to ordinary families, Ningguta Manchu embroidery could be found in what they wore and used. Therefore, Ningguta Manchu embroidery has become the most distinctive representative of the Manchu ethnic group and has endured over time. Ningguta Manchu embroidery stands alone in the treasure house of Chinese national art. After being passed down and carried forward by several generations of artisans, it has become a gem in the intangible cultural heritage of contemporary China and has strong dissemination and collection value.

I. Process Characteristics

Ningguta Manchu embroidery originated from the nail-stitching technique of the Jurchen people in the Jin Dynasty. Nail-stitching was a simple and rough folk handicraft used by Jurchen women to decorate hunting arrow bags and saddle cushions. At first, it was a "mark" to prevent people from taking the wrong hunting tools after resting and having meals during hunting. Later, it gradually developed into a handicraft art. Nail-stitching uses white coarse cloth and white leather as the backing. Coarse black lines are embroidered on the four edges of the material, creating a "sharp contrast between black and white". The patterns are distinct in black and white, with clear lines, a rough and powerful style, natural harmony and great charm.

Ningguta Manchu embroidery has strong and rich ethnic and regional characteristics. Its shapes are exaggerated and rough, yet gentle and kind. The colors are bright, with a contrast between warm and cold tones, expressing simple emotions. It often uses needles as brushes and threads as colors, with even stitches and clear textures. Its brushwork encompasses various painting arts such as Chinese painting, fine-brush painting, sketching and oil painting. The stitching techniques include flat stitching, long stitching, tapestry stitching, reverse stitching, chain stitching, gold-thread embroidery, double-satin stitching and so on.

II. Patterns

Ningguta Manchu embroidery inherits the folk art of Jurchen nail-stitching and has made new developments. In terms of color selection, it not only inherits the Jurchen's feature of using black threads but also learns and absorbs the Han people's feature of using a variety of colored threads. In the selection of backing materials and colors, Ningguta Manchu embroidery has changed the Jurchen's custom of using white coarse cloth and white leather as the backing and has learned to use colored cloth as the backing from Han embroidery. In the design of embroidery works, there are not only lace but also relatively complete patterns of flowers, birds, fish and water, forming its own embroidery characteristics.

The themes of Ningguta Manchu embroidery include landscapes, flowers and birds, insects, beasts, figures, characters, etc. The embroidered works are vivid and lifelike. The animals seem to be alive, the flowers appear fragrant and charming, the figures are extremely realistic as if they are about to step out, and the landscapes are vivid and beautiful.

Section VI Appreciation of Works

There are a total of six series of Ningguta Manchu embroidery works, including the humanities series, still-life series, lively-interest series, landscape series, flower series, and religious series. Here are several works by Ms. Jia Xiulan.

I. Humanities Series

Ms. Jia Xiulan is very good at embroidering figures. Her works include *Meditation, Tibetan Girl* (Figure 2-25), and *Mother* (Figure 2-26). In October 2017, the work *Tibetan Girl* won the special prize in the First-Session Creative Fine Arts Exhibition of "Innovation, Creation, and Entrepreneurship" in Mudanjiang.

Seeing off the Prince of Bohai on His Return to His Country (Figure 2-27) is selected from the poem of the same name by Wen Tingyun. As a local regime conferred by the Tang Empire, the Bohai State once established its capital in Aocheng (southeast of present-day Dunhua, Jilin). Aocheng was the initial political, economic, and cultural center of the Bohai State. There were frequent exchanges, learning, and trade between Bohai and the Tang Dynasty. In particular, Bohai was very yearning for Chinese culture. For example, "It sent many students to the Imperial College in the capital to learn about ancient and modern systems" (from *New Book of Tang: Biography of Bohai*). It sent literati to Chang'an many times to copy historical and political documents such as *Book of Han, Records of the Three Kingdoms, Book of Jin, Spring and Autumn of the Thirty-Six Kingdoms*, and *Rites of Tang*. Princes and noble children of Bohai flocked to the Central Plains to study, and some of them became officials in the Tang Dynasty after passing the imperial examinations. Most of the officials and envoys of Bohai were good at writing memorials in Chinese. In the close exchanges between Bohai and the Tang Dynasty, the affection of the people of the Tang Dynasty for the people of Bohai deepened. This picture depicts the scene when Wen Tingyun reluctantly bid farewell to the Prince of Bohai who was returning to his country after completing his studies. On September 29, 2015, *Seeing off the Prince of Bohai on His Return to His Country* won the first prize in the First-Session Creative Competition of Hand-knitted Cultural and Tourist Souvenirs in Mudanjiang.

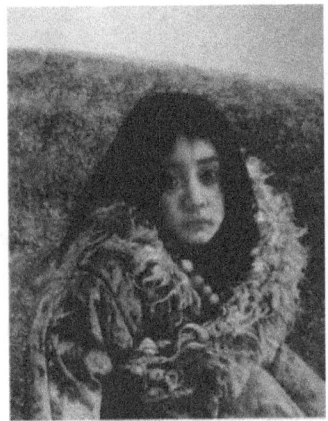
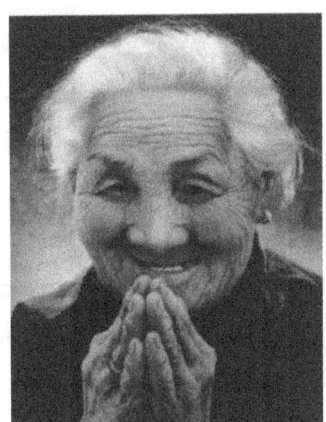

Figure 2-25 *Tibetan Girl*   Figure 2-26 *Mother*

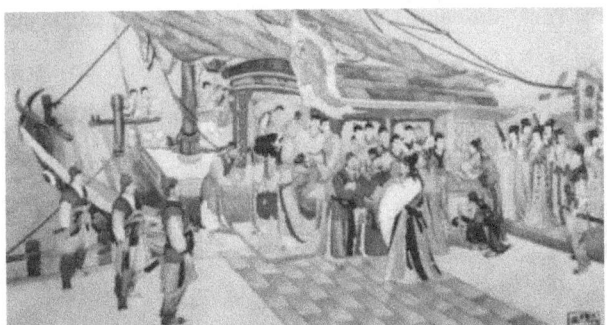

Figure 2-27 *Seeing off the Prince of Bohai on His Return to His Country*

II. Still-life Series

The Tripod (Figure 2-28) is one of Ms. Jia Xiulan's works. During the Bronze Age, the tripod symbolized power and was a significant national treasure. In the Zhou Dynasty, casting a tripod meant a major celebration or a court official receiving a reward from the king.

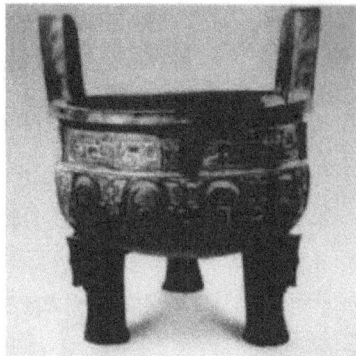

Figure 2-28 The Tripod

III. Lively-interest Series

In *Mother Monkey and Baby Monkey* (Figure 2-29), the baby monkey huddles tightly in the arms of the mother monkey, and the mother monkey encircles the baby monkey with her arms. The baby monkey shows a bit of fear but mostly looks innocent. This work makes people feel the strong motherly love. Bald Eagle (Figure 2-30), also known as the American eagle, is a large raptor and an endemic species in North America. It is the national bird of the United States. The bald eagle has very distinct features: pale-yellow eyes and beak, white head and neck, and a dark-brown body. It looks very majestic.

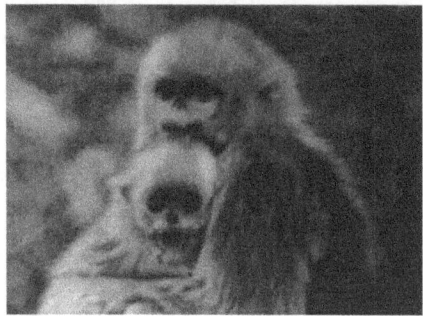 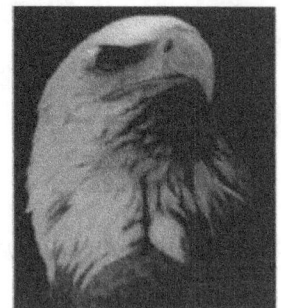

Figure 2-29 *Mother Monkey and Baby Monkey*   Figure 2-30 *Bald Eagle*

IV. Flower Series

Flowers in Full Bloom Bringing Prosperity (Figure 2-31): The inner diameter is 166cm × 83cm, and the outer diameter is 220cm × 120cm. It took

368 days to embroider, using the techniques of random-stitch embroidery and fine-flat embroidery. In this work, the stitches are short, there are many colors, with changes in light and shade, layers inside and outside, and a sense of distance. The distant part is hazy, while the near part is clear. The combination of real and imaginary embroidery techniques makes it vivid and pleasing to the eye. One flower in bloom does not make spring; only when all flowers are in bloom can it be called spring. This picture shows a variety of flowers in full bloom, filled with the breath of spring, symbolizing the beauty, happiness, good luck, prosperity, and peace of spring.

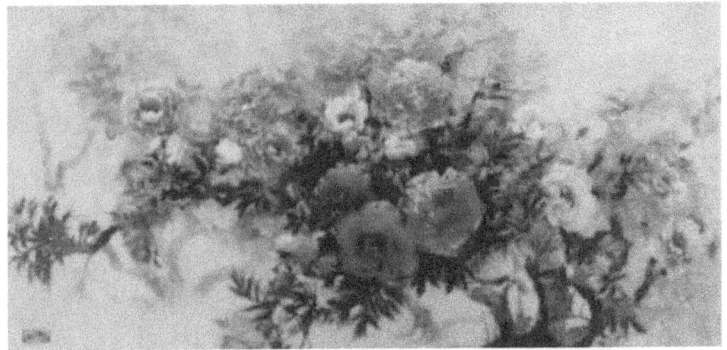

Figure 2-31 *Flowers in Full Bloom Bringing Prosperity*

V. Religious Series

Thousand-handed and Thousand-eyed Avalokitesvara (Figure 2-32): The inner diameter of the work is 84cm × 67cm, and the outer diameter is 120cm × 98cm. It took 198 days to complete, using a combination of flat-stitch embroidery and random-stitch embroidery, mainly the fine-flat embroidery technique. A total of 1315 different colors of threads were used for embroidery. "The Thousand-handed Avalokitesvara" is officially called "Thousand-handed and Thousand-eyed Avalokitesvara Bodhisattva" and is one of the six Avalokitesvaras in Buddhism.

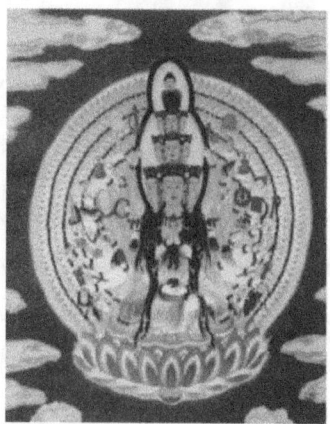

Figure 2-32 *Thousand-handed and Thousand-eyed Avalokitesvara*

Section VII Interviews with Inheritors

I. May I ask: How did you embark on the path of inheriting Ningguta embroidery?

Ms. Jia: I grew up in a family of Manchu embroidery. I started learning embroidery from my mother when I was 10 years old, and at 16, I became an apprentice to Zhang Xueqin, the second-generation inheritor of Manchu embroidery. This embroidery art looks beautiful, but learning it is really a tough job. For example, when embroidering a person's skin, you need to split a thin embroidery thread into 16 strands and use one of them for embroidery. There are also more than 70 different embroidery stitches that need to be constantly changed... Pricking your fingers with the needle and being scolded by the master are all common occurrences. I embroidered continuously for eight years like this. Nevertheless, I still love embroidery.

II. May I ask: Why did you leave the training class and start your own business?

Ms. Jia: In 2005, I stepped back from the front-line position, and my leader arranged for me to work in Dongjingcheng, Ning'an City. During that period, I noticed that many women in the surrounding area were idle at home, wasting their time chatting, wandering around, and playing mahjong. I thought that if we could organize these women and provide them with training to learn some skills, they would have a way to make a living. So, I decided to take action right away. With the strong support of the labor and employment department and the Municipal Education Bureau, our labor skills training class finally started in the empty classrooms of Jingcheng High School in Dongjingcheng. Over the past four years, we have provided re-employment skills training for laid-off workers and rural surplus labor in six townships and towns, namely Dongjingcheng Town, Shalan Town, Bohai Town, Mahe Township, Wolong Township, and

Jingbo Township. The training courses cover about seven or eight professional skills, including computer skills, pastry-making, cooking, maternity nursing, traditional Chinese massage, etc. A total of 3,536 person-times participated in 16 training sessions, and the employment rate reached 75%. Now, most of the trainees have found their own jobs. For example, Xu Haiying from the pastry-making class opened a steamed bun shop, and Zhang Fengying from the computer class opened a lottery ticket store. Many trainees from the maternity nursing class were sent to maternity nurse agencies in Beijing after graduation. They could earn 6,000 yuan in their first month, and some top-rated maternity purses could earn about 10,000 yuan a month. There are so many such success stories. In this way, the training base ignited my entrepreneurial passion. I felt much younger. It was this passion that later helped me achieve success with my Manchu embroidery workshop.

III. May I ask: What are some unforgettable experiences you had when establishing the Manembro Workshop?

Ms. Jia: To run the embroidery workshop well, I went to Dayilan Manchu Township many times to learn from the 82-year-old veteran embroiderer, Chen Yuhua. When I found the 103-year-old Ms. Wang Zhiyin, a folk master of Mudanjiang embroidery culture, I felt like I had found a precious treasure. The old lady has good hearing and eyesight and never needs to draw patterns when embroidering. I studied Manchu embroidery with her.

To make the embroidery workshop develop rapidly, I went to the south of the Yangtze River five times, visiting places like Shanghai and Suzhou to learn from them. At that time, relying only on a little information from the Internet, I rushed to a small village in the south for an inspection. I walked more than 40 li on foot in the heavy rain to reach the place. People in the south like to plant trees, and there were few people on the long shaded path. I really felt lonely and scared at that time. Everyone in that village was engaged in embroidery, and every family was doing embroidery work in the plastic sheds they built. I was shocked when I saw this scene. I went from house to house to observe and didn't even remember to eat. Once, I was so hungry that my stomach was sticking to my back and my legs were weak. Fortunately, a local person gave me two fruits to relieve my hunger.

Entrepreneurship is not always smooth sailing. The embroidery workshop encountered financial difficulties during its development. To pay the employees, I sold all my jewelry and used my husband's 120,000-yuan housing reform fund that he got after retirement. I distributed the money in just three days. My husband said helplessly, "Couldn't you let me hold the money for a while to feel its warmth?" Now, the sisters all regard the embroidery workshop as their home and share weal and woe with me. When there is a need for funds for new product research and development and marketing, the sisters contribute 30,000 yuan or 20,000 yuan from their private savings.

In fact, every entrepreneur's journey is difficult and bitter. However, with the passion for entrepreneurship and persistent perseverance, every entrepreneur starts from scratch and carves out their own path.

IV. May I ask: How do you cultivate inheritors of Ningguta Manchu embroidery?

Ms. Jia: Most of my embroiderers are rural women. They don't have a high level of education and no embroidery foundation at all. I treat them like primary school students and train and shape them from scratch. I hire experts and professors at high salaries to give lectures. For those with a little foundation, I take them to Jingpo Lake and the Underground Forest to sketch, so that they can personally experience the colors of nature. I teach them face-to-face and hand-in-hand.

To build a team of embroiderers with culture, good manners, and the ability to cooperate, I also hold etiquette training classes to spread the essence of traditional Chinese culture to them and teach them to respect the elderly and love their relatives. At present, we have trained more than 2,300 trainees, and there are more than 800 cooperative embroiderers. As the scale of the embroidery workshop grows and the overall quality of the embroiderers improves, I want our Manchu culture to go national and international. So I invited the professional team of Mudanjiang Haina Media to plan and produce a promotional video for the embroidery workshop, print brochures, and place free-learning advertisements on TV. I also lead the embroiderers to participate in major domestic and international exhibitions and various competitions. Our works have won awards from the municipal, provincial, and national levels to international awards. They are not only popular among domestic customers but also sold to countries such as Russia, the United States, Canada, Togo, and Japan. Our Manchu embroidery culture has finally gone global!

V. May I ask: Could you talk about the current development of the Manembro Workshop?

Ms. Jia: Since 2016, Ningguta Manchu embroidery has entered Ning'an Experimental Primary School. Over the four-year period, more than 200 primary school students have learned Ningguta Manchu embroidery skills. Since 2018, we have cooperated with Ning'an Vocational Education Center to recruit students for the Ningguta Manchu embroidery class. We have invested more than 700,000 yuan, and there is an 80-square-meter embroidery classroom, a 420-square-meter Ningguta Manchu embroidery exhibition hall, an 80-square-meter product storage room, a 60-square-meter seminar meeting room, and a Manchu embroidery inheritance classroom with 50 embroidery frames, equipped with multimedia teaching equipment, which can accommodate 50 students to have classes at the same time. Currently, there are 32 students learning, and the cumulative number of elective students has reached 530. It has formed a continuous and normalized vocational course for the teaching of intangible cultural heritage, effectively promoting the in-depth integration of intangible cultural heritage projects and education.

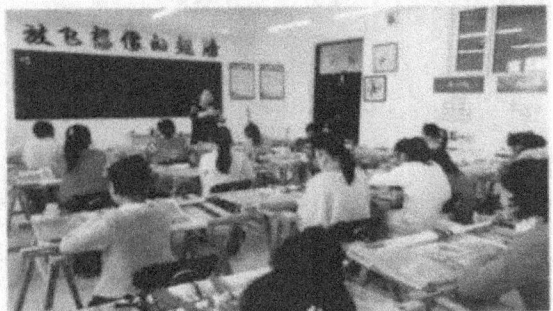

Figure 2-33 Jia Xiulan Having the Class

VI. May I ask: What are your expectations for the future development of Ningguta Manchu embroidery?

Ms. Jia: Over the past eight years, the Manchu embroidery workshop has grown from a small handicraft workshop with a registered capital of 1 million yuan to a brand-culture enterprise integrating operation, research and development, production, processing, and sales. Ningguta Manchu embroidery has been listed as an intangible cultural heritage of Heilongjiang Province. I believe this art will develop better in the future. I hope that more excellent embroiderers will join us in the future!

Section VIII Current Situation and Countermeasures of Inheritance

I. Current Situation of Inheritance

Under the leadership of Ms. Jia Xiulan, the prospects of the Manchu embroidery workshop are getting better and better. The workshop is located in Ning'an City, adjacent to the beautiful Jingpo Lake, which is the birthplace of the Bohai State culture and Manchu culture. In recent years, more than 4,800 trainees have been trained in Manchu embroidery, and there are more than 860 cooperative embroiderers. Currently, it is also cooperating with the Ning'an Vocational Education Center to recruit students for the Ningguta Manchu Embroidery Class.

Ms. Jia Xiulan's works have been exhibited at home and abroad many times and have been well-received by people from all walks of life. Although Ms. Jia has many apprentices, few can reach her level of embroidery.

II. Inheritance Problems

1. Insufficient Advertising and Promotion

To promote the Ningguta Manchu embroidery culture, not only inheritors but also advertising and promotion are needed. As major tourist provinces, the three northeastern provinces often promote their tourist attractions during TV advertising time, but rarely promote Ningguta Manchu embroidery as a tourist attraction. It is difficult to see relevant advertisements on TV or video apps, let alone the sponsorship of TV programs by Manchu embroidery enterprises such as the Manchu embroidery workshop. Moreover, there are few articles about Ningguta Manchu embroidery on websites or WeChat official accounts, not to mention interviews with its inheritors. There is also no use of modern new media for promotion. Although the embroidery products of Ningguta Manchu embroidery are of good quality, shine at various exhibitions, and have attracted the attention of some relevant people, they have not been popularized among the general public.

2. Inadequate Industrialization

Although the Manchu embroidery workshop has been established for nearly ten years and obtains some funds through the support of local schools and by providing works and customization services at major exhibitions, its current focus is on inheriting this traditional handicraft. It aims to let people know about the traditional handicraft of Ningguta Manchu embroidery by running training courses and school elective courses, and to increase its domestic and international popularity by participating in various competitions and relevant exhibitions, hoping that people will gradually understand Ningguta Manchu embroidery through these two ways. However, the training courses and elective courses are basically non-profit. In the short term, the company can sustain itself, but in the long term, it will be difficult to continue. In addition, the lack of a clear pricing standard for the works is also an urgent problem to be solved. Therefore, only by truly industrializing Ningguta Manchu embroidery can it be preserved in the long run.

3. Shortage of Successive Talents

One of the key points in the protection of intangible cultural heritage is the protection of inheritors. Oral transmission and living inheritance are the prominent features of the inheritance of handicrafts. Video and audio recordings and written records cannot fully represent the features of Ningguta Manchu embroidery. If there are no successors for Ningguta Manchu embroidery, the inheritance of this traditional handicraft will face the risk of a break. Moreover, the cultural level of inheritors also has an impact on the inheritance of intangible cultural heritage.

Currently, the Manchu embroidery workshop consists of Ms. Jia Xiulan, cooperative embroiderers, and interested students. Although Ms. Jia has her own apprentices, they are all relatively old. In addition, except for Ms. Jia, who studied music and aesthetics during her undergraduate and postgraduate years and has a relatively deep understanding of art and creative inspiration, there are few teachers who have both theoretical knowledge and skill literacy in Manchu embroidery. Therefore, an embroiderer team with high-level skills and a good theoretical foundation has not been established, and it is impossible to provide both theoretical and practical teaching and guidance. For an inheritance organization that needs long-term development, this unstable situation needs to be resolved urgently. Ningguta Manchu embroidery needs to balance product efficiency and ensure that each work has its own unique charm.

III. Countermeasures of Inheritance

1. Strengthening Promotion Efforts

To ensure that Ningguta Manchu embroidery is widely and deeply known to the public, it is recommended that: On the one hand, combine modern advanced technological media to ensure in-place online promotion and increase the popularity of Ningguta Manchu embroidery. First, produce some beautiful promotional videos on the website of the Manchu embroidery workshop, covering some basic knowledge of Manchu embroidery, and upload relevant pictures and production videos of Manchu embroidery art, so that younger people who are more proficient in online operations can access it. Second, insert some embroidery advertisements on the website to gradually increase people's familiarity with Manchu embroidery. An app about Ningguta Manchu embroidery can also be developed to provide a more convenient and modern way for people to learn about Ningguta Manchu embroidery and offer a good platform for people to get in touch with it. At the same time, platforms such as Weibo, WeChat, and Douyin can be utilized to popularize knowledge about Ningguta Manchu embroidery and release theme activities related to it. On the other hand, it can be combined with the tourism industry for offline promotion. In recent years, the tourism industry in Heilongjiang Province has been booming, which is a good sign. Since the tourism industry can develop, so can Ningguta

Manchu embroidery. First, a more commercialized Manchu embroidery street or a dedicated commercial street or tourist area full of Manchu embroidery can be built. Designs with Ningguta Manchu embroidery elements can be added to ubiquitous billboards, roadside publicity columns, and cultural activity squares. Second, the severe cold in the three northeastern provinces is well-known. Every winter, tourists from all over the country come to enjoy the snow scenery in the Northeast. On the basis of saving budget costs and showing the unique charm of the Northeast, themed exhibitions can be held. Beautiful embroidery works can be projected on ice sculptures to create a participatory and characteristic tourist landscape in the Northeast. During the exhibition, visitors can experience the charm of Ningguta Manchu embroidery, make Ningguta Manchu embroidery by hand, and the results of their participation can be displayed both online and offline. Third, the government can encourage relevant cultural departments to jointly hold art exhibitions, and jointly display with other Manchu embroidery works in the Northeast. At the exhibition site, the public can be encouraged to interact with Ningguta Manchu embroidery artists. Through live broadcasts or re-broadcasts, more tourists can be attracted to Heilongjiang and even the Northeast.

In addition, the media marketing of cultural and creative products can be learned from. For example, the cultural and creative products of the Forbidden City have been very popular in the past two years. The Forbidden City not only promotes its products in the cultural and creative museum but also on the Taobao online platform, thus expanding sales channels. The Forbidden City also creates Q-version dolls of many famous historical figures to attract public attention. Its WeChat official account not only conducts text promotion but also incorporates cultural and creative products, arousing readers' interest in purchasing. Moreover, the Forbidden City actively interacts with the audience to get closer to the public. Ningguta Manchu embroidery can also develop in this direction. By learning from successful cases like the Forbidden City and focusing on the quality of embroidery products, Ningguta Manchu embroidery will surely achieve long-term and good development.

2. Productive Protection

According to the *Classification of Cultural and Related Industries (2018)* standard issued by the National Bureau of Statistics, cultural and related industries are divided into eight categories. In the "Content Preservation Service" of "Content Creation and Production", the protection of cultural relics and intangible cultural heritage is included, indicating that intangible cultural heritage has been included in the field of cultural industries. This standard emphasizes the protection and management of heritage, and reasonable application is based on protection. Heritage is a non-renewable resource. If heritage is directly developed into a cultural industry, it is not conducive to the sustainable development of heritage. We should protect it rather than damage it. Cultural and creative industries can be developed, such as the industrialization of derivatives with heritage elements.

The author suggests planning a specific area to establish a Manchu embroidery handicraft base, which can include not only Ningguta Manchu embroidery. Professional embroidery masters can do on-site manual embroidery to create embroidery works that machines cannot match. There are three reasons for this: First, it can provide a venue for the production and sales of hand-embroidered products. Second, while allowing tourists to witness the whole process of manual Manchu embroidery production on the spot, they can also participate in making Manchu embroidery products by hand, hoping that tourists can fall in love with this traditional handicraft while experiencing the profound skills of Ningguta Manchu embroidery. Third, establishing a handicraft base can not only increase the income of the tourism industry but also encourage more people to join in the inheritance and learning of Ningguta Manchu embroidery and solve the employment problem of some people.

Break the single-mode of traditional tourism, increase the cultural connotation of tourism projects, and integrate cultural products of intangible cultural heritage into the tourism industry while tourists are enjoying the scenery. Since Ningguta Manchu embroidery is mainly developed in the Northeast, the three northeastern provinces should make every effort to develop Ningguta Manchu embroidery products, make the Ningguta Manchu embroidery culture well-known, and attract consumers with its unique artistic charm and distinct ethnic cultural characteristics.

3. Promoting Talent Cultivation

In view of the decreasing number of Ningguta Manchu embroidery craftsmen and their scattered and un-scaled state, as well as the lack of a systematic compilation of Manchu embroidery skills and stitches, the author suggests that: First, Ningguta Manchu embroidery craftsmen should be gathered as soon as possible. Combining their own embroidery experience, the embroidery methods of their predecessors, and the research results of experts, the skills of Ningguta Manchu embroidery should be systematically and completely recorded and bound into books for people to learn. Second, not only should laid-off workers be re-employed, but also college graduates, especially senior talents in art design, should be recruited into the Manchu embroidery workshop. Some general universities and vocational colleges offering cultural and creative majors should add elective courses on traditional skills such as Ningguta Manchu embroidery, so that more young people with innovative and creative design abilities can understand and love Ningguta Manchu embroidery and be committed to its inheritance, protection, and innovation.

References

[1] Yunjian dug out of mother-in-law's mother-in-law's old trunk [OL]. https://www.docin.com/p-322394938. html.

[2] Classification of cultural and related industries (2018) [OL].

http://www.stats.gov.cn/tjsj/tjbz/201805/t20180509_1598314. html.

[3] Zhang Jingming, Yang Chenxia. "Analysis of the Industrialization Prospect and Development Path of Intangible Cultural Heritage Derivatives of Arts: from the Development Status of Cultural Industry in Liaoning Province" [J]. *Journal of Tonghua Normal University*, 2016, 37 (3): 13-18.

Chapter III Xiuyan Manchu Folk Embroidery

Xiuyan Manchu Folk Embroidery is an embroidery art that has been passed down among the Manchu people in Xiuyan Manchu Autonomous County, Liaoning Province. It originated from Manchu embroidery and was influenced by Han culture during the more than a thousand years when the Manchus settled in Xiuyan. Eventually, it formed the unique Xiuyan Manchu folk embroidery. The techniques of Xiuyan Manchu folk embroidery are distinctive, and the embroidered works feature a bold and unrestrained style. They fully demonstrate the artistic creativity and enthusiasm of the Manchu people in Xiuyan and vividly showcase the local folk customs of the Xiuyan area. In June 2008, Xiuyan Manchu folk embroidery was officially included in the second batch of the National Intangible Cultural Heritage Representative Project List by the Ministry of Culture of the People's Republic of China, and it belongs to the category of traditional fine arts (Table 3-1). Ms. Wu Limei, the inheritor, was recognized as the municipal-level representative inheritor of the national intangible cultural heritage project of Xiuyan Manchu folk embroidery in June 2019 (Figure 3-1).

Table 3-1 Introduction to Xiuyan Manchu Folk Embroidery

Directory Name	Manchu Embroidery - Xiuyan Manchu Folk Embroidery
Directory Category	Traditional Fine Arts
Directory Level	National
Declaration Unit or Region	Xiuyan Manchu Autonomous County, Liaoning Province
Municipal Inheritance Representative	Wu Limei

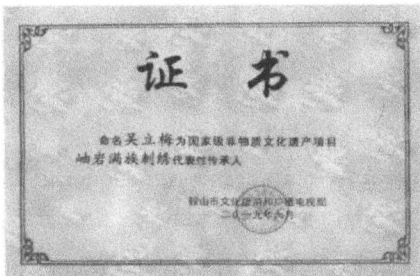

Figure. 3-1 Certificate of Representative Inheritor of Xiuyan Manchu Folk Embroidery

Section I Origin and Development

The Manchu folk embroidery in the Xiuyan area features a wide variety of patterns and emphasizes exquisite designs. It focuses on expressing the spirit rather than merely depicting the form, and pays attention to symmetrical and balanced compositions. The works not only boast a high-level of artistry but also showcase the simple folk customs of the Manchu ancestors and the life wisdom of Manchu women in Xiuyan. With needles as their brushes and threads as colors, Manchu women in Xiuyan have painted magnificent epic-like pictures and left a large number of artistic treasures for the world [2].

I. Origin and Development of Xiuyan Manchu Folk Embroidery

As one of the oldest ethnic minorities in China, the Manchu ethnic group has integrated the cultures of the Han, Mongolian, Hui and other ethnic groups during its inheritance process, forming a unique Manchu culture. According to historical records, in 1635, Huang Taiji proclaimed himself emperor in the Dazheng Hall, established the Qing Dynasty as the national title and changed the ethnic name to Manchu. Since then, court embroidery and folk embroidery have been collectively referred to as Manchu embroidery. Manchu embroidery emphasizes practicality and is mostly used for daily necessities and clothing. Among them, the most numerous surviving works are pillow-top embroidery. The main materials for Manchu embroidery are silk and satin, supplemented by homespun cloth. There is a wide variety of embroidery patterns, including the sun, moon, stars, flowers, plants, fish, insects, and stories from traditional operas, which express the worship of nature and the yearning for a better life[2].

Xiuyan Manchu folk embroidery originated and developed in Xiuyan Manchu Autonomous County, Liaoning Province, with a history of nearly four hundred years. In ancient times, Manchu girls learned embroidery from a young age. A girl with good embroidery skills was considered dexterous and virtuous.

Exquisite embroidery handicrafts were the best gifts for her husband's relatives and neighbors after marriage. Xiuyan Manchu folk embroidery fully demonstrates the main features of the Manchu social life in the Xiuyan area and has research value in sociology, ethnography, and other fields [3].

II. Origin and Development of the Skills Inherited by Inheritors

The Xiuyan Manchu folk embroidery technique has a long history. It evolved from Manchu embroidery and was passed down from generation to generation by Manchu women living in the Xiuyan area, thus forming the Xiuyan Manchu embroidery technique. Manchu girls in Northeast China learned embroidery when they were unmarried. On the one hand, they embroidered daily necessities for family use; on the other hand, they embroidered a large number of pillow-tops, insoles and other items for their dowries. In ancient times, a new bride's dexterity and virtue were judged by her embroidery skills. After a new bride married into her husband's family, she would give the embroidered dowries she made in her boudoir as gifts to her husband's relatives and neighbors. Firstly, it was to gain a good impression, and secondly, it was to show off her delicate embroidery skills. Over time, this embroidery technique has been passed down in the Xiuyan area, giving rise to the Xiuyan Manchu folk embroidery technique.

Ms. Wu Limei (Figure 3-2), the representative inheritor of the Xiuyan Manchu folk embroidery technique, was born in Anshan, Liaoning in 1964. Influenced by her family since childhood, Ms. Wu Limei loved and studied the Xiuyan Manchu embroidery technique. In her childhood, she learned embroidery skills from her grandmother. As an adult, out of her love for embroidery and with the idea of better developing and inheriting Xiuyan Manchu embroidery, Ms. Wu Limei went to Suzhou in 2002 to professionally further her study of embroidery skills. In 2003, she returned to her hometown and founded Limei Embroidery Workshop (Figure 3-3), integrating Suzhou embroidery with Xiuyan Manchu embroidery and creating a large number of exquisite works. Ms. Wu Limei gradually made a name for herself in the field of inheriting and developing Xiuyan Manchu embroidery. On the one hand, she opened courses in Xiuyan Autonomous County to train Manchu embroidery students (Figure 3-4) and has taught more than 400 disciples in total. On the other hand, she actively promoted Xiuyan Manchu embroidery to the outside world. In 2012, Ms. Wu Limei held an exhibition of works from Limei Embroidery Workshop, displaying more than 100 Xiuyan Manchu embroidery works. Her superb skills and exquisite embroidery works have not only been purchased and collected by entrepreneurs and folk collectors but also exported to countries such as the UK, France, Japan, Russia, and New Zealand.

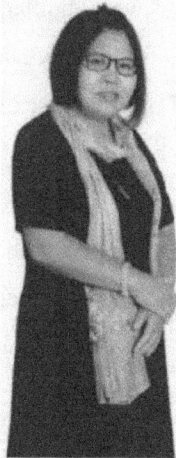

Figure 3-2 Ms. Wu Limei

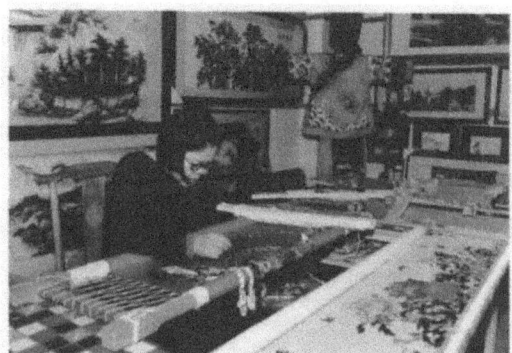

Figure 3-3 Ms. Wu Limei Embroidering in the Limei Embroidery Workshop
She Founded

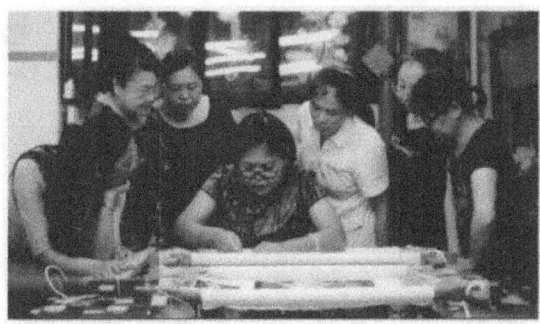

Figure 3-4 Ms. Wu Limei Teaching her Disciples to Embroidery

Ms. Wu Limei, with her positive attitude towards inheriting and developing the Xiuyan Manchu embroidery technique, was awarded the title of "Master of Arts and Crafts in Liaoning Province" by the People's Government of Liaoning Province in 2012. She is the vice-chairperson of the Anshan Arts and Crafts Association and the vice-chairperson of the Anshan Folk Artists Association. In addition, thanks to her excellent embroidery skills, her works have won many awards in major embroidery expositions. Among them, her work "Koi Carp" won the silver award at the Second "Hongshan Cup" Fine Arts Exposition in Liaoning Province in 2003, and "Oak Forest" won the silver award at the Third "Hongshan Cup" Arts and Crafts Exposition. In August 2016, her works participated in the "Splendor of Fingers" embroidery exchange activity between China and Russia and won an excellent award. Moreover, Ms. Wu Limei actively cooperates with universities to train inheritors of Xiuyan Manchu embroidery and showcases the charm of Xiuyan Manchu embroidery to university students. She has been employed as a special expert by Dalian University of the Arts, a guest professor at Liaoning Light Industry Vocational College, and a guest professor at Shenyang Normal University in Liaoning Province for the "Research and Training Program for Inheritors of Chinese Intangible Cultural Heritage". The "Xiuyan Manchu Embroidery Technique" courses she taught in many universities are popular among university students and have inspired their enthusiasm for the innovative development of Xiuyan

Manchu embroidery. On July 14, 2019, the unveiling ceremony of the "Manchu Embroidery Training Base of Wu Limei, Master of Arts and Crafts in Liaoning Province" was held at Liaoning Light Industry Vocational College (Figure 3-5) to carry out the cultivation work of Xiuyan Manchu embroidery, aiming to cultivate more high-quality talents who can combine Xiuyan Manchu embroidery with modern elements for innovative development in the future. See Table 3-2 for some of Ms. Wu's honors and award certificates.

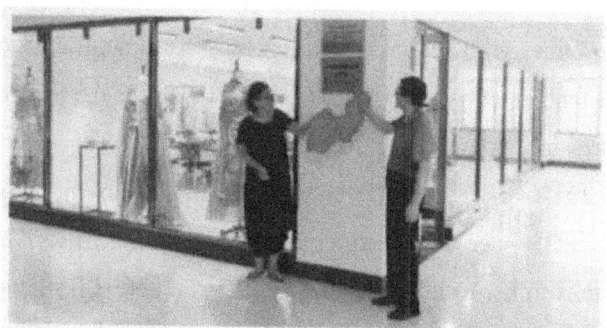

Figure 3-5 Bi Wanxin, Vice Dean of the Department of Textile and Apparel at Liaoning Vocational College of Light Industry and Wu Limei jointly are unveiling the Inheritance Base for Manchu Embroidery.

Table 3-2 Honors Awarded to Inheritor Ms. Wu Limei

Date	Awarding Institution	Award Description	Certificate Display
August 2010	Liaoning Arts and Crafts Industry Association	The work "Oak Grove" won an honorable mention at the 3rd "Hongshan Cup" Exposition of Fine Arts and Crafts.	
December 2012	Liaoning Provincial Economic and Information Commission	Ms. Wu Limei was awarded the title of Liaoning Arts and Crafts Master.	
October 2017	Dalian Art College	Ms. Wu Limei was invited to be a lecture expert for the 2017 National Art Fund Project "Training of Innovative Talents for Manchu Folk Handicrafts".	

October 2017	Dalian Art College	Ms. Wu Limei was invited to be a specially-appointed expert at Dalian Art College.	
June 2018	Wuhan Textile University	Ms. Wu Limei was rated as an outstanding trainee in the Folk Embroidery Training Class for Inheritors of Chinese Intangible Cultural Heritage.	
October 2018	Organizing Committee of the "New Journey, New Departure —— Contemporary Art Exhibition to Celebrate the 40th Anniversary of Reform and Opening up"	Ms. Wu Limei's works were selected to participate in the "New Journey, New Departure —— Contemporary Art Exhibition to Celebrate the 40th Anniversary of Reform and Opening up".	
June 2019	Organizing Committee of the Exhibition of Chinese Culture on World Stamps	The stamps themed on Ms. Wu Limei participated in the 2nd "Charming China Shines in the World —— Chinese Culture on World Stamps" exhibition.	

Section II Customs and Interesting Anecdotes

Over hundreds of years of inheritance, the Manchu embroidery technique in Xiuyan has accumulated profound cultural connotations. Xiuyan Manchu embroidery has been passed down and developed among the local people in Xiuyan, integrating with the local customs and folkways. It not only enriches the daily lives of the people in Xiuyan but also showcases the cultural charm and customs of this area.

I. When Willows Grow Long in March, Young Girls Embroider Mandarin Ducks by the Window

The saying "When willows grow long in March, young girls embroider mandarin ducks by the window" vividly depicts the real life of Manchu women in Xiuyan in the past. It is rumored that in ancient times, regardless of whether their families were rich or poor, Manchu girls in Xiuyan had to stay at home all day embroidering pillow tops, wedding dresses, shoes and other items from the age of thirteen or fourteen to prepare their dowries. Among them, embroidering mandarin ducks symbolized the girls' beautiful visions for their future marriages. They hoped to live in love and harmony with their future husbands and stay together forever. At that time, unmarried girls were not allowed to show themselves in public. Therefore, to know which girl was virtuous and dexterous, one had to see if the items she embroidered were exquisite. Although with the development of the times, girls are no longer evaluated by the quality of their embroidery, Xiuyan is located in a remote area with a relatively cold climate and relatively closed information flow, and there is a long idle time in farming. So embroidery has become the main way for women to kill time and communicate emotions during their leisure time. The Manchu embroidery technique in Xiuyan has been passed down from mother-to-daughter and between mothers-in-law and daughters-in-law, enabling this technique to be inherited from generation to generation.

II. Inspiration from a Cigarette

Ms. Wu Limei spent four years embroidering the oil-painting version of *The Drunken Concubine* (Figure 3-6) using 26 kinds of embroidery stitches. During this period, the most memorable thing was that Ms. Wu Limei always wanted to embroider a work that could best reflect the characteristic of the bright colors of Xiuyan Manchu embroidery. By chance, she saw the oil painting *The Drunken Concubine*. The color-matching of this oil painting was particularly suitable for showing the features of Xiuyan Manchu embroidery, so she decided to embroider a version of it. However, when she started embroidering, she was troubled by how to show the dynamic sense of Yang Guifei dancing gracefully after getting drunk. Thus, this work could never reach the effect that Ms. Wu Limei wanted. One accidental afternoon, Ms. Wu Limei was sitting in front of the embroidery frame, thinking about how to embroider this work. She lit a cigarette, and the smoke she exhaled dispersed in the sunlight. The swirling dynamic sense of the smoke gave Ms. Wu Limei inspiration. She thought that she could use the flowing air around the dancing sleeves of the concubine to show the dynamic sense of her dancing. Thus, this vivid *The Drunken Concubine* appeared in front of the public.

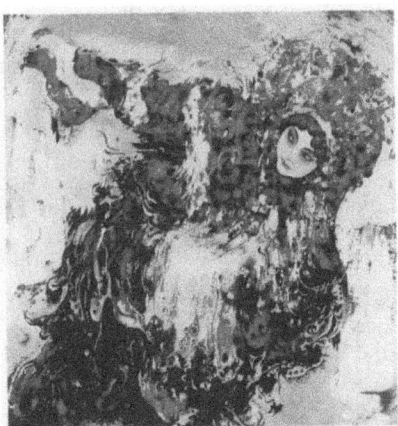

Figure 3-6 *The Drunken Concubine*

III. Artists on the Kang

Xiuyan Manchu embroidery originated from the rural folk life in Xiuyan. In the past, women embroidered items during their breaks in the fields. The embroiderers in Xiuyan are folk artists. But where does the term "artists on the kang" come from?

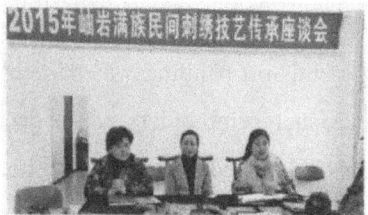

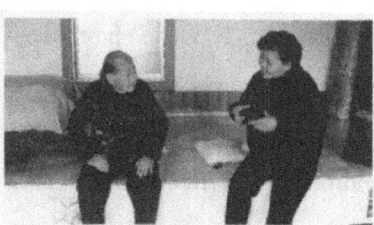

Figure 3-7 Symposium on the Inheritance of Xiuyan Manchu Folk Embroidery Technique in 2015 (Wu Limei, first from the left)

Figure 3-8 Field Trip in 2015. Ms. Wu Limei Visits an Elderly Embroidery Artist (Wu Limei, on the right)

This has something to do with the local customs in Xiuyan. Located in Northeast China, Xiuyan has the longest winter throughout the year, and it is extremely cold in winter. Every household in Xiuyan has a kang. A kang is a bed made of bricks and earth. There are holes under the kang, which are connected to the chimney, and it can be heated by burning fire. In winter, it is the slack season for farming in Xiuyan. So the elderly and women in the family sit on the warm kang, doing embroidery and chatting. This is a common sight in every household in Xiuyan in winter. Many exquisite embroidery works were created by the embroiderers sitting on the kang. Therefore, the embroiderers in Xiuyan can also be called "artists on the kang".

However, with the convenience of transportation, many young people go out to work, and the Xiuyan embroidery technique is gradually being lost. Only a few elderly people still keep this technique. In order not to let this technique be lost, in 2015, with the help of the Xiuyan Manchu Cultural Center, Ms. Wu Limei began to sort out the embroidery patterns and stitches of Manchu embroidery (Figure 3-7). She spent two and a half years visiting the relatively remote rural areas around Xiuyan. She visited the elderly people with good embroidery skills, sat on the kang with them, listened to their recalling the embroidery stitches, looked at the old embroidered items they made, embroidered with them, and sorted out the patterns and stitches of Xiuyan embroidery (Figure 3-8). At present, Ms. Wu Limei has sorted out 12 kinds of embroidery stitches of Xiuyan Manchu embroidery. She said that she will continue to sort out the remaining stitches and strive to sort out all 28 kinds of embroidery stitches of Xiuyan Manchu embroidery as soon as possible so that Xiuyan Manchu embroidery can be better inherited and promoted.

Section III Production Materials and Tools

The materials required for Xiuyan Manchu embroidery mainly include cloth, embroidery threads, embroidery needles, embroidery frames, hoops, scissors, tracing paper, toothpicks, and talcum powder (white powder).

I. Fabrics

Most of the Xiuyan Manchu folk embroidery products are practical items in daily life, mainly including clothes, shoes and hats, purses, tobacco pouches, waist pouches, pillow tops, tablecloths, bedspreads, and door curtains. The fabrics used are mainly satin, gauze, and hand-woven cloth, which are selected according to the purpose of the embroidery products.

Xiuyan Manchu folk embroidery originated in the villages around Xiuyan Manchu Autonomous County (referred to as "Xiuyan County"). Due to the backward economy and shortage of materials at that time, the embroidery products were mostly daily consumables such as pillow tops. Therefore, hand-woven cloth was mostly used as the fabric for embroidery at first. The advantages of hand-woven cloth are low price, softness and comfort, good moisture absorption and breathability, wear resistance, and durability. Moreover, since coarse cloth is woven from cotton threads spun from cotton, the raw materials are all-natural and pollution-free, and the whole process is handmade, so it is more environmentally friendly. Its disadvantages are few colors, lack of luster, and a relatively rough surface, which is not of high - end quality.

When embroidering wedding supplies such as wedding dresses and handicrafts that require high-quality appearance, satin fabrics are mostly used. Satin fabrics are colorful, with delicate luster, smooth and skin-friendly, and the finished products are noble and elegant. However, at the same time, satin fabrics are expensive, not durable, and difficult to maintain.

II. Embroidery Threads

According to the purpose of the products and different patterns, there are three types of embroidery threads selected for Xiuyan Manchu folk embroidery: cotton threads, silk threads (Figure 3-9), and gold threads (Figure 3-10). Cotton threads are spun from cotton fibers. Their advantages are soft texture, firm coloring, high strength, anti-aging, wear resistance, good elasticity, and low price. Silk threads are spun from silk. Their advantages are thinness, soft texture, smooth surface, and bright color, but the price of silk threads is relatively high. Gold threads are spun from synthetic chemical fibers. Their advantages are good luster, high strength, and the finished products are magnificent, but they are expensive and the thread quality is relatively thick and hard.

When embroidering daily necessities in Xiuyan Manchu folk embroidery, cotton threads are used for linear and relatively rough patterns, and the embroidered lines are relatively thick. Silk threads are mostly used when selecting silk fabrics, making handicrafts, and embroidering more delicate and realistic patterns. Gold threads are used when embroidering wedding dresses and for gold-coiling embroidery. Since gold threads are thick and hard, they need to be used with the gold-coiling embroidery stitch.

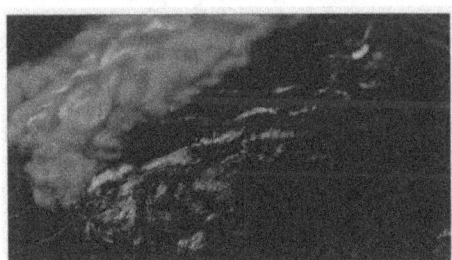 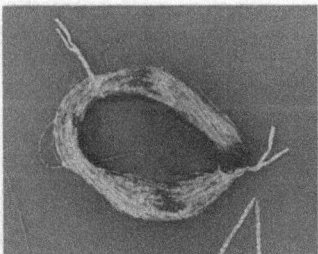

Figure 3-9 Silk Threads   Figure 3-10 Gold Threads

III. Hoops

The hoops used in Xiuyan Manchu folk embroidery are slightly different from those used in other types of embroidery. They are customized by inheritors according to their usage habits and are wooden frames measuring 20cm×20cm square (Figure 3-11). This is because Xiuyan Manchu folk embroidery is mostly used for folk pillow tops, and pillow tops are generally square fabrics measuring 15cm×15cm. Hoops are convenient for fixing the fabric and making the fabric surface flat for easy embroidery. Since women in the past had to work in the fields, the customized hoops needed to be easy to carry, so that women could use their free time for embroidery.

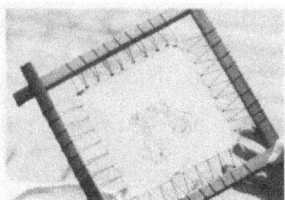

Figure 3-11 Hoops

IV. Scissors and Toothpicks

Small yarn scissors (Figure 3-12) are mostly used in Xiuyan Manchu embroidery. These scissors are small and lightweight, can be placed on the embroidery frame for easy access, and the blades are thin, making it easier to get close to the root of the thread, so the cut thread is not likely to leave a stub.

Toothpicks (Figure 3-13) are used to punch holes along the outline of the pattern on the tracing paper to transfer the pattern. Although pointed tools such as awls can also be used, toothpicks are more commonly used because they are cheap, easy to obtain, easy to carry, and relatively safe.

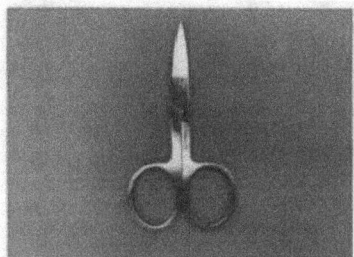 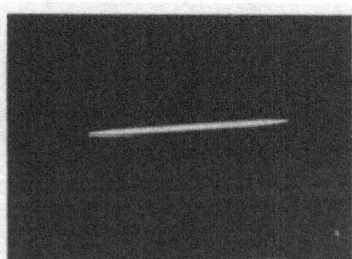

Figure 3-12 Small Yarn Scissors　　　Figure 3-13 Toothpick

V. Tracing Paper

Tracing paper is a semi-transparent paper used for professional drawing (Figure 3-14). It is made by specially treating paper with sulfuric acid. Its advantages are pure paper quality, high strength, transparency, no deformation, sun resistance, high-temperature resistance, and anti-aging, so it is widely used for manual drawing. The processed tracing paper patterns can be used repeatedly, which is convenient for batch-transferring patterns onto the fabric.

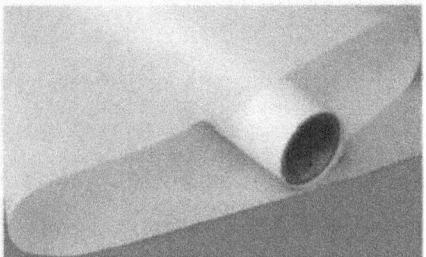

Figure 3-14 Tracing Paper

VI. Talcum Powder (White Powder)

First, lay the tracing paper with punched holes flat on the embroidery fabric, then sprinkle talcum powder on the tracing paper (Figure 3-15) to ensure that the powder leaks through each hole on the paper sample onto the fabric. Then, remove the tracing paper, and the pattern will be transferred onto the fabric. Of course, it is not necessarily talcum powder that is used here; other fine white powders can also be used. It's just that talcum powder is cheap, easy to obtain, and easy to shake off later.

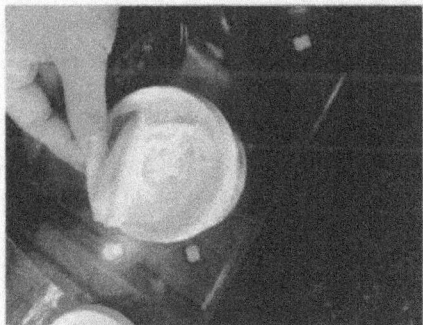

Figure 3-15 Talcum Powder

Section IV Production Process and Techniques

The folk embroidery technique of the Manchu ethnic group in Xiuyan reflects the wisdom of the Manchu working people. It requires simple tools and has a variety of stitching methods. The embroidered patterns are as free-flowing as floating clouds and running water, without being restricted by rigid forms. In this book, the production process of tea flags is taken as an example to demonstrate the manufacturing procedures of Xiuyan Manchu embroidery. Generally, the production process of tea flags can be divided into the following six steps.

I. Design Patterns

The traditional patterns of Xiuyan Manchu embroidery mainly fall into three categories: the sun, moon, stars, flowers, birds, fish, and insects, as well as drama stories from picture books. The patterns are relatively simple and bold, with a simple and natural style. With the development of the times and the changes in consumption habits and aesthetics, the embroidery patterns have become more diverse. Ms. Wu Limei, the inheritor, while preserving the traditional patterns of Xiuyan Manchu embroidery, also embroiders paintings by famous artists, and extracts some flower patterns from the masterpieces as embroidery patterns. As shown in Figure 3-16, the pattern on the round fan is part of the flower branches from the painting "Autumn Scenes".

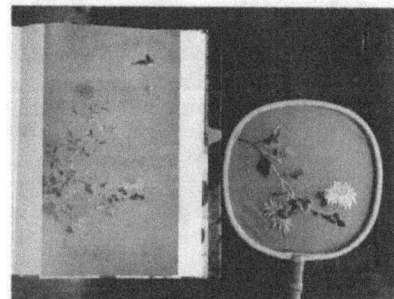

Figure 3-16 A Round Fan with Patterns from "Autumn Scenes"

II. Selection of Fabrics and Embroidery Threads

The selection of fabrics and embroidery threads should fully consider the requirements of the patterns and uses. Generally, when embroidering daily-consumable items, cotton fabrics are often used, and cotton embroidery threads are also suitable. When embroidering wedding supplies and decorative items, silk fabrics are used, and according to the patterns, silk threads or gold-plated threads are often used as embroidery threads.

III. Making Paper Patterns

Trace the patterns on tracing paper and use a toothpick to pierce holes along the outline of the patterns on the tracing paper. Tracing paper is semi-transparent, which makes it easy to trace patterns. Therefore, first transfer the designed patterns onto the tracing paper. To facilitate the transfer of the patterns onto the fabric and enable repeated use, in Xiuyan Manchu embroidery, a toothpick is used to pierce through the patterns on the tracing paper along the lines, as shown in Figure 3-17. When piercing, make sure to pierce the corners of the patterns, and the holes should not be too sparse or too small in area. It is necessary to ensure that talcum powder can pass through each hole later. The pierced paper templates can be reused, which not only saves labor but also ensures that the patterns remain consistent during mass production.

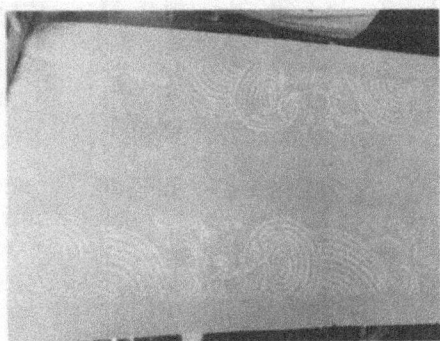

Figure 3-17 Paper with Pierced Patterns

IV. Transferring the Patterns

Lay the tracing paper flat on the fabric, ensuring that the paper template is aligned with the edge of the fabric, as shown in Figure 3-18. Sprinkle talcum powder on the pattern area of the tracing paper and press firmly to ensure that the powder passes through each hole and the pattern is printed on the fabric, as shown in Figure 3-19.

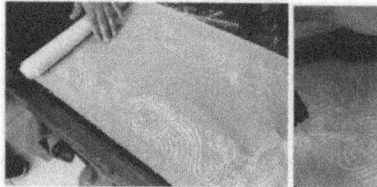

Figure 3-18 Laying the Paper Template on the Fabric

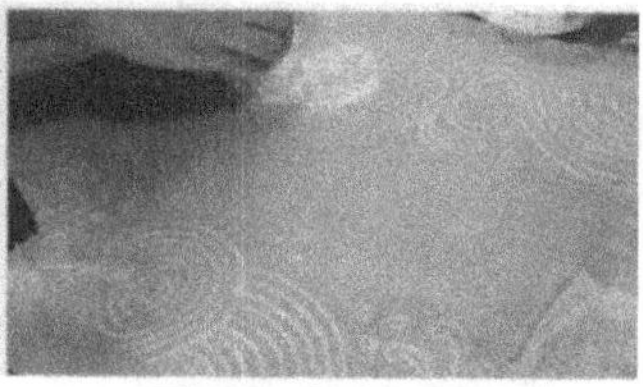

Figure 3-19 Pressing Talcum Powder onto the Paper Template

V. Outlining the Patterns

After ensuring that the pattern is printed on the fabric, the tracing paper can be removed, as shown in Figure 3-20. Use a white pen to smoothly connect the white dots on the fabric to outline the pattern, as shown in Figure 3-21. After the pattern is outlined, shake off the excess talcum powder on the fabric to keep the fabric clean, as shown in Figure 3-22.

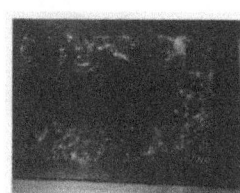 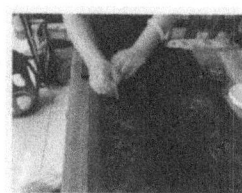 

Figure 3-20 Fabric with Printed White-dotted Patterns

Figure 3-21 Connecting the Pattern with a Pen

Figure 3-22 Cleaned Outlined Fabric

VI. Embroidering the Patterns

Embroider according to the outlined pattern. When embroidering, pay attention to making the stitches fine and dense to ensure smooth lines. After the embroidery is completed, clean the fabric, as shown in Figure 3-23.

Figure 3-23 The Finished Embroidered Work

Section V Process Characteristics and Patterns

Xiuyan Manchu embroidery vividly depicts the folk life of the Manchu people through the form of embroidery. The characteristics of Xiuyan Manchu embroidery are to portray shapes, spirits, and artistic conceptions. It features exaggerated shapes and bright colors. The patterns of Xiuyan Manchu folk embroidery mostly express the masses' worship of nature and their yearning for a better life.

I. Layer-by-layer Stripping, with Alternating Density, "A Horse Can Run in the Sparse Areas and It's Air- tight in the Dense Areas"

The embroidery skills of Xiuyan Manchu embroidery are characterized by being unrestrained. It combines boldness and exquisiteness. Compared with the four famous embroideries in China, Xiuyan Manchu embroidery has the unique ethnic characteristics of the Manchu people in the north. In terms of shape and composition, it emphasizes "layer-by-layer stripping, with alternating density, 'a horse can run in the sparse areas and it's air-tight in the dense areas'". As shown in Figure 3-24, in this embroidery work, embroidery threads are used as the "paint" for the "painting". According to the color changes, the thickness and density of the embroidery threads are adjusted, and the embroidery is done through layer-by-layer overlaying. The thickest part of this work has a total of 10 layers of embroidery.

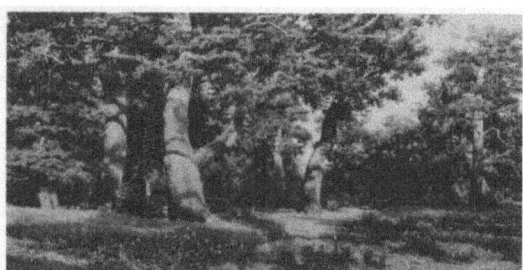

Figure 3-24 Pine Trees

II. Glittering and Colorful

According to the embroidery pattern, the gold thread is coiled and added to the edge of the embroidered or un-embroidered pattern. Since the thread direction follows the pattern for coiling embroidery, it is called coiled-gold embroidery, as shown in Figure 3-25 and Figure 3-26. It is mostly used on patterns with exaggerated and simple flower shapes, flat figures, and strong decorative effects. After being embroidered, the colors contrast strongly and are eye-catching [6]. Coiled-gold embroidery is generally used in combination with the stitch of nail-line embroidery, which is to nail the relatively stiff and hard-to-shape gold and silver threads onto the fabric surface. Its stitch is relatively complex and requires two needles. The thread on one needle is the main thread, that is, the gold thread, and the thread on the other needle is the auxiliary thread, which is used to nail the main thread. Generally, it is selected according to the color of the fabric or the pattern, and the color of the auxiliary thread should echo the embroidery color. Although the color of the gold thread is single, as long as the color of the auxiliary thread is changed, the gold thread can also have color changes. The denser the nail stitches of the coiled-gold embroidery are, the darker the color of the auxiliary thread appears, and vice versa. Choosing the appropriate color of the auxiliary thread to match the gold thread can well highlight the characteristics of coiled-gold embroidery.

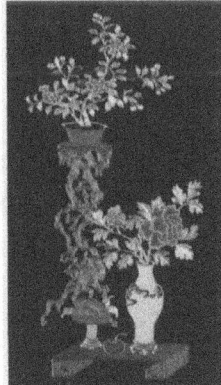 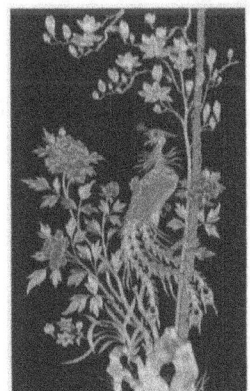

Figure 3-25 The Coiled-gold Embroidery Work(I) Figure 3-26 The Coiled-gold Embroidery Work (II)

III. The Sun, the Moon, the Stars, Mountains, Rivers, Lakes and Seas

In Manchu culture, Shamanism plays a crucial role. Shamanism also provides inspiration for Manchu embroidery. Shamanism believes in "animism". In Shamanism, things related to the sky, the earth, mountains, waters, animals, and plants are endowed with souls, and it is believed that these natural environments gave birth to their ancestors. These beliefs of nature worship, animal worship, and ancestor worship are deeply rooted in the minds of the Manchu ancestors from generation to generation and have a profound impact on the lives and customs of the Manchu ancestors. Therefore, patterns featuring natural landscapes, animals, and plants are common in Xiuyan Manchu embroidery works, as shown in Figure 3-27 to Figure 3-30. The charming and mysterious Shaman totems not only provide rich themes for Manchu folk embroidery but also offer inspiration and creative sources for Manchu folk embroidery art. Moreover, they have accumulated a rich cultural foundation for Xiuyan Manchu folk embroidery [7].

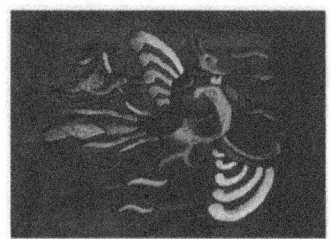
Figure 3-27 Phoenix Totems

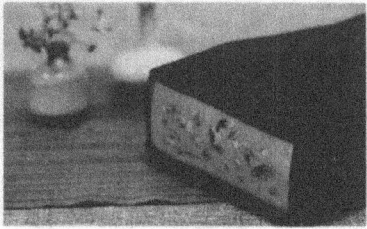
Figure 3-28 Animal and Plant Totems

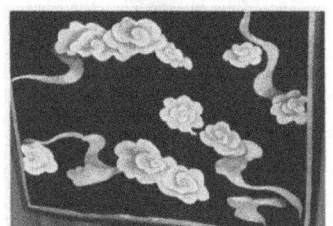
Figure 3-29 Auspicious Cloud Totems

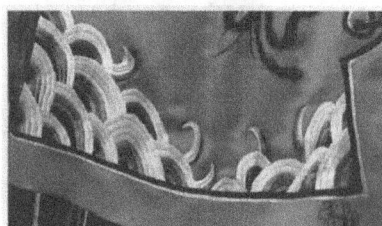
Figure 3-30 Wave Totems

Section VI Appreciation of Works

I. Dragon and Phoenix Wedding Gown

The Manchu bride's wedding gown in the late Qing Dynasty style shown in Figures 3-31 to 3-34 was personally designed with patterns and embroidered by Ms. Wu Limei, the inheritor. The color-matching of this wedding gown reflects the bold color-using characteristics of Xiuyan Manchu folk embroidery. Red, yellow, blue, and white complement each other, enhancing the overall beauty. There is a phoenix embroidered on the front and a dragon on the back of the gown. The dragon and phoenix on the gown seem to flutter in, vivid and lifelike, implying the auspiciousness of the dragon and phoenix together. It symbolizes that the bride and groom are outstanding people, and their future life will be prosperous and harmonious. The auspicious cloud and wave totems at the cuffs and the hem of the gown symbolize good fortune and peace. The hem and cuffs of the gown are decorated with delicate piped edges, and the collar opening is equipped with exquisite frog fasteners.

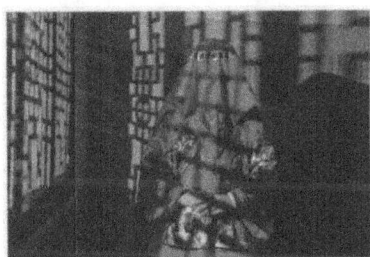

Figure 3-31 The Veil of the Traditional Xiuyan Manchu Wedding Gown

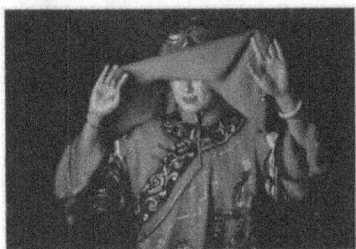

Figure 3-32 The Upper Garment of the Traditional Xiuyan Manchu Wedding Gown

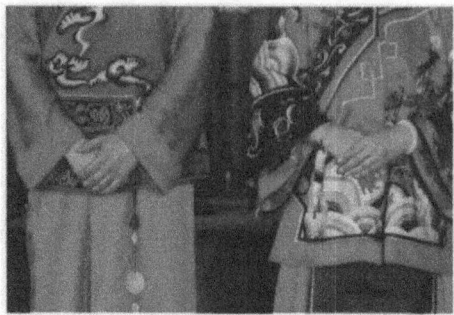

Figure 3-33 The Front of the Traditional Xiuyan Manchu Wedding Gown

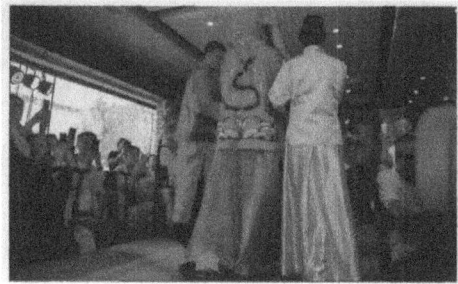

Figure 3-34 The Back of the Traditional Xiuyan Manchu Wedding Gown

II. Flowers, Birds, Fish, and Insects

The patterns of Xiuyan Manchu folk embroidery pay great attention to freehand brushwork. The patterns are simple and generous, with a relatively rough style. In order to better spread Xiuyan Manchu embroidery, Ms. Wu Limei combined Xiuyan Manchu embroidery with Suzhou embroidery. She used the stitching techniques of Manchu embroidery and combined them with the realistic features of Suzhou embroidery to embroider realistic decorative paintings of flowers, birds, fish, and insects. The representative works are shown in Figures 3-35 to 3-38.

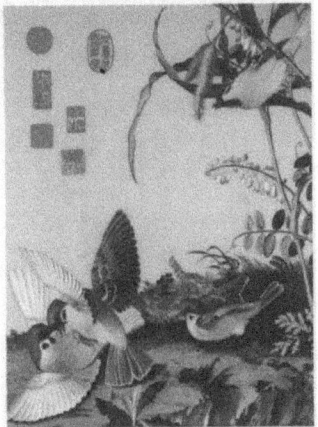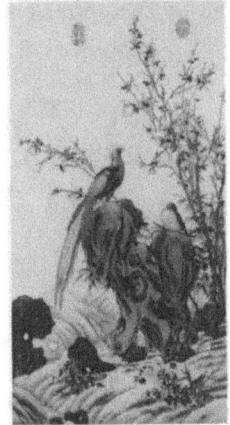

Figure 3-35 Bird Figure 3-36 *The Picture of Blooming Spring*

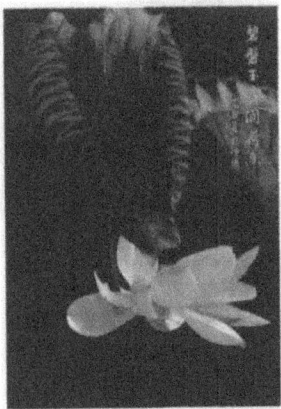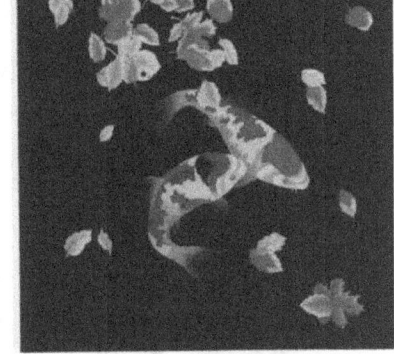

Figure 3-37 A Lotus Flower   Figure 3-38 Koi Carps

III. Gold-coiled Embroidery: Decorative Paintings of Plum Blossoms, Orchids, Bamboos, and Chrysanthemums

Plum blossoms, orchids, bamboos, and chrysanthemums are known as the "Four Gentlemen" in China, symbolizing the four excellent qualities of pride, elegance, perseverance, and modesty respectively. They are the most common themes for poets and painters in China and are deeply loved by the Chinese people. Ms. Wu Limei embroidered decorative paintings of plum blossoms, orchids, bamboos, and chrysanthemums using the gold-coiled embroidery technique. The finished products are noble, elegant, and magnificent, as shown in Figures 3-39 to 3-42.

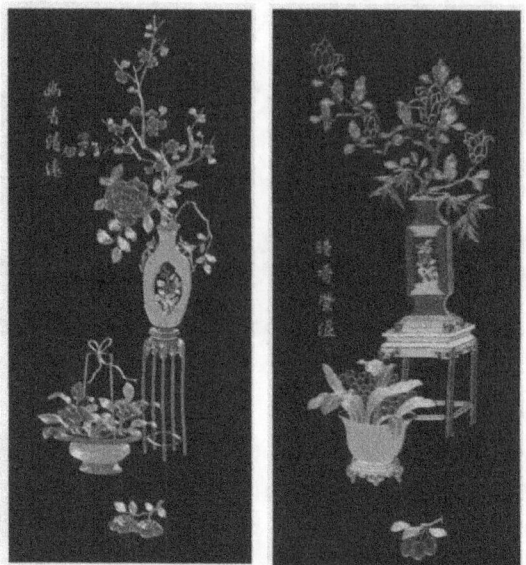

Figure 3-39 Plum Blossoms   Figure 3-40 Orchids

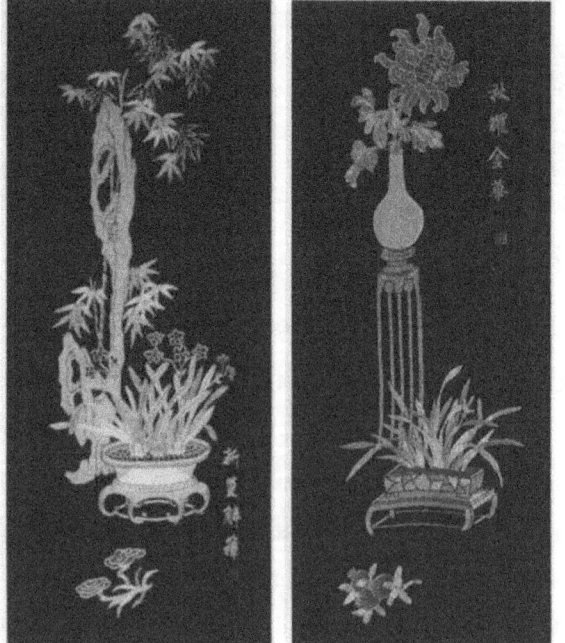

Figure 3-41 Bamboos   Figure 3-42 Chrysanthemums

IV. A Wide Variety of Handicrafts

Ms. Wu Limei has unique insights into the inheritance and development of Xiuyan Manchu embroidery. She believes that Xiuyan Manchu embroidery was initially used on pillow tops. With the improvement of living standards, few people use pillow tops nowadays. However, Xiuyan embroidery should not disappear. Instead, it should integrate different elements and use traditional patterns to create cultural and creative products that reflect the folk customs of Northeast China, so that Xiuyan Manchu embroidery can develop sustainably. Based on this idea, Ms. Wu Limei developed new types of popular consumer goods such as round fans, handbags, and notebooks with traditional Xiuyan Manchu embroidery patterns, as shown in Figures 3-43 to 3-45.

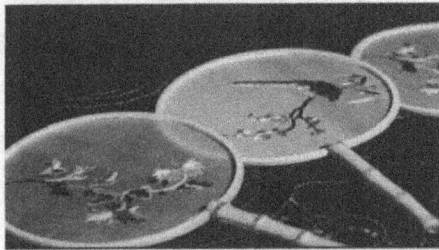

Figure 3-43 A Round Fan with Xiuyan Manchu Embroidery

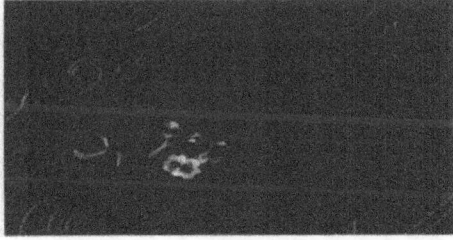

Figure 3-44 A Handbag with Xiuyan Manchu Embroidery

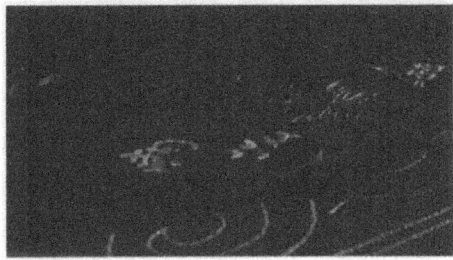

Figure 3-45 A Notebook with Xiuyan Manchu Embroidery

Section VII Interviews with Inheritors

After conducting on-the-spot research on Xiuyan Manchu embroidery, the author conducted an exclusive interview with Ms. Wu, having in-depth communication on aspects such as the cultural background, technical features, development status of Xiuyan Manchu folk embroidery skills, and the vision for the future development of Xiuyan Manchu embroidery. The following is the main content of this exclusive interview.

I. May I ask: As an inheritor of Xiuyan Manchu Embroidery, could you briefly introduce its characteristics?

Ms. Wu Limei: The patterns of Xiuyan Manchu embroidery are mostly animals and plants in nature. This is because the ancestors of the Manchu people in Xiuyan believed in Shamanism, which advocates that all things in nature have souls. Therefore, the patterns of Xiuyan Manchu embroidery are mostly in the forms of the sun, moon, stars, mountains, fires, trees, flowers, grasses, fish, and insects in nature. In addition, the works of Xiuyan Manchu embroidery pay more attention to practicality. The fabrics and patterns of early works were relatively rough, and the embroidery threads used were also thicker, because the embroidered items made in this way were wash-resistant and durable.

II. May I ask: What innovations have you made in inheriting and developing Xiuyan Manchu Embroidery?

Ms. Wu Limei: Xiuyan is located in Northeast China, and the local folk customs are enthusiastic and bold. Therefore, Xiuyan Manchu embroidery as a whole presents a relatively bold style. However, with the improvement of living standards, consumers prefer delicate and realistic styles. To ensure the continued inheritance of Xiuyan Manchu embroidery, we need to make improvements and innovations according to market demand. So, I tried to use the stitching methods of Manchu embroidery to express more delicate and realistic patterns, similar to Suzhou embroidery. In this way, it caters to the preferences of the market and consumers while retaining the traditional stitching methods of Xiuyan Manchu embroidery.

III. May I ask: During the process of inheriting and developing Xiuyan Manchu Embroidery, is there anything memorable for you?

Ms. Wu Limei: I've loved embroidery since I was a child. At that time, our family was poor, and embroidery threads were precious. So, when my sisters went out, I secretly embroidered their unfinished works. After I grew up, I felt that Xiuyan Manchu embroidery needed further inheritance, and I needed to learn embroidery skills more systematically. Therefore, I went to Suzhou alone to learn from a master. At that time, I was in a village in Suzhou, where I was unfamiliar with the place and there was no place to stay. So, I lived in the county town. I had to take a four-to five-hour bus ride every day, but I was not afraid of hardship and persisted in learning for a long time. After systematically learning embroidery skills, I returned to Xiuyan and founded the current Limei Embroidery Studio. On the one hand, it produces and sells Xiuyan Manchu embroidery handicrafts; on the other hand, it recruits apprentices to inherit and develop Xiuyan Manchu embroidery.

IV. May I ask: What are the main problems faced by the inheritance of Xiuyan Manchu Embroidery?

Ms. Wu Limei: The biggest challenge for Xiuyan Manchu embroidery is inheritance. Firstly, with the passing away of the old embroidery artists in Xiuyan, many traditional stitching methods and patterns are at the risk of being lost. Secondly, with the popularization of quality education, fewer children learn embroidery from a young age. Moreover, the embroidery industry doesn't pay well, so fewer people want to engage in it. Xiuyan embroidery is facing a shortage of inheritors.

V. May I ask: As the inheritor, how do you think these problems should be solved?

Ms. Wu Limei: When I founded the Limei Embroidery Studio, I had the idea of compiling a stitch pattern book for Xiuyan Manchu embroidery. In 2015, with the support of the county leaders, I conducted a three-year field survey. I visited every household in the villages around Xiuyan, sitting on the kang with well-known old embroiderers, embroidering with them, and helping them recall the stitching methods and patterns they often used in the past during our conversations. I'm still continuing to collect information and hope to complete the compilation of the Xiuyan Manchu embroidery stitch pattern book as soon as possible, providing reference materials for future generations to ensure that the stitching methods and patterns of Xiuyan Manchu embroidery won't be lost and there will be written records. In terms of cultivating inheritors, I've opened Xiuyan embroidery training courses and recruited disciples. In addition, I'm a specially-appointed expert at several universities and have opened courses on Xiuyan embroidery skills at these universities.

VI. May I ask: In terms of protecting the inheritance of Xiuyan Manchu Embroidery techniques, what efforts has the government made? Are there any aspects that need further improvement?

Ms. Wu Limei: The local government strongly supports the inheritance of Xiuyan Manchu embroidery. Financially, the government has provided us with certain subsidies. In terms of organization and management, the local government has organized embroidery seminars, opened embroidery training courses, and held symposiums on the inheritance of Xiuyan Manchu folk embroidery skills. If the government can organize more exchange seminars among embroidery artists from famous embroidery regions across the country, it will be more beneficial for the innovative development of Xiuyan Manchu folk embroidery. Through exchanges with professionals from outside, the outside world can also learn more about Xiuyan Manchu embroidery.

VII. May I ask: What is your vision and plan for the inheritance and development of Xiuyan Manchu Embroidery techniques?

Ms. Wu Limei: I want to build the brand of Xiuyan Manchu embroidery and make it a luxury brand in China. Xiuyan Manchu embroidery handicrafts range from a thousand yuan to hundreds of thousands of yuan. They require a lot of manpower and are exquisitely made, so they are actually a kind of luxury. Therefore, what we need to do is to carefully embroider each piece and innovate and develop Xiuyan Manchu embroidery according to market changes and aesthetic trends.

Section VIII Current Situation and Countermeasures of Inheritance

I. Current Situation of Inheritance

The folk embroidery skills of the Manchu people in Xiuyan embody the wisdom of the Manchu people over thousands of years. Xiuyan Manchu embroidery works not only reflect the optimistic and life-loving attitude of the people in Northeast China but also express their respect for nature and their yearning for a peaceful and happy life. After the folk embroidery skills of the Manchu people in Xiuyan were included in the national intangible cultural heritage, with the strong support of the state and the local government, many Xiuyan embroidery workshops were held, and inheritors taught villagers how to embroider. However, due to the gradual decrease in the number of people professionally engaged in the Xiuyan Manchu embroidery industry and the shrinking of the group purchasing Xiuyan embroidery products, the inheritance and development of Xiuyan Manchu embroidery are facing many difficulties. The author mainly analyzes the problems encountered in the development of Xiuyan Manchu embroidery from the following four aspects.

1. Single inheritance path of Xiuyan Manchu embroidery

Family inheritance is one of the most important ways of inheriting Xiuyan Manchu embroidery. This inheritance method means that the elderly in the family teach the young. Xiuyan is located in Northeast China, where information is blocked and the economic conditions are relatively backward. Children in the family lack entertainment. They have watched the elderly in the family embroider since childhood and regarded embroidery as a pastime, learning embroidery from an early age. Xiuyan embroidery is mostly passed down through word-of-mouth and influence within the family, and the embroiderers have not received formal training. In addition to family inheritance, master-apprentice inheritance is also a way of inheriting Xiuyan Manchu embroidery. As the younger generation in the family no longer learns embroidery, family inheritance has gradually decreased, and master-apprentice inheritance has taken its place. However, the number of students in these two inheritance methods is small, and their innovation ability is poor. Such inheritance methods are difficult to solve the problem of the decreasing number of inheritors of Xiuyan embroidery and cannot meet the demand for talents required to inherit this skill.

2. Difficulties in Industrializing Xiuyan Manchu Embroidery

The production of Xiuyan Manchu embroidery is mostly in the form of small-scale family workshops. This form has a low output, and the workshops are scattered, making it difficult to have a wide-ranging impact. Moreover, Xiuyan Manchu embroidery is located in the remote Northeast region, lacking technical exchanges with the outside world and developing slowly. With the rapid economic development and technological progress, famous embroideries such as Suzhou embroidery have large-scale and well-equipped embroidery factories, which can produce on a large scale and have independent brands. However, Xiuyan embroidery is still in the workshop-production mode. Xiuyan embroidery has insufficient exchanges with the outside world, and there are few embroidery products, making it difficult to open up the market. Therefore, the sales volume is low, resulting in fewer and fewer people engaging in the production of Xiuyan embroidery products. It is even more difficult for Xiuyan embroidery to form an industry. In the long run, a vicious circle has been formed, making it difficult for Xiuyan embroidery to build its own brand and develop industrially.

II. Countermeasures of Inheritance

Xiuyan traditional Manchu embroidery technique has been included in the national intangible cultural heritage protection list. It is a precious cultural heritage that requires planned protection and strong support for the inheritance of Xiuyan Manchu embroidery culture. In the new era, scientific and effective countermeasures are needed for the protection and inheritance of Xiuyan Manchu embroidery. The author mainly puts forward countermeasure suggestions from the following four aspects.

1. Promoting Xiuyan Manchu Embroidery Culture and Establishing Digital Document of Xiuyan Manchu Embroidery Techniques

To address the problems of a lack of understanding of the cultural background of Xiuyan embroidery in the inheritance and development of Xiuyan Manchu embroidery and the large-scale loss of Xiuyan Manchu embroidery stitches due to the passing away of the older generation of embroiderers, a large number of Xiuyan Manchu embroidery patterns and stitches should be collected to establish a digital picture library. This ensures that the stitches of Xiuyan Manchu embroidery will no longer continue to be lost and provides reference materials for subsequent inheritors. Meanwhile, the inheritance of Xiuyan Manchu embroidery requires the integration of modern design and Xiuyan Manchu embroidery culture. Only by meeting the needs of the times while inheriting its internal cultural connotations can Xiuyan Manchu embroidery be inherited and developed.

2. Expanding Inheritance Methods of Xiuyan Manchu Embroidery

The existing inheritance methods of Xiuyan Manchu embroidery are relatively single and have great limitations. The style of students completely depends on that of their teachers, and the learning resources for apprentices are quite limited. As a result, students have difficulty learning knowledge from various aspects, and their innovation ability is relatively weak. To solve this problem, Xiuyan Manchu embroidery needs to keep up with the trend of the times and expand new inheritance methods during the inheritance process. Primary and secondary school students have strong learning abilities and should be guided to learn and understand China's precious cultural heritage. Each region has its own characteristic cultural heritage, and amateur experience classes can be set up according to regional characteristics. In the Xiuyan area, embroidery inheritors can be invited to enter schools to offer Xiuyan Manchu embroidery experience courses and Xiuyan Manchu culture popularization courses. On the one hand, these courses can popularize the cultural connotations of Xiuyan embroidery to students; on the other hand, they can add hobbies for students and enrich their extracurricular lives. Effectively utilizing the excellent characteristics of college students, such as their strong learning and understanding abilities, innovation abilities, and broad horizons, is very beneficial for the further development of traditional culture. Xiuyan Manchu embroidery elective courses can be offered in local colleges and universities, and social practice projects for protecting the intangible cultural heritage skills of Xiuyan Manchu embroidery can be carried out. This allows students to gain in-depth understanding and hands-on experience, inspiring college talents interested in Xiuyan embroidery to participate in its inheritance. By integrating traditional skills into modern education, more high-quality talents with comprehensive qualities can be attracted to join the cause of innovating and developing Xiuyan Manchu embroidery.

3. Improving the Organizational Structure for the Inheritance of Xiuyan Manchu

Embroidery

At present, the inheritance of Xiuyan Manchu folk embroidery techniques is in a worrying situation, and it is difficult to ensure its inheritance through spontaneous inheritance channels. Therefore, government intervention and support for its development are needed. First, the protection of intangible cultural heritage requires a scientific and systematic management system. On the one hand, multiple departments such as culture, tourism, and education need to cooperate with the intangible cultural heritage protection center; on the other hand, regular learning activities should be organized to scientifically protect the inheritance and development of intangible cultural heritage projects. Second, grass-roots cultural service stations such as district and county libraries, Manchu cultural museums, and Xiuyan Manchu embroidery works and culture exhibition halls should be built in the Xiuyan area to popularize and promote Xiuyan Manchu culture among local people and display the charm of Xiuyan Manchu embroidery techniques. Finally, embroidery artist exchange meetings should be actively organized to provide a platform for embroidery artists to communicate with each other. This not only spreads the charm of Xiuyan embroidery techniques to the outside world but also benefits the innovative development of Xiuyan embroidery techniques through exchanges among masters.

4. Promoting the Unique Features of Xiuyan Manchu Embroidery and Persisting in Innovative Development

Due to the remote location of Xiuyan and its limited communication with the outside world, it is difficult to spread the characteristics of Xiuyan embroidery. To solve this problem, the popularity of Xiuyan Manchu embroidery techniques needs to be enhanced through various channels. First, keeping up with technological development, the Internet can be used to produce promotional materials and create work exhibition web pages to increase the popularity of Xiuyan Manchu embroidery techniques. Second, cooperation with the local tourism industry can be carried out. On the one hand, it can promote the sales of Xiuyan Manchu embroidery products and increase their popularity; on the other hand, Xiuyan embroidery work exhibitions and sales can be held to attract more tourists to travel in the Northeast region. Finally, the most important thing is to innovate the inheritance of Xiuyan embroidery. Inheritance means "preserving the original techniques" in the aspect of "transmission" and "using what is useful for oneself" in the aspect of "inheritance". Therefore, in the process of inheritance, while preserving the characteristics of Xiuyan embroidery techniques and the culture accumulated over thousands of years, it should be combined with modern design to achieve the "traditional modernization and design localization" development of Xiuyan embroidery techniques as soon as possible.

References

[1] Xiuyan Manchu Folk Embroidery: Sparse Enough for Horses to Run, Dense Enough to Block the Wind [OL]. [2018-10-09].

http://www.360doc.com/content/18/1009/15/31655491_793273287.html.

[2] Wan Wenjun, Tang Shouxiang. "Exploration of Traditional Techniques and Cultural

Essence of Manchu Folk Embroidery" [J]. *Theoretical Observation*, 2017(12): 22-24.

[3] Qi Zhi. "Liaoning Xiuyan Manchu Folk Embroidery: An Interview with the Inheritor Wu

Limei" [J]. *China National Expo*, 2017(3): 7-8.

[4] http://www.ihchina.cn/Article/Index/detail?id=14191.

[5] He Xiaohan. "Research on the Current Situation and Development of Manchu Folk

Embroidery as an Intangible Cultural Heritage" [D]. Shenyang: Shenyang Architecture University, 2018.

[6] Che Jixin. *Dictionary of Qilu Culture* [M]. Jinan: Shandong Education Press, 1989.

Chapter IV The Fish Skin Craftsmanship

of the Hezhe Ethnic Group

Chapter IV The Fish Skin Craftsmanship of the Hezhe Ethnic Group

The fish skin craftsmanship of the Hezhe ethnic group is a clothing-making skill of the Hezhe people, a northern ethnic minority in China. It is popular in the Hezhe-inhabited areas such as Tongjiang City, Fuyuan City, Raohe County in Heilongjiang Province and Aoqi Town in Jiamusi City. In 2006, the fish skin craftsmanship of the Hezhe ethnic group was included in the first batch of the National Intangible Cultural Heritage List, and its category in the list is traditional craftsmanship (Table 4-1). In 2017, when the first batch of the National Traditional Craft Revitalization Catalog was released, the fish skin craftsmanship of the Hezhe ethnic group was included, with the project number I-FSZZ-23. Fish-skin clothing is the main carrier of the Hezhe ethnic group's fish skin craftsmanship and an important symbol of Hezhe culture. The Hezhe people are the only ethnic group in China that has fish-skin clothing, and they are known as the "Fish-Skin Tribe". In 2007, Ms. You Wenfeng was named as the inheritor of the Hezhe ethnic group's fish skin craftsmanship by the Ministry of Culture (Figure 4-1). The fish-skin clothing made by Ms. You Wenfeng inherits the essence of the traditional Hezhe ethnic group's fish skin craftsmanship, and her works are collected by major museums. At the same time, Ms. You Wenfeng is also a provincial-level inheritor of Yimakan, a Hezhe ethnic group's rap story-telling art, and has made great contributions to the inheritance and promotion of Hezhe culture.

Table 4 - 1 The Fish Skin Craftsmanship of the Hezhe Ethnic Group

Directory Name	The Fish Skin Craftsmanship of the Hezhe Ethnic Group
Directory Category	Traditional Skills
Directory Level	National
Declaration Unit or Region	Raohe County and Fuyuan City, Heilongjiang Province
Representative Inheritor	You Wenfeng

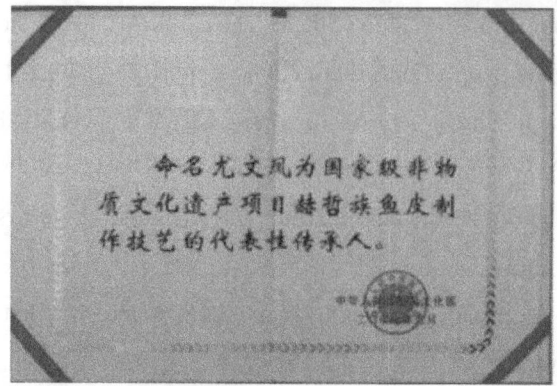

Figure 4-1 Certificate of Representative Inheritor of National Intangible

Cultural Heritage Project

Section I Origin and Development

I. Origin of Fish Skin Craftsmanship of the Hezhe Ethnic Group

The origin of the fish-skin craftsmanship of the Hezhe ethnic group can be traced back to the origin of the Hezhe people. According to historical records, the Hezhe ethnic group can be traced back to the Xinkaoliu period in Mishan over 6000 years ago. During the Shang and Zhou dynasties, they lived "north of Mount Buxian (Changbai Mountain)" and "east by the sea", and their territory extended north to the middle and lower reaches of the Heilongjiang River. In the pre-Qin period, they were called Sushen; in the Han and Wei dynasties, Yilou; in the Northern and Southern Dynasties, Wuji; in the Sui and Tang dynasties, Heishui; and in the Yuan, Ming, and Qing dynasties, Nüzhen. The name "Hezhe" first appeared in the *Veritable Records of Emperor Shengzu of the Qing Dynasty* during the Kangxi reign. According to the records, in that year, "on the Renchen day of the third lunar month, it was ordered that the tribute of sable furs from the people of the four-surname Kulicha area should be received in Ningguta according to the example of the Hezhe and other countries." At that time, the Qing Dynasty referred to the indigenous people living in the basins of the Heilongjiang, Songhua, and Wusuli rivers as "Hezhe". Currently, the Hezhe people are mainly concentrated in three townships and two villages, namely, Jiejinkou Hezhe Ethnic Township in Tongjiang City, Bacha Hezhe Ethnic Township, Sipai Hezhe Ethnic Township in Raohe County of Shuangyashan City, Aoqi Hezhe Ethnic Village in Aoqi Town of Jiamusi City, and Zhuaji Hezhe Ethnic Village in Zhuaji Town of Fuyuan City. The Hezhe ethnic group is the only northern ethnic minority in China that mainly relies on fishing. They have always led a life of fishing and hunting and have the habit of eating fish and wearing fish-skin clothes.

II. Development of Fish Skin Craftsmanship of the Hezhe Ethnic Group

The development of the fish-skin production technique of the Hezhe ethnic group is in line with the history of the Hezhe people. The materials in the Heilongjiang Provincial Ethnic Museum show that in history, people in other countries also ate fish and wore fish-skin clothing. Unfortunately, these practices were lost during the turbulent years of war, and only the Hezhe ethnic group has continued to inherit this technique. This is due to the wisdom, firm beliefs, and the arduous struggle spirit of the Hezhe people in difficult circumstances. Due to historical reasons such as diseases and wars, the Hezhe ethnic group was once on the verge of extinction, and the fish-skin production technique was also facing disappearance. At this critical moment, Ms. You Wenfeng's mother, the elderly You Cuiyu (Figure 4-2), inherited the fish-skin craftsmanship and was the main person to save this technique. According to historical records, from 1941 to 1942, under the pretext of "maintaining public order and suppressing political dissent" and "strengthening public security", the puppet Manchukuo regime under Japanese control implemented a reactionary policy of "scorched-earth and village consolidation". They forcibly relocated 237 Hezhe people living along the Huntong River to the swamps 40 - 50 km away from the riverbank, namely the so-called First, Second, and Third Tribes. At that time, due to the extremely harsh living environment and the spread of diseases, 72 people died during this process. After the founding of New China, there were only more than 150 Hezhe people left, and fish-skin clothing declined rapidly, only remaining among these more than one hundred Hezhe people.

According to Ms. You Wenfeng, during the process of being relocated to the First, Second, and Third Tribes, most of the Hezhe people died due to Japanese persecution, and only more than one hundred people survived. The elderly You Cuiyu was one of them. After being driven into the deep mountains, she still wore the fish-skin clothes she made herself. In that situation, seeing that the entire nation was on the verge of extinction and fish-skin clothing was about to disappear, the elderly You Cuiyu resolutely started making fish-skin clothes again. After the founding of New China, the elderly You Cuiyu passed on the fish-skin production technique of the Hezhe ethnic group from the old society to the new society. In this way, the fish-skin craftsmanship of the Hezhe ethnic group had a foundation for continuation and development in the new era. The current styles of Hezhe fish-skin clothing are passed down by the You family. Ms. You Wenfeng's mother, grandmother, and great-grandmother were all experts in the fish-skin craftsmanship of the Hezhe ethnic group. Ms. You Wenfeng started learning to make Hezhe fish-skin clothing from her mother, the elderly You Cuiyu, when she was eight or nine years old. As her skills became more and more proficient, Ms. You Wenfeng also helped her mother with some fish-skin clothing orders from museums. Nowadays, a large part of the fish-skin clothes preserved in local museums in Jiamusi, Heilongjiang, and Beijing are made by You Cuiyu and You Wenfeng. Museum collection has become the primary destination for contemporary Hezhe fish-skin clothing.

As for how the fact that the Hezhe people wear fish-skin clothes was discovered and protected, it has to start with You Zhixian, the second uncle of Ms. You Wenfeng. Ms. You Wenfeng has four uncles. Her father is You Zhibin, and You Zhixian is her second uncle. You Zhixian's daughter, Ms. You's cousin, went to university in Beijing. During her university days, she spread the news that the Hezhe people had the habit of wearing fish-skin clothing. Then, the news spread from one to ten and from ten to a hundred. More and more people learned about the Hezhe fish-skin clothing and its maker, the elderly You Cuiyu. The news reached the National Museum of Ethnicities in Beijing, and the museum found the elderly You Cuiyu and ordered a set of fish-skin clothes. While the elderly You Cuiyu was making the fish-skin clothes, it happened that a central cadre group and the Ethnic Affairs Commission were conducting a survey on the clothing and ornaments of the 56 ethnic groups. When the research group came to Jiejinkou to investigate the clothing and ornaments of the Hezhe ethnic group, the fish-skin clothes sewn by the elderly You Cuiyu were not finished yet and were in the stitching stage. When the leaders of the research group saw the fish-skin clothes, they were amazed and constantly praised the wisdom of the ethnic minorities. They said that it was really remarkable that the Hezhe people could develop fish-skin to make clothes in a situation of extreme material shortage, which fully reflected the wisdom of the Hezhe people in life. Before leaving, the research group repeatedly told the Hezhe people: "You must teach this technique to your children and let more people learn it. The technique of making fish-skin clothing and ornaments of the Hezhe ethnic group must be continued and passed down."

Nowadays, with the country's strong advocacy of protecting intangible cultural heritage, the fish-skin craftsmanship of the Hezhe ethnic group has not only been selected as a national-level intangible cultural heritage but also has received more effective publicity and protection. You Wenfeng said, "Every time we participate in an exhibition, our Hezhe exhibition hall is crowded with people because many people have never seen fish-skin clothing. Usually, from the beginning of the exhibition, we need to constantly introduce this technique to everyone and answer various questions. Although we are very tired, we feel very happy in our hearts. Because our ethnic group is small and the publicity is not strong, thanks to the country for publicizing our technique, more and more people know about the fish-skin craftsmanship of the Hezhe ethnic group. So, it is really not easy for this technique to be preserved." Ms. You Wenfeng's feelings show that with the joint efforts of all sectors of society, the fish-skin craftsmanship of the Hezhe ethnic group has regained new vitality. It also makes us more confident that in the new historical period and the new era, the fish-skin craftsmanship of the Hezhe ethnic group will be better inherited and developed.

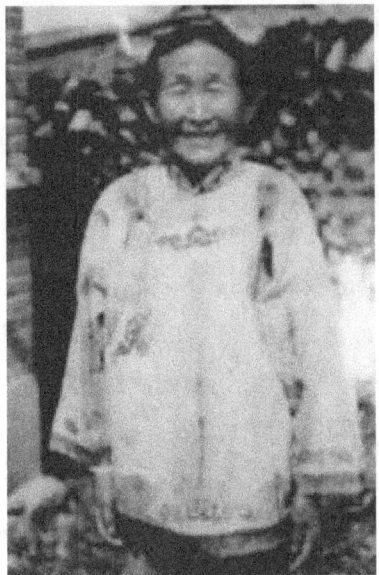

Figure 4-2 You Cuiyu

Section II Customs and Interesting Anecdotes

I. Shamanic Culture of Polytheistic Worship[3]

The term "Shaman" originated from the Tungusic language, meaning "a crazy person". This is because a shaman would enter a state of frenzy before performing magic, and only then could they cast spells smoothly, hence the term "crazy". Shaman culture is a form of culture and a primitive religious belief of the Hezhe ethnic group, which is polytheistic worship. The Hezhe people believe that all things have spirits. In the eyes of the Hezhe people, the mountains, rivers, trees, and flowers in nature can be regarded as gods as long as they believe so. The saying "Believe in something and it will exist" is fully reflected in the Hezhe people's Shaman culture.

Legend has it that there are 96 gods in the Hezhe people's belief, generally in the form of wooden carved god idols. Currently, the Heilongjiang Provincial Museum of Nationalities has custom-made 48 god idols, which are collected in the museum. Each god has its own functions, in charge of different fields. According to the forms of the god idols, the gods worshipped by the Hezhe people can be divided into four categories. The first category is related to natural phenomena. The Hezhe people have a deep-seated worship of natural phenomena. They have lived and thrived in the Heilongjiang River Basin for generations, living a self-sufficient life. Naturally, they need to obtain daily necessities from nature. The Hezhe people believe that the power of nature is irresistible. Therefore, when facing unyielding natural environments, they rely on their faith in gods to seek spiritual comfort. For example, there are gods of the sky, the earth, the sun, the moon, the wind, the rain, the mountains, the rivers, the water, the fire, and the gods of the four seasons (spring, summer, autumn, and winter). The second category is related to natural creatures. Among these god idols are those of bears, deer, tigers, horses, etc. Since hunting is one of the main means of livelihood for the Hezhe people, their actions during hunting are subject to the will of the gods. For instance, the god in charge of animal skins is responsible for hunting-related matters involving skins. The third category is related to disease-prevention and disaster-relief. The worship of these gods reflects the Hezhe people's strong desire to get rid of diseases and disasters. When they encounter serious diseases that cannot be cured, they can only rely on their faith in disease-related gods to seek health. The fourth category is related to evil-repelling and blessing-bestowing. This reflects the Hezhe people's longing for good wishes, praying for the gods to protect the safety of individuals and families. For example, there are the god of the house ridge, the evil-repelling god, and the lucky-star god.

The Hezhe people's worship of gods is manifested in all aspects of their lives. For example, when going up the mountains, they would worship the mountain god; when fishing, they would worship the river god, praying for the gods' blessings so that they can have a smooth journey and a good harvest when hunting in the mountains or fishing in the rivers. The shaman is considered to be the incarnation of the gods, and the Hezhe people communicate with the gods through the shaman. According to Ms. You Wenfeng, with the progress of society, these superstitious activities have gradually disappeared. The shamans among the local people are now mainly actors, whose main task is to promote the traditional Shaman culture of the Hezhe ethnic group, and there are no real shamans left.

II. The Traditional "New-Year Pictures" of the Hezhe People

The Hezhe people celebrate the Spring Festival together with the Han people. During the Spring Festival, they make dumplings with fish fillings, stir-fry fish flakes, deep-fry raw fish, eat frozen fish slices, and make fish balls, all of which are mainly fish-based. They also have the custom of pasting "New-Year pictures", and of course, these "New-Year pictures" are also related to fish. In the early years, the Hezhe people recorded their fishing and hunting lives and expressed their emotions through carving fish-skin paintings (Figure 4-3). The content includes daily life scenes such as hunting and carrying wood from the mountains, which are carved on fish skins and pasted on windows, just like the Han people's New-Year pictures. Traditional fish-skin paintings are made from large fish skins. In the past, there were no cloth or picture frames. They would cut large fish skins into small pieces and create paintings depicting the Hezhe people's hunting, fishing, storytelling, and singing "Yimakan". Among them, the most beloved scene by the Hezhe people is the budding of willow trees and the return of swallows in spring. The Hezhe children used to like making such paintings. In spring, whether it is the Han people or ethnic minorities, everyone looks forward to spring with the same feeling.

As the weather warms up and everything comes back to life, the temperature in Northeast China also gradually rises, and people can go outdoors, making life more cheerful. Spring symbolizes hope, so the Hezhe people make fish-skin paintings about spring every year and paste them on windows and walls in spring. How did they paste the fish-skin paintings on the walls when there were no wall nails in the past? The Hezhe people are very ingenious. They would break off some small branches of the Mongolian oak. Since Mongolian oak is strong and corrosion-resistant, they would carve them into the shape of nails. Because the walls in the past were made of mud, it was easy to drive these oak nails into the walls, and then the fish-skin paintings could be pasted on the walls.

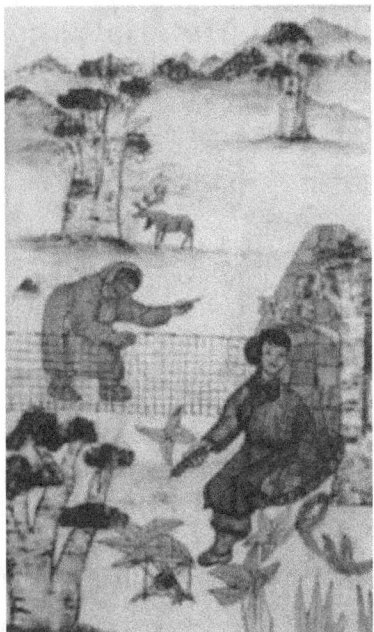

Figure 4-3 A Fish-skin Painting

Section III Production Materials and Tools

The main material for the Hezhe ethnic group's fish-skin making technique is fish skin. To make the fish skin soft, various tools are needed for curing, mainly including knives, wooden presses, and cornmeal. In the process of making fish-skin clothing, unique fish-skin strips and threads are also essential parts.

I. Fish skin

Fish skin is the fabric for making Hezhe ethnic group's fish-skin clothing. In the Hezhe ethnic group's fish-skin making technique, the fish skin (as shown in Figure 4-4 and Figure 4-5) mainly comes from the chum salmon, also known as the salmon. Adult chum salmon are about 60 cm long and weigh about 10 catties. They are cold-water fish. The day of White Dew marks the beginning of the chum salmon fishing season. The life habits of chum salmon are very interesting. They are born in rivers, grow in the ocean, and are fish that can survive in both fresh-water and salt-water systems. Every autumn, chum salmon swimming in the vast Pacific Ocean gather in the Tartar Strait, struggle to swim back up the Heilongjiang River for thousands of miles, and finally reach the middle reaches of the Heilongjiang River and spawn in the gravel riverbed of the Wusuli River. [6]

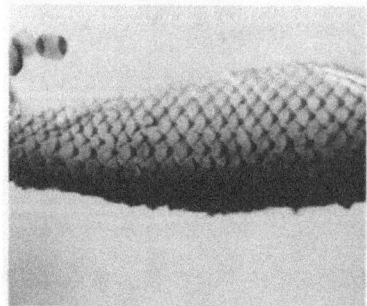 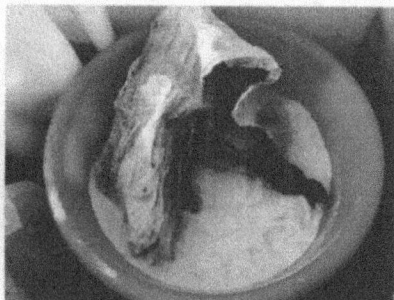

Figure 4 - 4 Freshly skinned fish skin   Figure 4 - 5 Fish skin being cured

II. Knives

Knives are tools used for skinning fish. Traditionally, the Hezhe people used wooden knives to skin fish. These knives were made from local materials, usually carved from oak. They were shaped like a crescent moon, with one side thin and the other thick, about 15 cm long. The blade was relatively blunt, so it was not easy to damage the fish skin when using it. With the development of social industry, iron knives gradually entered the lives of the Hezhe people and also became indispensable tools in the process of skinning fish (as shown in Figure 4-6).

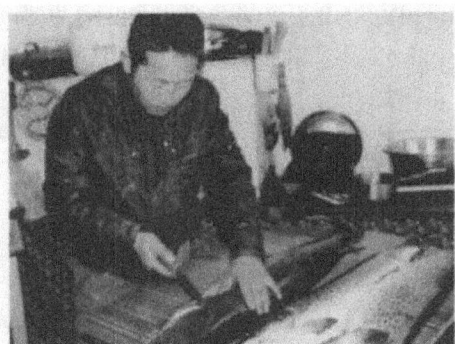

Figure 4 - 6 Fu Shanyong, the son of You Wenfeng, demonstrating fish-skinning

III. Wooden Presses

Wooden presses are important tools for curing fish skin. After the fish skin is skinned and dried, its texture is very hard, like a steel plate, and it cannot be directly used to make clothing. It needs further curing to make it soft. At this time, the wooden press (as shown in Figure 4-7) is used. In the Hezhe language, it is called "ge ji ge". The main part of the wooden press consists of two parts: the bottom trough and the press blade. The bottom trough is made of relatively thick wood, with a hollow in the middle and serrations on both sides. The press blade is also made with serrations. Its head is fixed on the bottom trough, and there is a handle at the tail, which can move up and down.

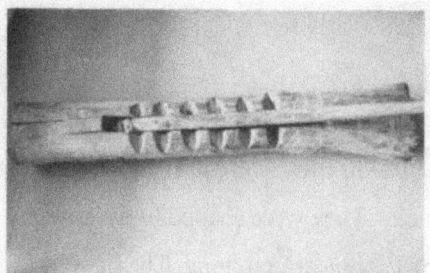

Figure 4-7 A Wooden Press

IV. Cornmeal

The cornmeal in the basin shown in Figure 4-8 has two functions in the Hezhe ethnic group's fish-skin making technique. One is to cure the fish skin, and the other is to clean fish-skin clothing. During the process of curing fish skin, cornmeal is used to remove the grease from the fish skin. Only when the grease in the fish skin is completely absorbed can the fish skin be preserved for a long time, up to a hundred years without deterioration. However, if there is residual grease that is not completely removed, the fish skin will be infested with insects and rot.

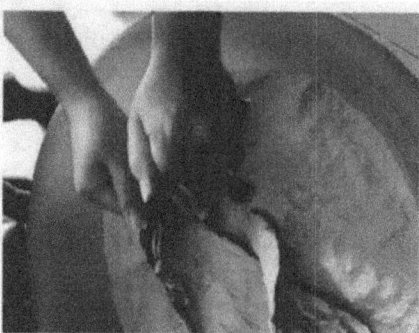

Figure 4-8 Cornmeal

V. Fish-skin Strips

Fish-skin strips are thin strips cut from fish skin. They function like cloth strips and are mainly used for making frog fasteners and decorating details. Figure 4-9 shows the scene of making fish-skin strips, and Figure 4-10 shows the frog fasteners made of fish-skin strips.

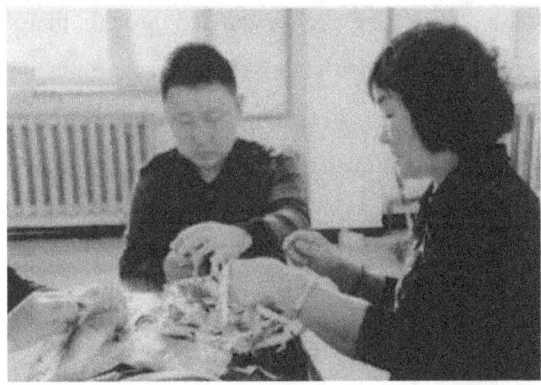

Figure 4 - 9 You Wenfeng's third son demonstrating cutting fish-skin strips

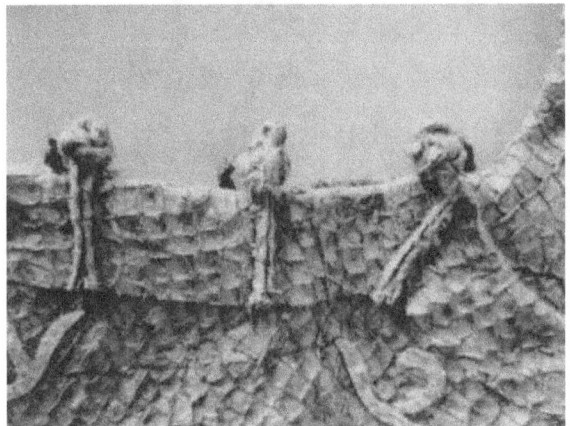

Figure 4 - 10 Frog-knot Buttons Made of Fish-skin Strips

VI. Threads

The most primitive threads for sewing fish-skin clothing by the Hezhe people were mainly fish-skin threads, roe deer tendons, and deer tendons. To make fish-skin threads, first, the fish skin was peeled off, spread out, and dried. Then, the uneven corners were cut off. A layer of fish liver oil was applied to the fish skin to make it moist, and then it was rolled up. A small wooden board was used to press it tightly, and a sharp knife was used to cut it into thin threads. One end of the thread should be thinner for easy threading. Then, it was dyed into various colors with wild flowers and could be used to sew clothes as needed. When using these "threads" to sew fish skin, it seemed that one thing could control another. Roe deer tendons and deer tendons could fasten the fish skin very well. Generally, when a needle was passed through, there was no need to pull hard to tightly close the fish skin. When disassembling, it could only be done stitch by stitch; otherwise, it couldn't be disassembled. However, now roe deer and deer are protected animals, so the Hezhe people use cotton threads (as shown in Figure 4-11) to replace traditional materials such as roe deer tendons and deer tendons. When sewing with cotton threads, one must pull hard for each stitch to sew the fish skin well.

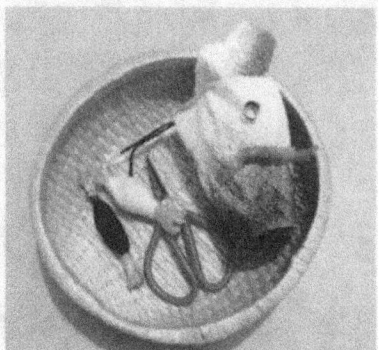

Figure 4 - 11 You Wenfeng's Sewing Basket

Section IV Production Process and Techniques

The traditional craftsmanship of making fish-skin clothing by the Hezhe ethnic group mainly consists of six major steps: fishing, skinning the fish, drying the fish skin, softening the fish skin, splicing, and sewing (Figure 4 - 12).

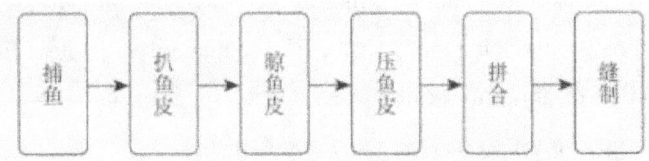

Figure 4 - 12 The Craftsmanship Process of the Hezhe Ethnic Group's Fish Skin

I. Fishing

Fishing was the primary and essential step in the past for the Hezhe people to make fish-skin clothing. However, with the development of the market economy, numerous fish markets and fish-skin markets have emerged, greatly facilitating fish-skin makers. As a result, fishing is no longer a necessary step for them.

There are about 70 species of fish in the Heilongjiang River, among which around 10 are suitable for making fish-skin clothing. The fish required for making fish-skin clothing are relatively large, weighing about 10 catties. Currently, the fish-skin materials used for Hezhe fish-skin clothing mainly come from the chum salmon, which is a migratory fish. The local Hezhe people usually fish in Fuyuan. In the Hezhe language, Fuyuan means "a golden fish beach". It is located at the confluence of the Heilongjiang and Wusuli Rivers, with Russia across the river to the northeast. The river mouth is in Russia. Every year, when the chum salmon migrate from the ocean, they pass through this area in large numbers. Therefore, the Hezhe people often go fishing in Fuyuan. The locals know very well that if they fish in Jiejinkou, they can hardly catch any fish throughout the year. If a boat can catch two or three fish in a year, it is considered a great harvest. Around September 20th each year is the migration period of the chum salmon, which is also the fishing season for catching them.

With the development of the Hezhe fish-skin making craftsmanship, professional fish-skin markets have emerged in the local area, specializing in selling dried fish skins. When making fish-skin clothing, people can directly purchase fish skins from vendors, which saves more time and energy compared to fishing directly. It is also more cost-effective than buying whole fish, with a price reduction of about two-thirds. The development of the fish- skin market has brought good news to fish-skin handicraftsmen.

II. Skinning the Fish

After fishing or buying fish, the next step is to skin the fish. Generally, it is much easier to skin a freshly caught fish. If the fish is not fresh, the flesh and skin will stick tightly together, making it difficult to separate them. However, this has no impact on the quality of the fish skin. The process of skinning the fish starts by making incisions on both sides of the back and abdomen, cutting from under the gills to the tail. Then, start peeling from under the gills towards the tail to remove the entire fish skin. After removing the skin, use a knife to clean all the remaining flesh on the fish skin, and the skinning process is completed.

III. Drying the Fish Skin

Drying the fish skin refers to the process of pasting the removed fish skin onto a wooden board to dry. This step follows the previous one. After the fish skin is removed and the attached flesh is cleaned, wash it thoroughly and then paste it onto a wooden board. Make sure to paste the fish skin flat. At room temperature, it usually takes one night to dry the fish skin. Once dried, the fish skin becomes very hard, as hard as an iron sheet, as shown in Figure 4-13.

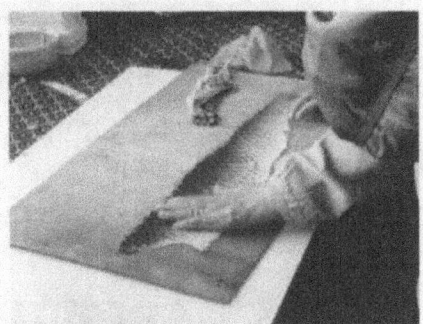

Figure 4-13 Drying the Fish Skin

IV. Softening the Fish Skin

Softening the fish skin is also called "pressing the fish skin" or "tanning the fish skin". The toughness of well-tanned fish skin can reach 2-3 times that of cowhide, and its wear resistance and tensile strength are several times that of ordinary leather. The freshly dried fish skin is very hard and plate-like. It needs to go through the "softening" process to become soft.

The ancient method of softening was to wrap small fish skins with large fish skins because there were no other materials available for wrapping fish skins in the past. The wise Hezhe people came up with this method. The specific method is to first lay a layer of large fish skin, sprinkle cornmeal on the inner side of the fish skin, then place a slightly smaller fish skin on it, and sprinkle cornmeal again. Repeat this process, layering fish skins from large to small with cornmeal in between (Figure 4-14). After stacking, roll all the fish skins into a long roll (Figure 4-15). Then, two people work together. One person holds both ends of the fish-skin roll and puts it into a wooden press. The other person holds the handle of the wooden press and presses down hard (Figure 4-16), then lifts it. After the wooden press is lifted, the person holding the fish-skin roll tightens it again and puts it back into the press, and then presses it in the same way. Press harder on the harder parts and repeat this process until the stiff fish skin gradually becomes soft. After pressing, do not shake off the cornmeal inside the fish skin. Then, rub the fish skin (Figure 4-17). Hold a piece of fish skin with both hands and rub it like washing clothes until it becomes fuzzy. This step further removes the grease from the fish skin. Pressing the fish skin is the most time-consuming process in making fish-skin clothing. It takes about two months to make a piece of fish-skin clothing, and the process of just pressing the fish skin alone lasts nearly a month.

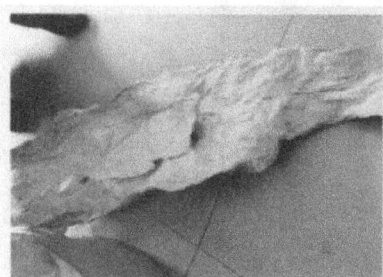 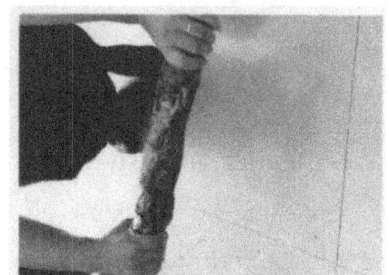

Figure 4 - 14 Stacking Fish Skins   Figure 4 - 15 Rolling up Fish Skins

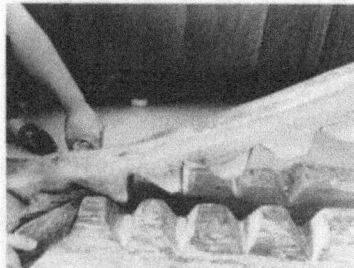 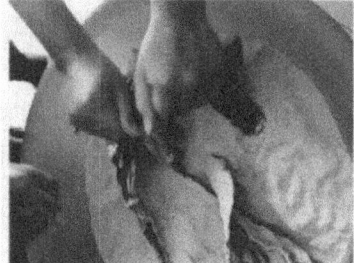

Figure 4 - 16 Pressing Fish Skins Figure 4 - 17 Rubbing Fish Skins

V. Splicing

Due to the shape and area limitations of fish skins, the well-cured fish skins cannot be directly cut for making clothes. They need to be further spliced. Splicing is the process of joining small pieces of fish skin into large fish-skin materials. However, this is not a simple stitching process. Instead, it requires an artistic splicing according to the natural color shades, scale sizes, and grain directions of the fish skins. In this way, the spliced large-piece fish- skin material has natural patterns and is very beautiful.

VI. Sewing

The spliced fish-skin material can be used to make clothes just like ordinary fabric. Sewing is the process of cutting and sewing the spliced large-piece fish skin into clothes. Generally, after the whole piece of clothing is sewn, unique Hezhe patterns are sewn on it for decoration. Thus, a piece of fish-skin clothing is completed. Figure 4-18 shows You Wenfeng teaching her three daughters-in-law to sew fish-skin clothing.

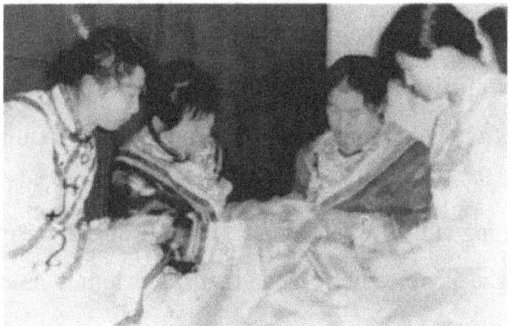

Figure 4-18 Sewing Fish-skin Clothing

Section V Process Characteristics and Patterns

I. The Hezhe Fish Skin Craftsmanship Representing an Innovation in Clothing Fabrics

The development of clothing fabrics has generally gone through several stages, including leaves, animal furs, silk, hemp, and cotton. Among them, animal furs were one of the earliest clothing fabrics used by humans. Historically, the Hezhe people lived a life of fishing and hunting with little agricultural activity. Therefore, the clothing fabrics of the Hezhe ethnic group were mainly animal furs, such as deer and roe deer skins. In addition, the Hezhe people also developed fish-skin fabrics using fishery resources. Besides the common characteristics of general leather products, fish-skin fabrics are wear-resistant, tear-resistant, lightweight, and warm-keeping. This further expands the scope of clothing fabrics and is of great significance to the research of textile fabrics. The Hezhe people often wear fish-skin clothes in summer for their lightness and coolness. In winter, they first wear fish-skin leggings as the inner layer and add an animal-fur outerwear on the outside to resist the cold. Using fish skins as fabrics to make clothing and accessories makes the Hezhe ethnic group's clothing unique and stands out among the ethnic minority clothing.

II. The Patterns of Hezhe Fish Skin Clothing Exhibiting Natural Characteristics

The fish-skin clothing of the Hezhe ethnic group often uses fish-skin strips to cut into patterns, which have natural colors and are unique. Due to the limited area of fish skins, making a piece of fish-skin clothing usually requires multiple fish skins. The Hezhe people take advantage of the light and dark color changes between the back and abdomen of fish to cut and splice them. The resulting clothing has natural patterns and a symmetrical style. This decorative style of clothing patterns maximizes the characteristics of natural materials, which is not found in the clothing of other ethnic minorities in China. In addition, there are also other patterns used as decorations on the Hezhe ethnic group's clothing. These patterns are usually cut from fish skins and then sewn onto the corresponding parts. Traditionally, men's clothing is generally cut with S-shaped patterns (Figure 4-19). The patterns on women's clothing are significantly different from those on men's clothing and are more diverse. They are mainly cloud patterns, as well as animal patterns such as fish patterns, water-wave patterns, and antler patterns (Figure 4-20 to Figure 4-22).

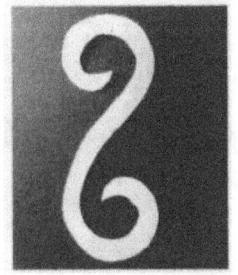

Figure 4-19 S-shaped Pattern   Figure 4-20 Cloud Pattern

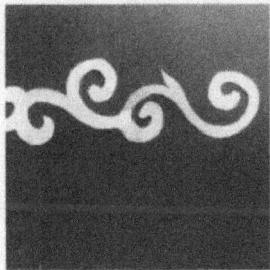 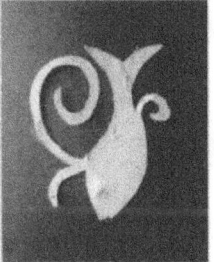

Figure 4-21 Water-wave Pattern   Figure 4-22 Fish Pattern

III. Cleaning Fish-skin Clothes with Cornmeal

Due to the special fabric used in making fish-skin clothing, there is a specific cleaning method. When fish-skin clothes get dirty, they are not washed with water or chemical detergents, but with cornmeal. The specific method is also very simple. Simply sprinkle cornmeal on the dirty parts of the fish-skin clothes and rub them with hands. The stains on the clothes can be absorbed by the cornmeal. Then shake off the cornmeal, and the cleaning of the fish-skin clothes is completed. After being cleaned with cornmeal, the fish-skin clothes look as good as new and are as clean as when they were first made.

Section VI Appreciation of Works

The application of the Hezhe ethnic group's fish-skin making technique mainly includes fish-skin clothing, fish-skin paintings, fish-skin bags, and fish-skin small pendants. Fish-skin clothing is the most primitive and widespread application of the Hezhe ethnic group's fish-skin making technique. Fish-skin paintings fully demonstrate the Hezhe ethnic group's painting and calligraphy art. Fish-skin bags are an innovative application of fish-skin fabric at present. Fish-skin small pendants were mainly used for the decoration of fish-skin clothing in the past and are now mainly sold as handicrafts.

I. Fish-skin Clothing

Fish-skin clothing is the traditional clothing of the Hezhe ethnic group. Fish-skin clothes are characterized by being light, warm, wear-resistant, tear-resistant, and waterproof. In terms of style, they are greatly influenced by Manchu clothing, mostly long clothes, similar to Manchu clothing. As the daily clothing of the Hezhe ethnic group, Hezhe fish-skin clothes are also keeping pace with the times and constantly innovating.

1. Adult clothing

Adult fish-skin clothes are mainly suits and gowns, with distinct features for men and women (Figures 4-23 to 4-25). The collar style of suits is mostly round-cornered standing collars, and gowns mostly have no collars. The most common opening styles are right-lapel slant openings and front openings. The edges of the clothes are designed with binding. The binding emphasizes the contrast between light and dark colors. Dark binding is used for light-colored parts, and white binding is used for dark-colored parts to enhance the visual effect through contrast. Various patterns are often pasted and sewn on the cuffs, collars, both sides of the opening, the back, and the hem of the clothes. The pasting and sewing methods also reflect the characteristics of light-dark contrast and symmetry everywhere. For suits, the sleeves of fish-skin clothes are fat and slightly short, and the overall style is loose. The style of women's fish-skin clothes is similar to that of cheongsams. Some also have shells, copper bells, or Yingluo beads (pendants made of pearls and precious stones) sewn on the hem of the clothes to show uniqueness and beauty. Due to the natural and excellent characteristics of fish-skin clothes, wearing them during winter hunting can be wear-resistant and cold-resistant, and wearing them during spring and autumn fishing can be waterproof and protect the knees. According to the memories of local elders, fish-skin clothes have very good thermal insulation effects. When Hezhe people went hunting in the mountains in winter, they first wore fish-skin clothes and then put on roe-deer leather clothes and trousers outside. They could lie in the snow one-meter deep all night until dawn, and the hunters would be sweating all over their faces.

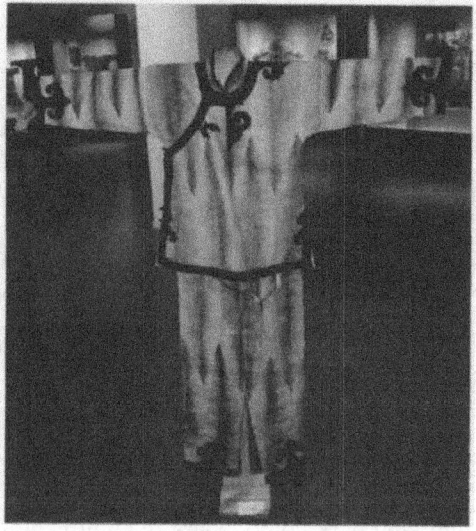

Figure 4-23 The Right-front-opening Suit

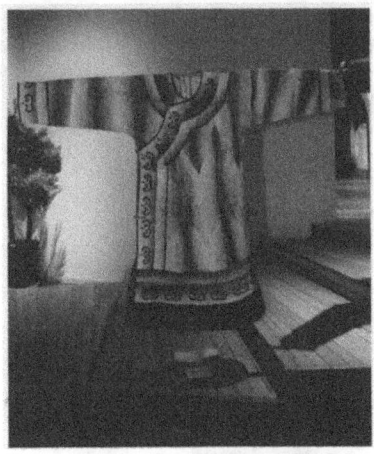

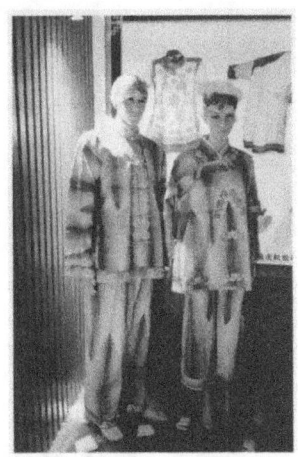

Figure 4-24 Long Robe

Figure 4-25 Men's and

Women's Outfits

2. Dresses

Dresses are mostly for girls' clothing. As shown in Figure 4-26, it is a traditional suit-style girls' dress of the Hezhe ethnic group. The whole dress set consists of three pieces of clothing, namely a shawl, a vest, and a half-skirt. The edges of the shawl are decorated with bead tassels, adding a sense of liveliness to the whole dress set. Various patterns are pasted and sewn on the front and back of the vest, and the waist and hem of the half-skirt to express good wishes. The most distinctive feature of the dress shown in Figure 4-27 is that it uses red fabric for binding and pastes and sews red cloud patterns on the abdomen. The rest is made of fish skin, perfectly combining tradition and modernity. The half-skirt shown in Figure 4-28 is not much different from the current A-line skirt in style, but it is made of traditional fabric, making it more distinctive.

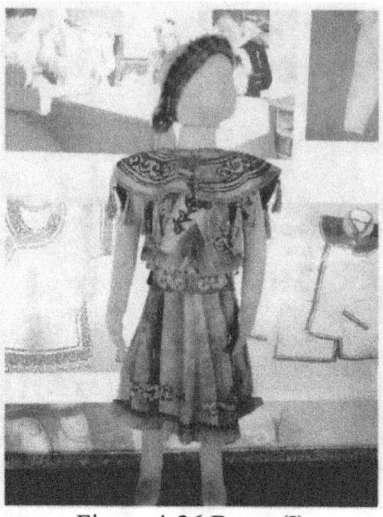

Figure 4-26 Dress (I)

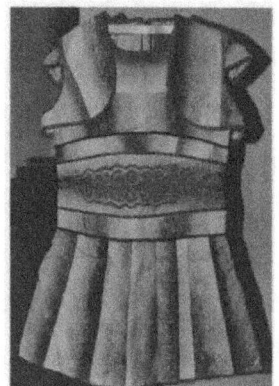 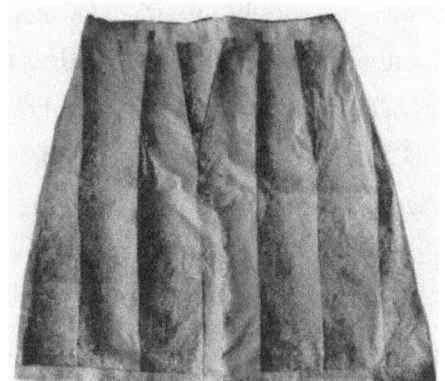

Figure 4-27 Dress (II)   Figure 4-28 Skirt

3. Children's Clothing

Children's clothing is basically the same as adult clothing in terms of style. The biggest difference lies in the patterns on the clothes. Dragon patterns can be seen on boys' hats. Usually, a dragon is sewn on the front first, and then it evolves into a fish. On the one hand, it expresses the hope that the son will become a dragon (In China, a dragon is used to represent an outstanding person), and on the other hand, it also represents the fishing and hunting life of the Hezhe ethnic group. Animal patterns such as deer and roe deer are often used on girls' clothing. For the Hezhe ethnic group, deer and roe deer represent beautiful girls and imply good luck. Figures 4-29 to 4-34 show children's clothing.

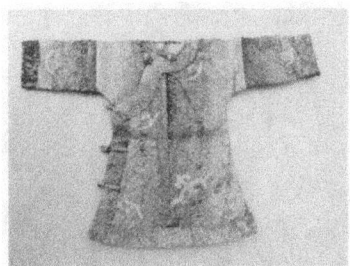
Figure 4-29 Front View of Children's Clothing with Right-slanting Front Opening

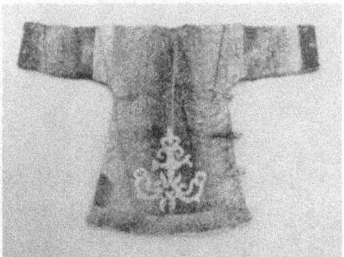
Figure 4-30 Back View of Children's Clothing with Right-slanting Front Opening

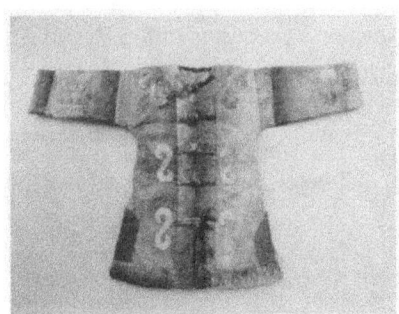
Figure 4-31 Front View of Children's Clothing with Front Opening

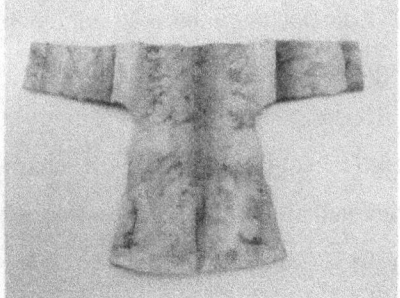
Figure 4-32 Back View of Children's Clothing with Front Opening

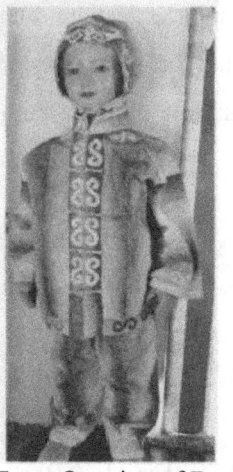 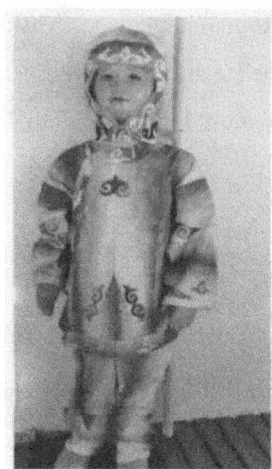

Figure 4-33 Front Opening of Boys'
Clothing

Figure 4-34 Right-slanting Front
Opening of Girls' Clothing

II. Fish-skin Paintings

Fish-skin paintings are traditional New Year paintings of the Hezhe ethnic group. Traditional fish-skin paintings are mostly used to depict the daily life of the Hezhe people, such as hunting and fishing. With the improvement of people's living standards, the content of fish-skin paintings has also become richer, and all content and themes related to the development of the times can be fully reflected. The works in this part are made by Ms. Gao Yarong and Ms. Huang Yuan. The two are apprentices of You Wenfeng, a national-level inheritor of the Hezhe ethnic group's fish-skin making technique. Since they became apprentices, they have studied assiduously and made efforts to inherit the Hezhe ethnic group's fish-skin making technique. As shown in Figure 4-35, it is Ms. Gao Yarong's work *Flowers in Full Bloom and Wealth*, which contains two elements, namely peonies and peacocks, symbolizing peace and wealth. The peacock's feathers are the difficult part of the production. Each feather is cut out of fish skin and then pasted layer by layer to finally get a lifelike peacock. As shown in Figure 4-36, it is Ms. Huang Yuan's work *Descendants of the Dragon*. Using fish skin to make the dragon, the scale pattern of the fish skin more realistically reflects the shape of the dragon's scales. Then, dyed fish skin is used to express the facial makeup, reflecting the idea that all Chinese people are descendants of the dragon.

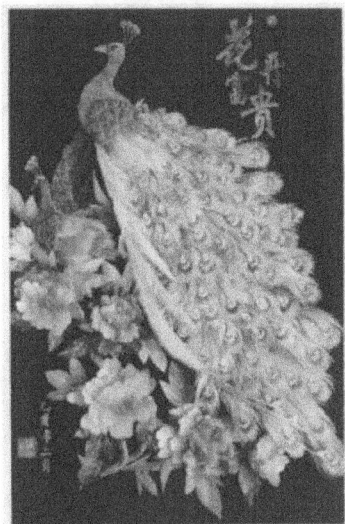 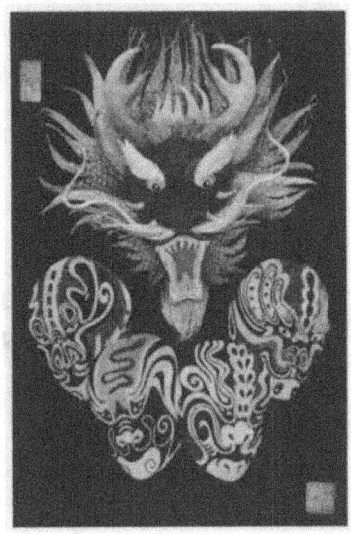

Figure 4-35 "Flowers in Full Bloom and Wealth" by Gao Yarong

Figure 4-36 "Descendants of the Dragon" by Huang Yuan

III. Fish-skin Bags

Fish-skin bags are another important application of fish-skin fabric and have great application prospects in contemporary life. The Hezhe ethnic group's cultural industry base cooperated with the chief designer of LV to combine special fish- skin fabric with fashionable bag bodies to design fashionable handbags at present, as shown in Figures 4-37 to 4-40. The pictures in this part were taken at the Hezhe ethnic group's cultural industry base.

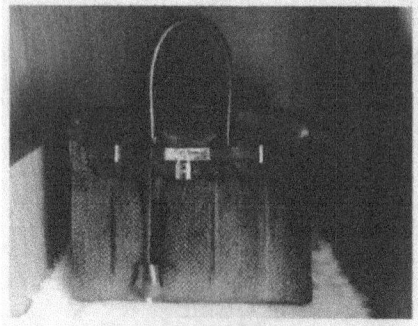

Figure 4-37 Sapphire-blue Fish-skin
Handbag

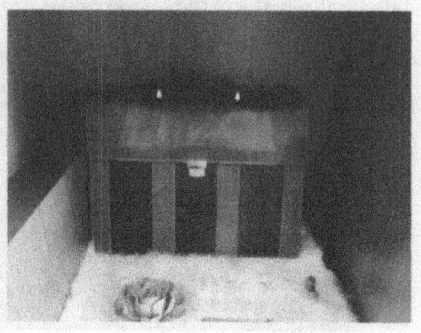

Figure 4-38 Brown Fish-skin Bag

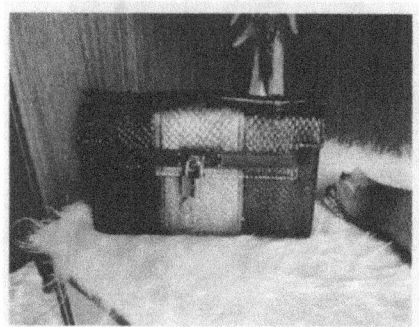

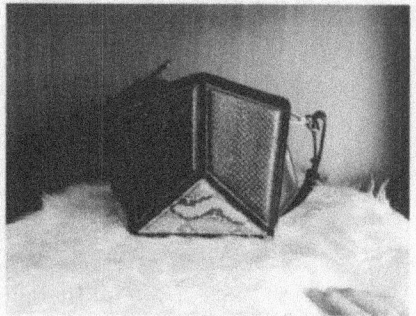

Figure 4-39 Small Fish-skin Satchel   Figure 4-40 Fish-skin Shoulder Bag

IV. Small Fish Handicrafts

When the Hezhe people make small fish pendants, they have a belief of coexisting with nature. In their lives, they not only eat fish but also wear fish-skin clothes. So they feel sorry in their hearts. Then they will make all kinds of small fish and sell them as handicrafts, hoping that these small fish can come back to life. The small fish handicraft pendants are shown in Figure 4-41.

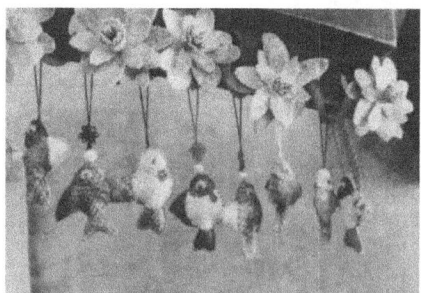

Figure 4 - 41 Small Fish Handicraft Pendants

Section VII Interviews with Inheritors

I. May I ask: Are you still making fish-skin clothes?

Ms. You Wenfeng: Most of the fish-skin clothes I make are for museum collections. No one wears them in daily life anymore. So, if a museum needs a collection, they will come to me for a custom made one, and I'll make it. I usually don't make them otherwise because the Hezhe ethnic group's fish-skin clothes can't be mass-produced like ordinary clothing. It takes a long time to make one. However, in recent years, some merchants have also bought them. The price of a women's Hezhe fish-skin dress I make is 16,000 yuan, and that of a men's is 18,000 yuan. Since men's clothes are longer, they require five or six more fishes, so they are a bit more expensive.

II. May I ask: Are there any local exhibition and exchange activities about the Hezhe fish-skin clothing?

Ms. You Wenfeng: We have exchanges and learning sessions at the Wurigong Conference. "Wurigong" in the Hezhe language means "auspicious festival". The Hezhe ethnic group's Wurigong Conference was held every three years before 1997. Since 1997, it has been held every four years in late June. On the festival day, we first offer incense, then light the sky lanterns to summon all the gods, and then report our lives in the past few years to them. After that, everyone sings and dances. This is when we exchange ideas about fish-skin clothes. For example, if I made particularly good clothes this year, I'll bring them to the Wurigong Conference. Three years later, when my skills have improved and I've made new clothing styles, I'll bring them again. So, the Hezhe ethnic group's fish-skin clothing is developing and innovating every year. The fish-skin clothes presented each time are different. Other aspects of the Hezhe culture, such as dance and Yimakan, also develop through such exchanges. The Wurigong Conference provides a platform for the Hezhe ethnic group to communicate and innovate. Therefore, our Hezhe clothing is becoming more and more beautiful. However, the items sent to museums remain the same as before. They can't be changed casually. The clothing we usually make is always in the process of innovation, trying to keep up with the current market trends.

III. May I ask: Have you made any innovations in the process of inheriting the fish Skin craftsmanship of the Hezhe ethnic group?

Ms. You Wenfeng: The Hezhe ethnic group's fish skin craftsmanship has always been evolving. These fish-skin clothes date back thousands of years. The Hezhe people led a fishing and hunting life. They lived at the foot of the mountains, with a river below. This kind of environment made it convenient for them to hunt in the mountains and fish in the river. They wouldn't live anywhere else that wasn't surrounded by both mountains and water. Without mountains or without water, it was uninhabitable. The mountains and waters nurtured the Hezhe people. In the past, when there were no clothes, our ancestors peeled the fish skins, dried them, and then used the "konggu" to press the fish skins. They could only press one or two skins at a time, which was very time-consuming. Later, the wooden press was gradually invented. Although the wooden press had many teeth, in actual use, only the two teeth close to the person were used. But it was still the most practical one, and it could press six or seven fish skins at a time. The other teeth were just for the aesthetic appearance of the wooden press. Now, there have been some improvements in the tools for pressing fish skins. New tools have emerged on the market to replace the traditional wooden press. I bought one for my home, but the effect of pressing fish skins with it is not as good as that of the traditional method. The fish skins pressed by the traditional wooden press are of better quality.

IV. May I ask: How do you cultivate the next generation of inheritors?

Ms. You Wenfeng: It is mainly through family inheritance and taking in apprentices. In family inheritance, the skills have been passed on to my daughters-in-law. My youngest daughter-in-law is a provincial-level inheritor, and my second daughter-in-law is also very good at it, almost as good as me. I have three daughters-in-law. The eldest one is in business and didn't learn the skills, but the other two have learned very well. Taking in apprentices is also an important way of inheritance. I have taken in six or seven apprentices now. Two of them are from the Hezhe ethnic group, and the others are the Han people. At that time, I took in these Han apprentices because they had good painting skills and were very interested in the Hezhe ethnic group's fish skin craftsmanship. I thought that once they got involved in the Hezhe fish skin craftsmanship, they would be non-Hezhe people with a heart for the Hezhe culture and could all inherit our Hezhe ethnic group's fish skin craftsmanship. My hope is to pass on this skill by any means possible.

In addition, I also hold training classes. There are more than 60 people in the training classes in Tongjiang, Jiejinkou, Bacha, Fuyuan, and Yaohe. Some classes have more than 10 people, and some have more than 20 people. These students are all very serious in their learning. Sometimes, I am also invited to give lectures at universities. Once, I gave a lecture at a university in Harbin. It was a training class funded by the state, and the students were all from areas like Tongjiang, Bacha, Fuyuan, and Yaohe, including both Hezhe and Han people. There were more than 50 students in one class. The students were very interested in listening and liked to do hands-on work. The lectures at Mudanjiang University were also very popular. Last autumn, around August, Chinese students from various cities studying in the UK saw fish-skin clothes in the UK. Their British teacher brought them to China to learn how to make fish-skin clothes. They stayed in Jiejinkou, Tongjiang for half a month, and I taught them all. After all, they are Chinese college students. My thought is that if they are willing to carry on this skill after graduation, it will be a continuation of this skill. If not, at least they have learned about this handicraft. When I first taught them to press fish skins, the students were very happy at first. But after a few days of pressing, they said to me, "Teacher, this is really tiring." I told them, "This is the Hezhe ethnic group's fish-skin making skill. If you want to learn it, you have to be prepared to work hard."

V. May I ask: What do you think of the innovation of intangible cultural heritage?

Ms. You Wenfeng: Now, I also hope to make innovations, that is, to create things that meet the contemporary people's aesthetic and practical needs. This is also the innovation of our traditional skills, and I strongly support this kind of innovation. We are also working hard on it ourselves. The intangible cultural heritage skills left by our ancestors in the past are very valuable, and we should pass them down from generation to generation. But for us, we can't just stick to the old ways and always make the same things as in the past. In the past few years, scientific research has also been changing the fish-skin craftsmanship. We went to Guiyang to watch the performances of ethnic minorities. When I came back, I was thinking about whether we could also have a "new inheritance of old skills" for the Hezhe ethnic group's fish skin craftsmanship. This is the future development trend of the Hezhe ethnic group's fish skin craftsmanship.

Section VIII Current Situation and Countermeasures of Inheritance

I. Current Situation of Inheritance

For thousands of years, the Hezhe ethnic group's fish-skin craftsmanship and fish-skin culture have developed along with society. At the end of the 19th century, fish-skin clothing still held an indispensable position in the daily lives of the Hezhe people. By the late Qing Dynasty, cotton cloth had become popular among the ethnic minorities in Northeast China, and the production and use of fish-skin clothing gradually decreased. In 1934, Ling Chunsheng published *The Hezhe People in the Lower Reaches of the Songhua River*, in which he wrote, "Today, fish-skin clothes are rarely seen, but fish-skin leggings, shoes, overalls, and bags are still commonly used." Today, after years of ethnic integration and changes in the mode of production, the Hezhe people have shifted from fishing to agriculture. These changes in the mode of production have led to corresponding changes in people's lifestyles and production techniques. The Hezhe fish skin craftsmanship has gradually faded out of people's lives, and the younger generation has become increasingly unfamiliar with traditional skills. Traditional handicrafts such as skinning fish, curing fish skin, cutting, and sewing fish-skin clothing are also gradually being lost. Currently, fish-skin clothing is mainly collected in some museums at home and abroad. The Hezhe fish skin craftsmanship has become an ethnic cultural heritage in urgent need of protection, facing the following inheritance dilemmas.

1. Discontinuity in the Inheritor Population

With the development of society, the popularization of textile fabrics, and changes in the traditional living environment of the Hezhe people, fish-skin clothing has withdrawn from the lives of the Hezhe people, and the fish-skin craftsmanship has also been gradually forgotten. Currently, very few Hezhe people can master this technique, and those who can are mostly elderly people from the older generation. The younger generation has not developed a deep cultural attachment to this technique, and few are willing to learn it. As a result, there is a discontinuity in the inheritor population of the Hezhe fish skin craftsmanship.

2. Small Market Scale

The Hezhe fish-skin products, including fish-skin clothes, fish-skin paintings, and fish-skin bags, have a certain market but have not yet formed a scale. Fish-skin clothing is only limited to the collectibles market. Fish-skin paintings and fish-skin bags are not produced on a large scale due to their complex production processes and high prices. Overall, the market scale of products associated with the Hezhe fish skin craftsmanship is very small and needs further development.

3. Severe Cultural Loss

As a national intangible cultural heritage, the Hezhe fish skin craftsmanship, in addition to its unique production methods, reflects the Hezhe people's outlook on life, values, and world-view. Rooted in the traditional life of the Hezhe people, it bears unique ethnic imprints. However, the change in lifestyle has deprived this culture of its nurturing ground and gradually lost its vitality. The development of commerce has further impacted the traditional fish-skin culture, resulting in a severe loss of the cultural value of the Hezhe fish skin craftsmanship.

II. Countermeasures and suggestions

In view of the difficulties in the process of inheriting the above fish skin craftsmanship of the Hezhe ethnic group, we can start from the following aspects.

1. Exploring New Uses of the Hezhe Fish-skin Products and Expanding the Market of Fish Skin Derivatives

Fish-skin clothing is the most original and primary use of the Hezhe fish-skin craftsmanship. Currently, museum collection is almost its only market. Fish-skin paintings, which evolved from traditional New-Year paintings and window grilles, still retain their vitality today and are the most promising part of Hezhe fish-skin products. However, due to insufficient promotion, the market for fish-skin paintings remains small. In the 21st century, with the rapid development of the economy and society, products without a market will soon be forgotten. To solve this problem, the market for fish-skin derivatives should be developed. Expanding the market for fish-skin derivatives is a feasible way to promote the inheritance of the Hezhe fish skin craftsmanship. Derivatives such as fish-skin backpacks, handbags, and hats will be the focus of future market exploration. In addition, the inheritor You Wenfeng dressed the mold dolls used in the performance of "Yimakan" in fish-skin clothing, which was well-received. Fish-skin toys are also worth exploring.

2. Establishing a Team of Intangible Cultural Heritage Brokers

The Hezhe ethnic group has a small population, which makes it difficult to inherit intangible cultural heritage. To address the disadvantage in the number of inheritors, it is recommended to establish a team of brokers for the Hezhe fish-skin craftsmanship. The team will package the Hezhe fish-skin craftsmanship into a business, be responsible for its operation, packaging, promotion, and marketing. The inheritors and those who are proficient in fish-skin making will focus on producing fish-skin related products, inheriting the fish-skin technique, and continuing the Hezhe fish-skin culture. This approach allows inheritors to devote as much energy as possible to inheriting the intangible cultural heritage skills and culture, improves market efficiency, and ultimately achieves a win-win situation of obtaining market benefits while better preserving the authenticity of the intangible cultural heritage.

3. Establishing a Cultural Ecology for Hezhe Fish-skin Culture

The term "cultural ecology" generally refers to the situation and environment of the material and spiritual wealth created by humans in social and historical practice. With the decline of the Hezhe fishing industry, the traditional fishing and hunting culture behind the Hezhe fish-skin craftsmanship has also suffered a sharp decline, and the entire cultural ecology has become very fragile. Culture is the core and foundation of a nation and an important source of its vitality and perseverance. Therefore, the government can reconstruct the Hezhe fish-skin culture in the new era through policy design. For example, it can stipulate that people wear fish-skin clothing when participating in major events, restore traditional customs during traditional festivals, and encourage ethnic cultural exchanges.

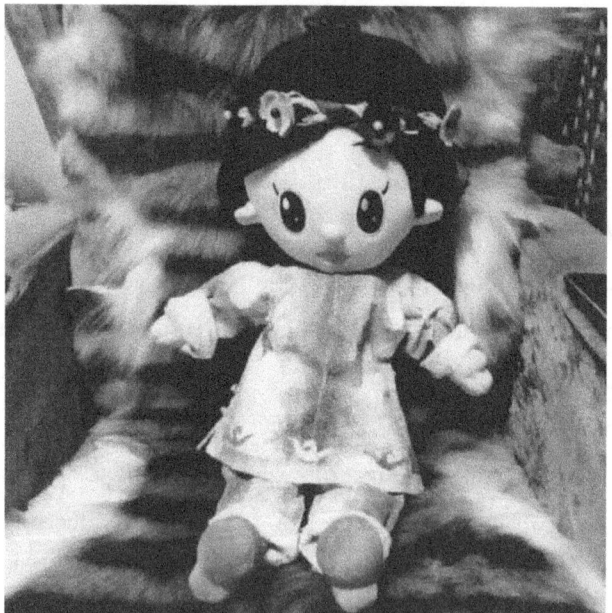

Figure 4 - 42 A Doll Wearing a Fish-skin Coat

References

[1] Cong Shubing. "Exploration of Fish Skin Skills and Handicrafts of Hezhe Nationality" [J]. *Journal of Social Sciences of Jiamusi University*, 2006 (5): 93-94.

[2] Hezhe nationality. https://baike.baidu.com/item/Hezhe/158839?fr = aladdin.

[3] Li Chenglong. "Shamanic Culture in the Polytheistic Worship of Hezhe Nationality" [J]. Art and Technology, 2017, 30 (3): 31.

[4] He Chunyan. "The Animistic Belief of the Hezhe People: A Glimpse into the Spiritual Faith of the Hezhe Ethnic Group from the Museum's Collection of Spirit Dolls" [J]. *Identification and Appreciation of Cultural Relics*, 2017 (11): 50-52.

[5] Zhang Yangguang. " 'Fishing Tribes' in the Sanjiang River Basin (Part 2): An Exploration of the Life of Hezhe People" [J]. *Environment*, 2002 (7): 36-37.

Chapter V: Mongolian Clothing

Mongolian clothing is recognized as a provincial-level intangible cultural heritage item in Jilin Province. It was included in the second batch of provincial-level intangible cultural heritage lists of Jilin Province on June 5, 2009 (Table 5-1), and the category of the list is folk festivals. Mongolian clothing originated in Qianguoerlos Mongolian Autonomous County, Jilin Province. "Guoerlos" is a transliteration of the Mongolian tribal name "Huoluolasi", meaning "rivers and streams". Qianguoerlos is located on the south bank of the Songhua River, so in Mongolian, Qianguoerlos means "south of the river". There are currently more than 70,000 Mongolians in the local area, and Mongolian clothing is mainly popular among the local Mongolian population. In 2011, Ms. Wuyin (Figure 5-1) was recognized as the inheritor of Mongolian clothing by the Department of Culture of Jilin Province. Wuyin National Clothing Co., Ltd., established in 2006, is the inheritance base for the intangible cultural heritage of Mongolian clothing designated by the Department of Culture of Jilin Province, and also the internship base for students' clothing design and production designated by the School of Art of Northeast Electric Power University. The Mongolian clothing produced and processed by Wuyin National Clothing Co., Ltd. not only inherits the culture of traditional Mongolian clothing but also integrates modern design into the Mongolian robe. It has distinct regional characteristics, rich ethnic features, and advanced contemporary characteristics, enabling Mongolian clothing to enter the wardrobes of more people.

Table 5-1 Mongolian Clothing

Directory Name	Mongolian Clothing
Directory Category	Folk Festivals
Directory Level	Provincial
Declaration Unit or Region	Qianguoerlos Mongolian Autonomous County, Songyuan City, Jilin Province
Representative Inheritor	Elut Wuyin

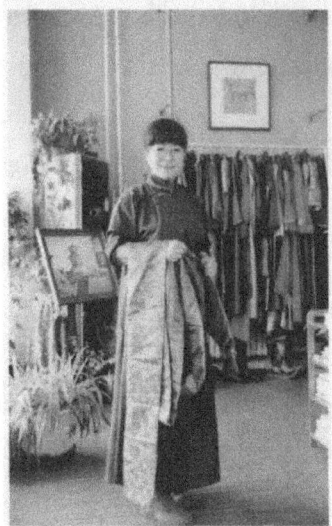

Figure 5-1 Wuyin, the Inheritor of Mongolian Clothing

Section I Origin and Development

I. Origin

The Guoerlos Mongolians belong to the Horqin tribe. The origin of the Mongolian clothing with tribal characteristics can be traced back to the Qing Dynasty. Historically, Guoerlos was one of the nomadic areas under the jurisdiction of Khaghatu Khasar, the second-younger brother of Genghis Khan. In 1206, Genghis Khan unified the Mongol tribes, and for the first time, the Mongolian ethnic group emerged in northern China. At that time, the Mongolian robes of various tribes had similar characteristics. After the establishment of the Yuan Dynasty, the production techniques, fabrics, and styles of Mongolian robes also witnessed significant development. In 1368, after the fall of the Yuan Dynasty, the Mongolians scattered across the grasslands. Due to the Ming court's embargo on the grasslands, Mongolian robes became simpler and more elegant, and the characteristics of tribal clothing began to emerge. During the Qing Dynasty, the imperial court adopted a policy of "divide and rule" towards the Mongolians. On the premise of retaining the enfeoffment system of the Mongolian nomadic people, a new league-banner system was established, advocating differences in clothing between banners. This promoted the formation of different styles of robes among various Mongolian tribes, such as the Horqin, Chahar, Buryat, and Barghu tribes with distinct characteristics. By the end of the Qing Dynasty, the characteristics of tribal clothing were basically finalized. Among them, the Horqin tribal clothing was greatly influenced by Manchu clothing, incorporating many features of cheongsams, especially the women's robes, which were more characteristic of cheongsams. This was mainly due to the inter-marriage between the Qing government and the Horqin tribe to stabilize the regime and strengthen the rule over the Mongolian region. The Guoerlos Mongolian clothing, on the basis of inheriting the characteristics of the Horqin tribal clothing, has integrated with the local people's living habits, forming a unique style of Mongolian clothing.

II. Development

The development of the production techniques of Mongolian clothing has been a bumpy journey.

During the Qing Dynasty, most of the Mongolians living in the Guoerlos area were ordinary people, with few high-ranking officials and nobles. The local Mongolian people simply wore plain robes, which were very simple in style and rather plain in color. Due to historical reasons, the Qianguoerlos Banner was one of the earliest banners in eastern Inner Mongolia to carry out agricultural development. The pastures were turned into farmlands, and the nomadic culture was transformed into an agricultural culture at an early stage. After the founding of the People's Republic of China, the natural, social, and cultural environments on which Mongolian clothing depended gradually disappeared, and the production techniques of Mongolian clothing were on the verge of being lost. Only in the Chaganhua Grassland, where the local Mongolians were most concentrated, could one occasionally see traces of Mongolian robes. Today, with the development of social and cultural life, the attention paid to intangible cultural heritage and ethnic culture has been greatly enhanced, and Mongolian clothing has once again come into the public view.

As a provincial-level inheritor of Mongolian clothing, Ms. Wuyin and her family have played a pivotal role in promoting the inheritance and development of Mongolian clothing. Ms. Wuyin's grandparents were native Mongolians from the Chaganhua Grassland. Ms. Wuyin's initial impression of Mongolian robes came from that generation. At that time, when the economic development level was relatively low, people basically made their own Mongolian robes, and family inheritance was the most important way. Her grandmother passed on the production techniques of Mongolian clothing to Ms. Wuyin's mother, Ms. Qimuge. Ms. Qimuge is now 84 years old. When she was 17, she became a professional solo singer in a song-and-dance troupe. Every time she performed, she needed to wear Mongolian clothing. However, after leaving the countryside, it became extremely difficult to order Mongolian performance costumes. Due to the rapid disappearance of the production techniques of Mongolian clothing, hardly anyone in the local area wore or made Mongolian robes. So, the Mongolian robes that Ms. Qimuge needed for her performances had to be ordered in Beijing. This phenomenon directly reflected the rapid loss of Mongolian robes. During the "Cultural Revolution", Ms. Wuyin's father, Suhebalu, was sent to the Chaganhua Grassland because of his family's historical issues. Ms. Qimuge was required to draw a clear line from Suhebalu, otherwise, she would be dismissed from her public-service job. Despite the severe situation, Ms. Qimuge resolutely chose to follow her husband to the countryside. So, the couple of Suhebalu took their eldest daughter Wulan, second daughter Wuyin, and Wuyin's twin sister Shandan back to the countryside. In this way, Ms. Wuyin's family returned to the Chaganhua Grassland, which was half-flowered and half-grassy. After returning to the countryside, facing the hard times and simple food, clothing, housing, and transportation, Ms. Qimuge had to pick up needlework and the production techniques of Mongolian clothing passed down from the previous generation. Since there were many daughters in the family, Ms. Qimuge was constantly doing needlework all year round. When the girls in the family were eleven or twelve years old, they all had to learn needlework from their mother. Ms. Wuyin learned to make small items, shoes, and cotton-padded clothes from her mother in this situation and gradually mastered the production techniques of Mongolian robes. The life on the Chaganhua Grassland did not last forever. A few years later, Ms. Wuyin's family returned to Songyuan City. Songyuan was established as a city in 1992. With a short urban history and slow economic development, the ethnic culture had not recovered yet. In the urban life at that time, there was no longer a need to wear Mongolian robes, and gradually, Mongolian clothing was forgotten again. Today, Ms. Wuyin's ability to revive and continue the tradition of Mongolian clothing is closely related to the revival of the local ethnic culture.

Behind the revival of ethnic culture is the effort of a generation. According to Wuyin, her decision to make Mongolian clothing a career has been greatly influenced by Secretary Aruhan and her father. Aruhan served as the Party secretary of Qianguoerlos County from 2005 to 2007. During his tenure, he was committed to restoring the local folk culture. His representative works include the historical document *A Brief Account of Songyuan Culture* and the songs such as *Girl of Hongjila* and *Mongolian Plateau*. Her father, Suhebalu, is also a scholar enthusiastic about cultural research. He has been studying the history and culture of the Mongolian ethnic group and has unearthed a lot of valuable information. Thanks to their efforts, the ethnic culture in the Guoerlos area has gradually recovered, and the requirements for the public in ethnic activities have also gradually increased. Mongolian clothing, as an intangible cultural heritage, has also shown new vitality.

Before that, Mongolian robes could only be seen when actors were performing, and only actors needed them. Other people no longer needed Mongolian robes. In response to these problems, the county government has introduced many policies and measures beneficial to the inheritance of ethnic culture. To protect traditional Mongolian clothing, Mongolians are required to wear Mongolian robes on various important occasions, such as when attending the Two Sessions (the National People's Congress and the Chinese People's Political Consultative Conference), Political Consultative Conferences, the People's Congress meetings, and other important festivals.

Most of Ms. Wuyin's family members work as actors in art troupes, so they have a greater need for Mongolian robes. However, they had to go to Inner Mongolia or Beijing to order a Mongolian robe. Considering making Mongolian robes for her family, Ms. Wuyin, who was working in Inner Mongolia at that time, had the idea of picking up the production techniques of Mongolian clothing again. Ms. Wuyin quickly put her idea into action. Besides consulting her mother, she often went out to learn and communicate with local Mongolians about the production techniques of Mongolian robes during her spare time. When she returned to Songyuan City four years later, her original intention was just to make Mongolian robes for her family. But after actually starting to make them, she found that more and more people needed Mongolian robes. So in 2006, Ms. Wuyin established her own studio-Wuyin Ethnic Clothing Studio, which is dedicated to the production, sales, and inheritance of Mongolian clothing. She has been doing this for 15 years. During this period, Wuyin has been constantly learning, combining tradition with modernity to create Mongolian clothing with contemporary features and has achieved certain results. Her clothing works won the gold medal in the first Mongolian clothing and adornment competition among eight provincial- level regions. In 2016, she was employed as a senior researcher at the Jilin Ethnic Clothing Research Institute of Northeast Electric Power University (Figure 5-2), and in 2019, she won the title of "Excellent Instructor for Graduation Projects" from Northeast Electric Power University (Figure 5-3).

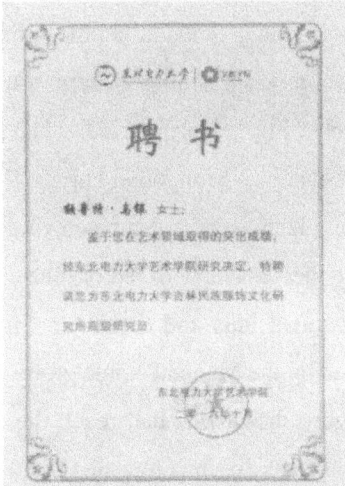 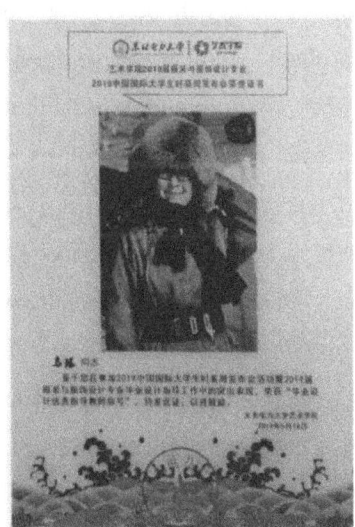

Figure 5-2 Appointment letter from Northeast Electric Power University   Figure 5-3 Certificate of Excellent Instructor for Graduation Projects

Section II Customs and Interesting Anecdotes

Mongolian ethnic clothing is a symbol of the identity of the Mongolians in the Guoerlos region, reflecting the local people's love for life and worship of the grassland. In the era of ethnic integration, Mongolian descendants showcase Mongolian culture by wearing Mongolian robes on specific occasions and express their affection for Mongolian robes through poetry, songs and odes.

I. The Surprise Brought by a Wedding

When Ms. Wuyin first started her Mongolian ethnic clothing studio, there were few customers apart from her family members, and the business was not booming. The turning point can be attributed to a wedding in 2007. At that time, a couple of overseas-Chinese students who were getting married planned to hold a traditional Mongolian wedding in Germany and invited Ms. Wuyin to design and make their wedding dresses.

The Mongolian wedding dresses in the Guoerlos region mainly consist of long gowns, along with belts, boots and jewelry. This primarily stems from the fact that the Mongolian people are a horse-riding nomadic ethnic group, and their robes are designed to facilitate horseback riding. There are slight differences in styles due to different regions. In the Horqin tribe, when getting married, men wear gowns with accessories such as Mongolian knives, flint and snuff bottles, and also carry tobacco purses. They wear soft-tube cowhide boots that reach the knees. Women usually wrap their heads with red or blue cloth. In winter weddings, like men, they wear conical hats and some fur. Since the Horqin tribe's clothing is greatly influenced by the Manchu ethnic group, during weddings, most people wear wide, straight-tube gowns that reach the ankles, with slits on both sides, and the collars and cuffs are in contrasting colors.

When the newly-weds appeared in the Mongolian wedding dresses designed by Wuyin, the whole audience was amazed. The fame of Wuyin's studio spread in the local area, orders came in one after another, and the business gradually thrived. Nowadays, for Mongolians in the Guoerlos area getting married, the gorgeous Mongolian ethnic clothing is still an indispensable part. In the second act "Song of Welcoming the Bride" of *The Wedding Song of Guoerlos*, there is a song called "Song of Dressing Up" which vividly describes the characteristics of men's clothing in Mongolian weddings: "Wearing a hat with colorful plumes and red tassels, dressed in a long gown with colored edges and rolled-up sleeves. Putting on long boots embroidered with eagles, with a long belt around the waist. Hanging a Hatt knife (a curved blade used by Mongolian herders for skinning and crafting) on the left and a beautiful purse on the right. Tucking a hada and an arrow cloth behind the back, and the arrow quiver holds auspicious omens…"

Jewelry is an important part of women's clothing. The second song "Sisters' Hearts" in the *Suite of Mongolian Wedding Songs* reveals the characteristics of the bride's magnificent attire: "There are ninety-nine fresh flowers in your coiled hair. There are ninety-nine shining pearls on your hairband. Ninety-nine colorful ribbons are attached to your sleeves full of lotus flowers. Ninety-nine lotuses bloom on your lapel full of green leaves. There are ninety-nine shining pearls on your hairband. Even if it takes a hundred days' journey, I'll accompany you all the way…"

II. Writing Poems for Mongolian Clothing

Apart from inheriting the craftsmanship of making Mongolian ethnic clothing, Wuyin, who was born into a family of scholars, is also quite talented in literary creation under the influence of her family. She has published poems in many magazines such as *Poetry Journal, Chinese Poets, Selected Poems, Stars*, and *Poetry Monthly*, and has also published books like *Legends of Chagan Lake* and *A Sketch of Guoerlos History* and *Wuyin's Poems*. Writing poems about Mongolian robes has become her way of expressing her affection for traditional

Mongolian ethnic clothing. The poem *Nothing Can Stop* conveys Ms. Wuyin's feelings towards Mongolian robes. When Ms. Wuyin received the wedding dress from her mother, she made a lifelong commitment to the Mongolian robe, and nothing could stop her from protecting it.

Nothing Can Stop

When I say I love you, when I give myself to you, and when you accept me.

The heart I unfold shimmers with such tenderness under your gentle gaze, just like the time

When my Mongolian mother personally handed me

The wedding dress of happiness made of colorful silk brocades

Embroidered with dragons and phoenixes, echoing with the songs of bees and butterflies

Where rhododendrons and sarilang flowers bloom one after another

Nothing can

Be like the magnificent heart I unfold for you at this moment.

III. The "Kind-hearted" Stitching Method Reflecting the Friendliness of the Mongolian People

When sewing Mongolian robes, a special stitching method called the barbed-hook stitch is used. The direction of the needle is inward instead of straight outward. This is the same as the way people in Tibet sew their clothes. "When I was a child, I always thought everyone sewed like this. When I grew up, I found that only we did it this way. So I asked my father the reason. My father has been studying Mongolian customs and culture, and he told me that this is a kind of ethnic wisdom. Since the needle is a sharp tool, we are afraid of pricking others when sewing, so the needle should go inward. On the one hand, it prevents pricking others; on the other hand, it is also a way to show friendliness. It means that we would rather hurt ourselves than hurt others. This kind of courtesy is also reflected in the way Mongolian people hold knives when eating beef and mutton, which is always towards themselves. It's the same principle," Ms. Wuyin told us.

Section III Production Materials and Tools

Mongolian ethnic clothing consists of four main parts: hats, robes, boots, and accessories. The materials and tools used are all carefully selected. The main materials and tools are listed as follows:

I. Fabrics

Fabrics are the most fundamental materials in the production of Mongolian robes. Traditionally, a wide variety of fabrics were used for Mongolian robes, including sheepskin, mink fur, otter fur, beaver fur, lynx fur, ermine, black fox fur, white fox fur, brocade, velvet, figured satin, and silk. These were mainly used for keeping warm and were not easy to clean. Nowadays, the functionality of traditional Mongolian robes is no longer a necessity. In Wuyin's studio, trendy and fashionable fabrics are the most popular, mainly including satin and cotton (as shown in Figure 5-4 and Figure 5-5). These fabrics are mainly purchased from other regions.

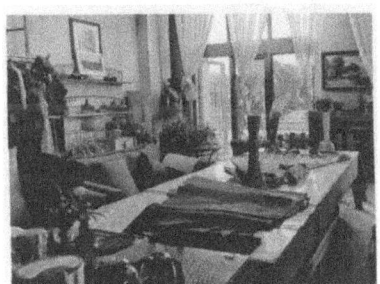

Figure 5-4 Satin

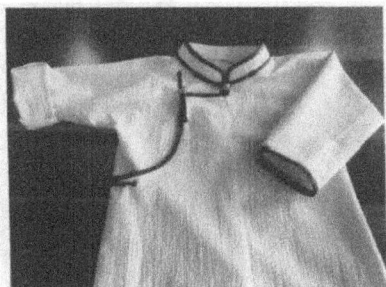

Figure 5-5 Cotton Robes

II. Accessory Materials

Mongolian ethnic clothing includes a large number of accessories, which are important embellishments of Mongolian clothing. The main materials for making these accessories are gold, silver, pearls, agate, coral, turquoise, and jadeite. Among them, coral and turquoise are the most widely used. Common earrings, rings, etc., are generally made of coral, silver, and turquoise (as shown in Figure 5-6).

Although the Mongolian people love turquoise and coral very much, the gathering area of the Horqin Mongolian tribe is located on the plain, neither close to mountains nor the sea, so there are no local sources of turquoise and coral. These materials are all purchased from other places. The Mongolians love turquoise and coral because turquoise is blue, which is considered the luckiest color in the hearts of the Mongolians. And coral is a kind of trophy, symbolizing beauty, bravery, and loyalty. In the past, when the Mongolians went on expeditions to the seaside and obtained coral, they brought it back to their hometown as a trophy. Since then, beautiful coral has become a symbol. As for silver, all ethnic minorities in the north like silver. Compared with gold, most ornaments prefer to be inlaid with silver.

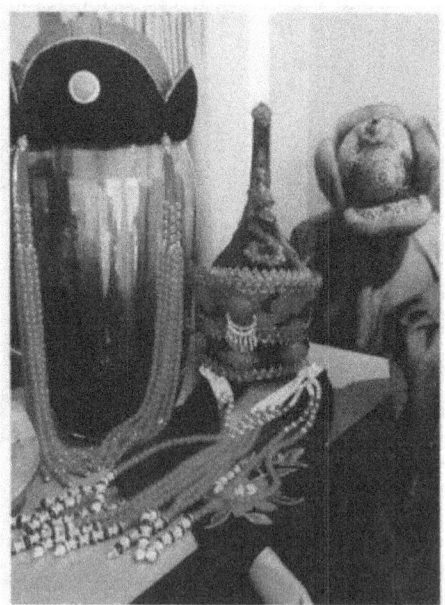

Figure 5-6 Coral Beads on a Hat

III. Scissors, Rulers, and Irons

These tools are the same as those required for ordinary clothing production. Figure 5-7 shows scissors and rulers, and Figure 5-8 shows the toolbox of inheritor Ms. Wuyin.

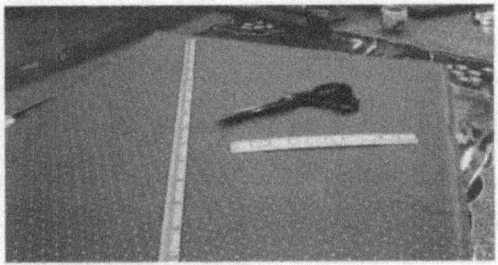

Figure 5-7 Scissors and Rulers

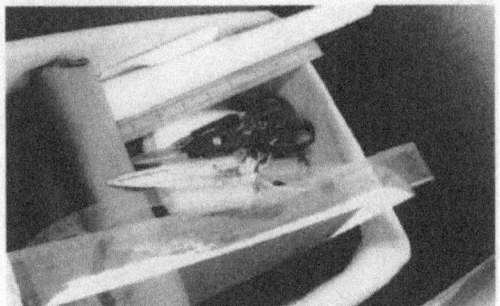

Figure 5-8 Ms. Wuyin's Toolbox

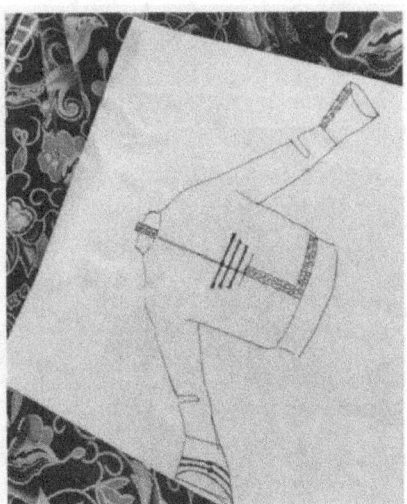

Figure 5-9 Drawn Pattern

Section IV Production Process and Techniques

The production process of Mongolian ethnic clothing involves several steps: pattern- making, fabric cutting, sewing, embroidery, and bead-threading and rope-braiding.

I. Pattern-making and Fabric Cutting

This step involves drawing the original pattern of the clothes on the fabric according to the customer's measurements and customization requirements, and then cutting the required fabric according to the shape of the pattern. Figure 5-9 shows the drawn pattern.

II. Sewing

Sewing refers to the process of stitching the cut fabric together, and it also includes the sewing of decorative elements such as edges. Traditionally, all Mongolian robes were sewn by hand (as shown in Figure 5-10 and Figure 5-11). With the development of technology, the invention of sewing machines has made mass production possible. Now, except for some detailed parts that are still sewn by hand, most of the sewing work is done by sewing machines.

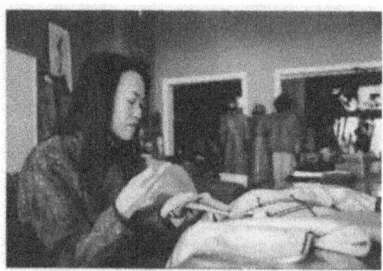

Figure 5-10 A worker sewing frog fasteners

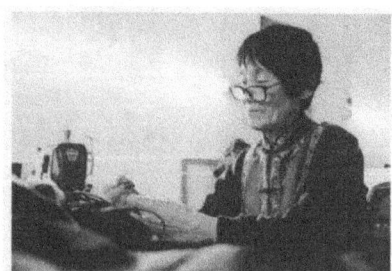

Figure 5-11 A worker sewing a Mongolian robe

III. Embroidery

One of the prominent features of the clothing of the Horqin tribe is large-scale embroidery. In the Guoerlos area, there were fewer nobles, so the embroidery area on Mongolian robes is relatively small. Patterns are mainly embroidered on the front opening and sleeves for decoration. The embroidery patterns are mostly based on flowers, plants, insects, birds, and the totems believed in by the ethnic group, and they all carry profound meanings. Apricot blossoms symbolize early spring; peonies represent wealth and happiness; grape patterns are a blessing for a successful career and fruitful results; scrollwork patterns symbolize prosperity; plum blossoms, as plants that bloom in winter in the north, represent nobility and carry the meaning of good luck in five aspects; intertwined-intestine patterns symbolize unity; coiled- dragon patterns symbolize good fortune; and flame patterns symbolize fulfillment. When Mongolian women embroider, they generally do not use an embroidery frame. Instead, they hold the satin directly in their hands. The main stitching methods used include parallel stitches, uneven stitches, stepped stitches, and scattered stitches. Figure 5-12 shows Ms. Wuyin embroidering.

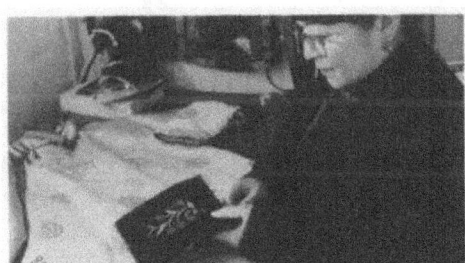

Figure 5-12 Ms. Wuyin Embroidering

IV. Bead-threading and Rope-braiding

Jewelry is an important part of Mongolian ethnic clothing, and there are a large variety of bead strings, which are used on hairpins, hats, headbands, waist ornaments, etc. Bead-threading and rope-braiding are the main techniques for making accessories. Figure 5-13 and Figure 5-14 show hats using bead-threading and rope-braiding techniques.

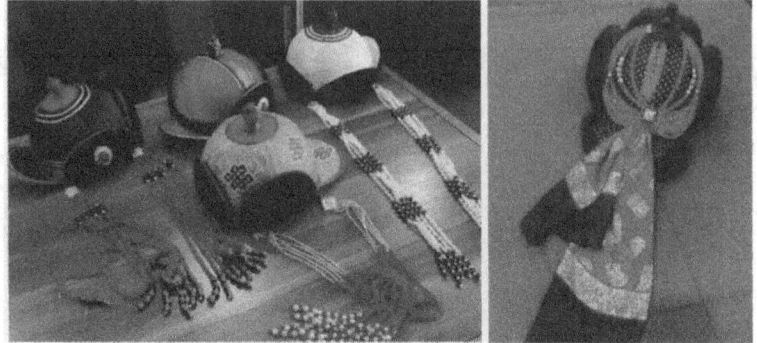

Figure 5-13 Bead Strings on a Hat

Figure 5-14 A Hat with Red Coral Beads

Section V Process Characteristics and Patterns

I. The Water Ripple Element Symbolizing Guoerluos

Since the Guoerlos Mongols live in communities along the Songhua River, the local Mongolian people highly revere water. Coincidentally, the beginning of the Mongolian letters of "Guoerlos" looks just like a water ripple, which the Mongols call "Shuige". Gradually, the Shuige pattern has become a symbol of the Guoerlos Mongols and is the most commonly used and distinctive graphic in the area. Therefore, this symbol can often be seen in Mongolian ethnic clothing. According to Wuyin, this pattern is used when representing Guoerlos in competitions and exhibitions. The Shuige pattern is shown in Figure 5-15.

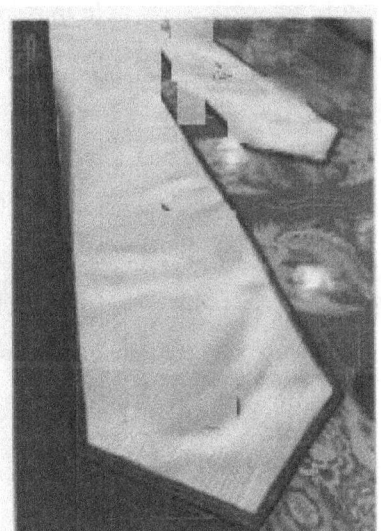

Figure 5-15 "Shuige" Pattern

II. Emphasis on Accessory Art, Reflecting the Aesthetic Taste of the Nomadic People

The Mongols attach great importance to clothing art, especially the decoration of the head. The Mongols believe that the head is the representative part of a person's body, symbolizing dignity. The most obvious manifestation is the headdresses of Mongolian women. Some luxurious headdresses are made of gold and can weigh dozens of catties, which reflects the labor characteristics, life emotions, and aesthetic tastes of the nomadic people. In addition, when Mongolian women wear robes, they must have red coral as accessories. The coral is usually decorated with silver, and coral and silver are used in earrings, accessories, and hairpins. This also reflects the economic situation of a family. Whether a family is wealthy or not is reflected in the headdresses and ornaments worn by Mongolian women.

III. Bright Colors Reflecting the Open-minded Nature of the Mongols

The Mongolian people are particularly bold in color matching. When she was a child, Wuyin was often curious about why Mongolian robes were so bright. Wuyin explained, "My mother said that we play on the grassland every day. The grassland is so vast. If we wear gray clothes, it would be hard to find us. So we must dress the children in bright colors. The grassland is too vast and people can feel lonely. So we need these bright-colored things to adjust the monotonous visual experience and resist the feeling of fatigue." This fully reflects the Mongolian people's open-minded and optimistic attitude of living in harmony with nature.

Section VI Appreciation of Works

Mongolian ethnic clothing consists of four parts: hats, robes, boots, and accessories. Each part has its own characteristics, representing the temperament of the Mongolian people.

I. Mongolian Hats

The most prominent feature of Mongolian hats is their "height". On the one hand, in ancient times, Mongolian hats were a symbol of status. The higher the status of a person, the taller the hat they wore. Therefore, Mongolians generally prefer tall hats. On the other hand, hats should be placed in a "high" position. That is, when placing hats, they should be put in the highest place, and other clothes should not be placed on top of the hats. In addition, Mongolian hats also pay attention to decoration. It is the most common decoration for a Mongolian hat to have agates and turquoise inlaid around it and coral strings hanging on both sides. As shown in Figure 5-16, it is a set of Mongolian formal clothing designed by Ms. Wuyin, an inheritor of Mongolian ethnic clothing. The hat in the formal clothing has a brimless design, with a round cap and a tall, flower-plume-like pointed top. Both the circumference and the pointed top are inlaid with jewels, and bead strings hang on both sides.

According to the design of the brim, the hats of the Guoerlos Mongols can be divided into brimless, semi-standing brim, and standing brim. The first two types are more commonly seen in women's hats, while the last type is more common in men's hats. Figures 5-17 to 5-19 show brimless women's hats, Figure 5-20 shows a semi-standing brim women's hat, Figure 5-21 shows a conical-top standing brim men's Mongolian hat, and Figure 5-22 shows a round-top semi-standing brim men's hat. Both of these two types of men's Mongolian hats have a frog fasteners design at the top.

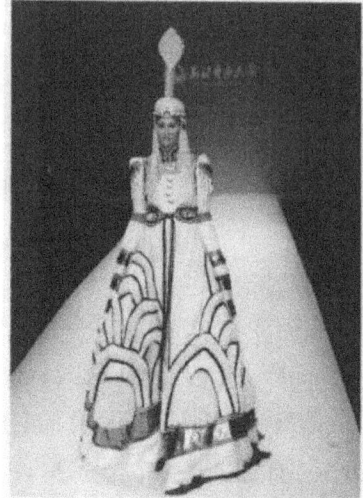
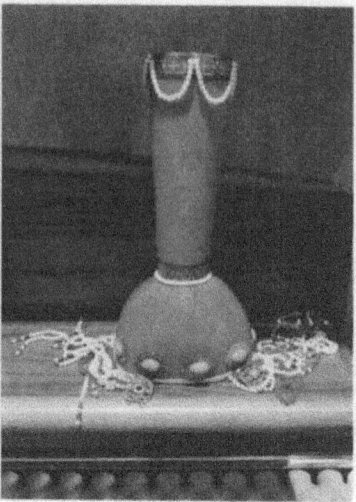

Figure 5- 16 Mongolian Formal
Clothing

Figure 5-17 A Red Gem-inlaid
Women's Hat

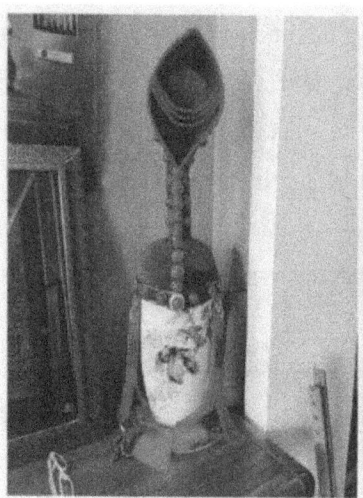
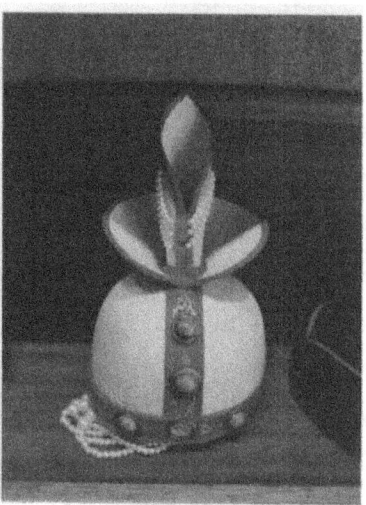

Figure 5-18 A Women's Hat with
Semi-upright Brim

Figure 5- 19 A White Women's Hat

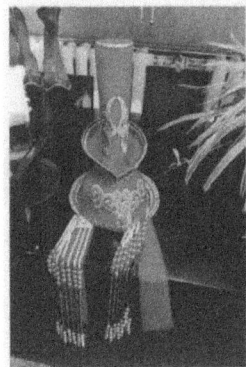 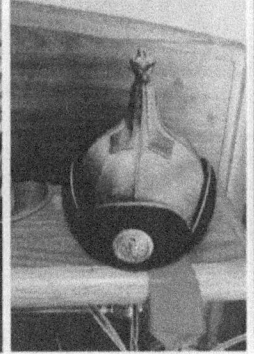 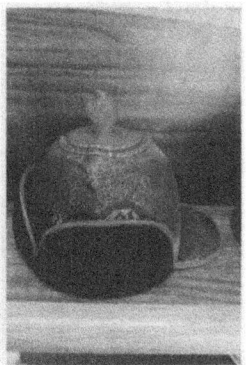

Figure 5-20 A Sapphire Blue Women's Hat

Women's Hat Men's Hat

Figure 5-22 A Semi-standing Women's Hat

II. Mongolian Robes

Mongolian robes are divided into men's robes and women's robes. Due to the inter- marriage between the Mongols and the Manchus, women's clothing is slightly similar to Manchu cheongsams. The style features a rounded stand-up collar, an arc-shaped right-front cross-over placket, and obvious high slits on both sides. Some women's robes have a front- opening placket, while there are fewer front- opening men's robes. Traditional men's clothing usually has side-opening plackets. Since the Mongols have always been a nomadic people on horseback, for the convenience of horse-riding and archery, Mongolian robes are designed with open hems. In addition, men's Mongolian clothing generally has nine buttons. In the eyes of the Mongols, "9" is the largest single-digit number, so it is an auspicious number. Nowadays, there are also some changes in some men's robes. For example, buttons may be added to the sleeves, but traditional men's Mongolian robes have exactly nine buttons. Figures 5-23 to 5-27 show various types of Mongolian robes.

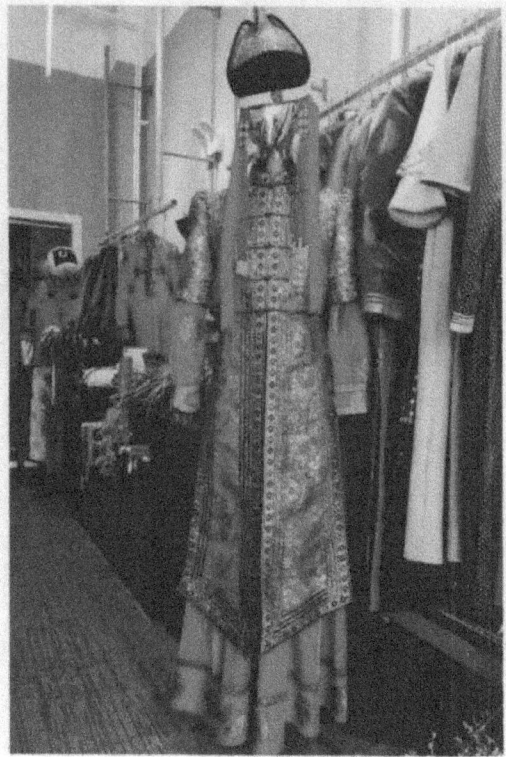

Figure 5-23 A Long-waistcoat Women's Robe

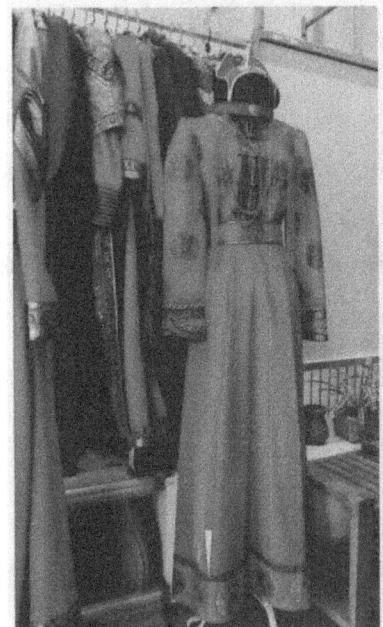
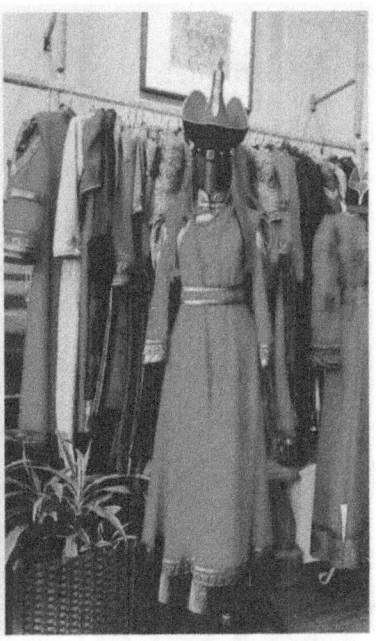

Figure 5-24 A Front-opening Women's Robe

Figure 5-25 A Cross-over Placket Women's Robe

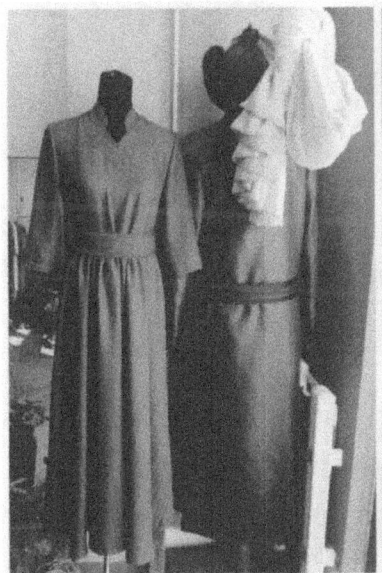
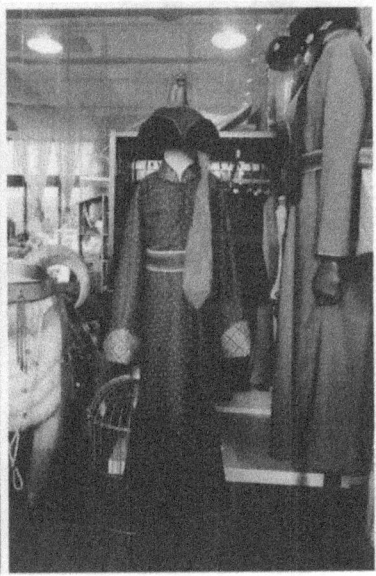

Figure 5-26 A Women's Mongolian-style dress

Figure 5-27 A Polka-dot Men's Robe

III. Mongolian Boots

The soles of Mongolian boots are generally made of materials such as felt and leather, and the uppers are also mostly made of leather. The production of boots is all handmade and cannot be mechanized, so it is very time-consuming. As a result, few people wear boots nowadays. In summer, the traditional way of wearing Mongolian boots is to wear a felt boot inside a leather boot. Figures 5-28 and 5-29 show two types of Mongolian boots.

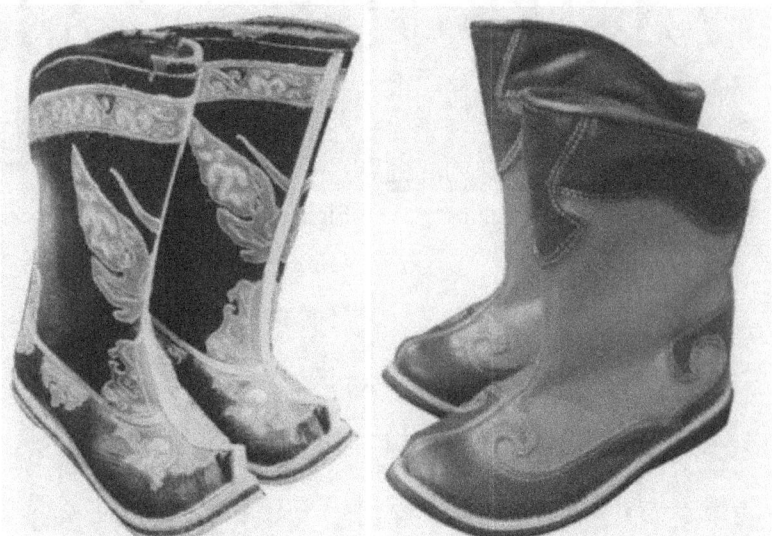

Figure 5-28 Black Mongolian Boots   Figure 5-29 Red Mongolian Boots

IV. Mongolian Accessories

Mongolian ethnic clothing includes a variety of accessories. Hairpins, headbands, coral strings on hats, earrings, necklaces, rings, pouches, waist ornaments, etc., are all indispensable parts of Mongolian robes, adding a bit of liveliness to the robes. The accessories of the Mongolian hats shown in Figures 5-30 and 5-31 include coral strings and turquoise inlaid on the front of the forehead. The turquoise on the front of the Mongolian hat shown in Figure 5-32 is decorated with silver around it, designed in a cluster-flower shape.

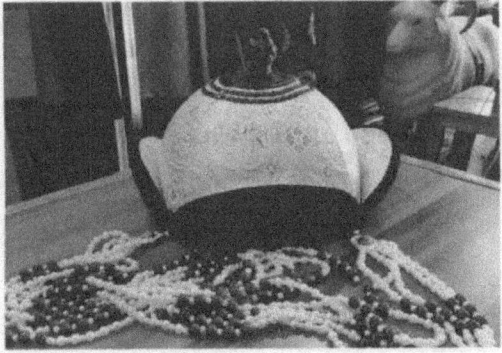

Figure 5-30 Accessories for Mongolian Hats (Blue-and-white Bead Strings)

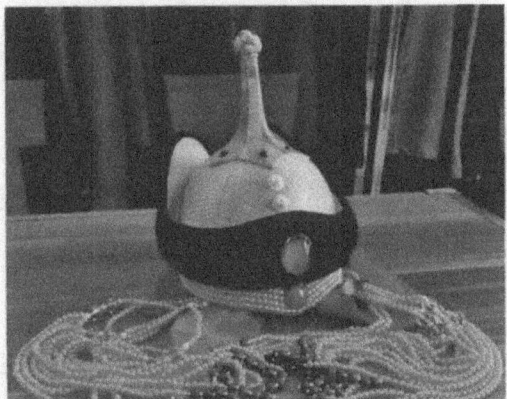

Figure 5-31 Accessories for Mongolian Hats (Orange-and-blue Bead Strings)

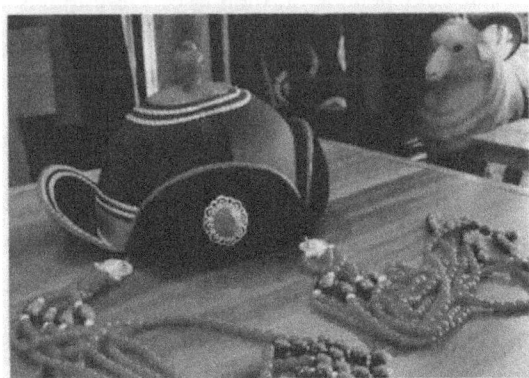

Figure 5-32 Accessories for Mongolian Hats (Red-and-green Bead Strings)

Section VII Interviews with Inheritors

As an intangible cultural heritage at the provincial level in Jilin Province, Mongolian clothing is of great significance for enriching textile-related intangible cultural heritages and ethnic minority clothing. To further study, inherit and innovate this intangible cultural heritage, this research interviewed Ms. Wuyin, an inheritor of Mongolian clothing.

I. May I ask: People like your generation have lived in an intangible cultural heritage environment since childhood, and have deep feelings for intangible cultural heritage. However, as far as we are concerned, we rarely touched intangible cultural heritage when we were young, so when we grow up, many of our peers have difficulty understanding intangible cultural heritage, and even think that intangible cultural heritage things are outdated. What do you think of this phenomenon?

Ms. Wuyin: This is actually due to the influence of the environment. We grew up being exposed to these things, so we regarded them as part of our lives. It's quite normal that your generation didn't see these things when you were young and thus don't understand them. But the more you see, the more you'll understand. Take myself as an example. I have a daughter who graduated from an art college early and majored in music. At the age of 15, she became a music teacher at a public school. When I was running my studio, she had saved some money and opened her own clothing store. At that time, it mainly focused on high-end clothing. She was not yet 20 years old and went to Hong Kong and Shenzhen to source goods by herself. Sometimes, she could make a profit of over a thousand yuan from selling one piece of clothing. At that time, she was not optimistic about the Mongolian clothing I was making. But a few years later, her business couldn't survive and closed down. However, my studio gradually became better and more appealing without me even realizing it. She also found it very interesting. Slowly, she started learning on her own, could calm down to make a Mongolian robe, communicate with the workers in the workshop, had her own ideas, and could understand our Mongolian clothing.

II. May I ask: What are the main difficulties you have encountered in making Mongolian clothing?

Ms. Wuyin: The main difficulty now is that few people are willing to continue this work. In fact, I've regarded it as a way to support my family, so for me personally, there aren't really any difficulties. Over the years of making Mongolian clothing, I have always done the most conscientious processing. As far as my current situation is concerned, survival is not a problem. But I wonder if there will still be people willing to continue this work when our generation gets old and can no longer do it. This is, I think, the biggest difficulty in the inheritance of Mongolian clothing.

III. May I ask: What innovations have you made in the process of making Mongolian clothing?

Ms. Wuyin: Actually, none of the current ethnic clothing is 100% in the traditional style. With the development of society, ethnic clothing is also evolving. Everyone can learn from others. For example, if you see a nice cuff design on someone else's clothes, you might apply it to your own clothes. Or if you see someone wearing a nice waistcoat, you might also incorporate it. There is more or less a fusion of other elements. The biggest feature of traditional Horqin clothing is the extensive use of hand-embroidered patterns. Its style is greatly influenced by Manchu culture and is quite similar to Manchu clothing, including the hats. People also wear mandarin jackets and don't need to wear belts. However, there are very few people in our local area who can do hand-embroidery now, and there are also few people making Mongolian robes. The youngest worker in our company is over 50 years old. So now, many patterns on the clothes are the base patterns on the fabric or are made by computer-controlled embroidery machines, and there is very little hand-embroidery.

The most significant innovations are probably in the style and fabric. The current direction of innovation is to make some daily-wear clothing with the mark of Mongolian robes. I often learn some fashion design knowledge and design Mongolian robes into styles that people can wear in daily life. The improved Mongolian robe has a shorter body, a straight-tube and large-front-opening design, similar to a dress. The belt is replaced with a cloth one that can be tightened. People can directly wear it as a dress. This kind of improved robe is very popular in summer because traditional Mongolian robes don't have summer styles, and people have to wear thick clothes even in summer. After the improvement, lighter fabrics are used, which are suitable for summer wear. Moreover, the fabrics we use now can be directly washed in the washing machine. Traditional Mongolian robes are made of satin, which is very difficult to clean and will break easily after washing. Now, we mainly choose some wear-resistant and easy-to-clean fabrics, and the fabric selection has become very modern.

IV. May I ask: When is there a higher demand for ordering Mongolian robes?

Ms. Wuyin: Our company has a relatively good sales volume. There are new orders almost every day, and we always have customers. There are currently 8 people in our studio, and we're busy all year round. Excluding large-scale events, we sell an average of six or seven thousand pieces per year just through daily sales. Our workers are always very busy. Except for the Spring Festival, I don't even have time to take a vacation. In our local area, Mongolian clothing is required for many occasions. As long as they are Mongolians, most people will order Mongolian robes. First of all, all young people wear Mongolian robes when they get married. This has become a custom. If the bride and groom don't wear Mongolian robes, they will feel very sorry for the guests at the wedding. They'll think that as Mongolians, they should wear Mongolian robes for their weddings. Also, many people give Mongolian robes as gifts to children on their birthdays. The elderly also wear Mongolian robes. In addition, when attending large-scale meetings or events, such as the Chinese People's Political Consultative Conference and the Nadam Fair, ethnic minority cadres must wear Mongolian robes. Nowadays, many people also wear Mongolian robes in daily life. So we always have customers.

V. May I ask: How do you cultivate the next generation of inheritors?

Ms. Wuyin: First of all, it's through family inheritance. The youngest inheritor now is my daughter. She is also a music teacher and a morin khuur player in the dance troupe. I teach her how to make frog fasteners, cut fabrics, design, and embroider, starting from the basics. Secondly, we also train inheritors by recruiting apprentices. We recruit apprentices all year round and teach them for free. In fact, in the past six or seven years, more than 10 college students have come to learn. They are all local students majoring in fashion design or related fields. After graduation, they know that the country attaches great importance to intangible cultural heritage, so they want to come and learn. However, the longest one persisted for two months, and the shortest one quit after just a few days. At the beginning, they all start with basic sewing and then gradually learn design. They find it completely different from what they imagined and very boring. When they think that it might take two years before they can make a Mongolian robe on their own, they don't want to persevere and leave. So this method doesn't have very good results. Thirdly, we also train through giving lectures in schools. Our company has a cooperation with

Northeast Electric Power University. Sometimes, the students from the school come here to learn about the production of ethnic handicrafts. I also take our workers to the school for exchanges, and I myself give lectures to the students, including courses on folk customs and intangible cultural heritage. Finally, there are also some other ways of training, such as teaching basic techniques in communities. We'll bring some fabrics and teach the children in the community to make Mongolian flower-button pillows, small waistcoats, and Mongolian embroidery.

VI. May I ask: What did you gain from participating in the seminar for intangible inheritance held by colleges and universities?

Ms. Wuyin: I've participated in several training courses for inheritors of intangible cultural heritage organized by Donghua University in Shanghai. I think it's extremely beneficial, especially for people like us living in relatively remote areas. The inheritors who come to participate in these training courses all have unique skills, and every time I'm really impressed and learn a lot. We are relatively conservative people. Through communicating and learning with others outside, we'll have some new ideas when we come back. For example, the clothing we designed for the Beijing College Students' Art Festival in cooperation with Northeast Electric Power University this year was inspired by what I learned during the training courses.

VII. May I ask: What materials for making Mongolian robes need to be purchased from other regions?

Ms. Wuyin: The main one is fabric, such as silk and some more modern fabrics, which are not available locally. As far as I know, the silk used by Mongolians in Inner Mongolia and Tibet in China, as well as in Mongolia, has local ethnic-characteristic patterns on it and can be customized in the Jiangsu and Zhejiang areas. But we don't have such fabrics here. Our city is very small. It was established only 25 years ago. Before that, it was just a small ethnic autonomous county merged with two other counties. The city has a short history and a relatively underdeveloped economy. There is no market or store for the fabrics needed for making ethnic clothing here. So up to now, these raw materials still have to be purchased from other places. And the local transportation is not well-developed. So overall, the source of raw materials for making Mongolian robes is very restricted, and we mainly have to go out and select them ourselves.

VIII. May I ask: What measures has the local government taken to support the development of Mongolian attire?

Ms. Wuyin: The local government attaches great importance to the protection of intangible cultural heritage and has taken a series of supportive measures. An incubation base for intangible cultural heritage has been established in the Faya area. In April 2018, all national-level, provincial-level, and county-level intangible cultural heritage projects were moved to the incubation base. Here, the government provides factories and studios. The preferential policy for us is that the rent is completely waived, and the heating and property management fees are also paid by the government. We only need to pay for electricity and water. The government spends about 30 million yuan a year renting this place for these intangible cultural heritage projects. The support for us is very strong.

Section VIII Current Situation and Countermeasures of Inheritance

I. Current Situation of Inheritance

With the advancement of the intangible cultural heritage protection work in Jilin Province, the development of ethnic culture in the Guoerlos region, and the establishment of the Mongolian clothing inheritance base, Mongolian clothing has been effectively inherited and protected. The awareness of clothing culture and its popularity in the market have been gradually increasing. However, due to the constraints of the local economic development level, the further inheritance and development of Mongolian clothing still face a series of problems, mainly manifested in the following three aspects:

1. Lack of Talents and Difficulties in Cultivating Inheritors

The production process of Guoerlos Mongolian clothing is cumbersome, requiring the mastery of multiple skills such as design, sewing, embroidery, and bead-stringing and rope-weaving. It takes a lot of time to learn and practice, and it is difficult to get direct material rewards in the short term. This is the most direct reason for the difficulties in talent cultivation. On the one hand, it is difficult to retain middle-aged talents in this industry. These people experienced the prosperous period of Mongolian clothing development in their childhood and have a certain foundation in its production and wearing. However, most of them gradually abandoned it with social development and changes in living habits. On the other hand, it is difficult to attract young people to engage in the production of Mongolian clothing. For the younger generation, material rewards are particularly crucial. An industry without sufficient financial incentives is often not attractive.

2. Small Number and Scale of Production Enterprises

Although the Guoerlos region is an area where Mongolians gather, there are very few Mongolian robe production enterprises, and large-scale production has not been formed. According to the inheritors of Mongolian clothing, there were originally three Mongolian clothing production enterprises in the local area. In recent years, more and more people are wearing Mongolian robes, and the market situation for Mongolian robes is good. One of the enterprises expanded its production scale, but due to its overly aggressive approach, it went bankrupt soon after. Another enterprise switched to producing yangko costumes and other items after operating for a while and no longer produced Mongolian robes. As of now, only Wuyin National Clothing Co., Ltd. is still specializing in the production and operation of Mongolian clothing.

3. Untapped Raw Material Market and High Production Costs

The main raw materials for making Mongolian clothing are silk and cotton cloth. However, there are no local enterprises producing specialized fabrics, so the main raw materials are basically all purchased from other places. The upstream raw material market is completely untapped. Coupled with the underdeveloped local transportation and high transportation costs, the production cost has increased directly, which restricts the production and operation of enterprises. This has forced the Mongolian clothing industry to become an industry with high costs and high risks, reducing the possibility of enterprises entering and expanding their scale and is not conducive to subsequent development.

II. Countermeasures of Inheritance

Inheriting excellent intangible cultural heritages of textile categories, protecting the clothing and ornaments of ethnic minorities, and innovatively developing Mongolian clothing require the unremitting efforts and exploration of the entire society, the government, enterprises, and relevant individuals. In response to the above-mentioned problems encountered in the inheritance and development of Mongolian clothing, the author believes that the following three aspects can be considered: excavating middle-aged craftsmen and cultivating young inheritors; integrating resources and establishing an online sales platform; guiding the market and improving the industrial chain.

1. Excavating Middle-Aged Craftsmen and Cultivating Young Inheritors

"People" are the soul of all intangible cultural heritages of textile categories, and Mongolian clothing is no exception. Behind the inheritance and development of Mongolian clothing are the perseverance of a group of inheritors and craftsmen. Therefore, excavating craftsmen and cultivating inheritors is the primary and key task. First, excavate middle-aged craftsmen. Conduct a census of those who can make Mongolian robes in the Guoerlos region, especially in rural areas, and establish a talent file for subsequent support of enterprises as a talent reserve. These people are generally middle-aged and above, and the skills they have mastered are mostly inherited from the previous generation. They have a solid foundation and can easily get started. Second, cultivate young inheritors. Currently, Mongolian clothing is not attractive enough to young talents. The root cause is the low short-term remuneration. Therefore, government departments can support local vocational colleges and technical schools to offer majors related to Mongolian clothing, enabling the younger generation to master skills through school learning. When they graduate and directly enter the workforce, there will be no long learning period. In addition, such schools can guide and support including Mongolian clothing in college students' entrepreneurship projects, thereby inspiring the younger generation to learn about Mongolian clothing and inherit intangible cultural heritage skills.

2. Integrating Resources to Establish Online Sales Platforms

For clothing enterprises, online sales can not only save costs but also expand the market. The author believes that the government should take the lead in promoting the establishment of an online sales platform for Mongolian clothing. Enterprises should enter the online platform under the name of their physical companies. The platform is responsible for reviewing and approving the enterprises entering the platform, promoting and publicizing enterprises with high-quality products, and removing enterprises with low-quality products. At the same time, relevant enterprises can upload videos on the product pages to promote the culture behind Mongolian clothing, achieving a win-win situation of promoting products and spreading culture.

3. Guiding the Market and Improving the Industrial Chain

One of the problems faced by Mongolian clothing is the imperfect market development, the underdevelopment of upstream and downstream enterprises, and the lack of an industrial chain. Therefore, government departments can guide from the following aspects. First, support the development of upstream production enterprises. On the one hand, preferential policies can be used to encourage the establishment of new enterprises. On the other hand, investment promotion can be carried out to attract textile enterprises from the Jiangsu-Zhejiang region to build factories. Second, guide downstream production and operation enterprises to expand their scale. First, in combination with mass entrepreneurship, guide start-up enterprises to flow into the Mongolian clothing and ornament industry, and provide policy preferences such as tax incentives for start-up enterprises to encourage the establishment of new enterprises. Second, make full use of the talent file to provide technical guidance for the problems that arise in the development of enterprises.

References

[1] Chengge. "Craftsmanship and Research on Horqin Mongolian Robes" [J]. *Popular Literature and Art*, 2017(8): 98-99.

[2] Characteristics of Guoerluosi Mongolian Costumes [OL]. [2012-3-23]. http://blog.sina.com.cn/s/blog_521311270102dzsx.html.

[3] Menghebaoyin. "Research on the Opening-up of Mongolian Land and the Anti-Reclamation Struggle in Horqin Front Banner" [J]. *Yinshan Academic Journal*, 2011, 24(3): 87-90.

[4] Bo Shaobu. "A Study on the Koulasi Tribe" [J]. *Journal of Inner Mongolia University for Nationalities (Social Sciences Edition)*, 2002(4): 20-24.

[5] Wulan. "A Brief Discussion on the Protection and Inheritance of Horqin Mongolian Costumes" [J]. *Inner Mongolia Education (Vocational Edition)*, 2013(4): 71-72.

Chapter VI: Traditional Craft of Manchu Cheongsam

There is a local traditional handicraft in Jilin City, Jilin Province that has been handed down from ancient times to the present, that is, the traditional craft of Manchu cheongsam. The traditional craft of Manchu cheongsam was included in the second batch of the Jilin Intangible Cultural Heritage List in June 2007, and is categorized as a traditional handicraft (Table 6-1 and Figure 6-1), and in 2011, Liu Shufen was recognized as the provincial representative inheritor of the traditional craft of Manchu cheongsam (Figure 6-2), As the only inheritor of the traditional craft of Manchu cheongsam in Jilin Province, Liu Shufen continues the hand-sewing craft of the Qing Dynasty court cheongsam to this day.

Table 6-1 Introduction to the Traditional Craft of Manchu Cheongsam

Name of the List	Traditional Craft of Manchu Cheongsam
Category of the List	Traditional Handicraft
Level of the List	Provincial
Declaration Unit or Region	Jilin City, Jilin Province
Provincial Representative Inheritor	Liu Shufen

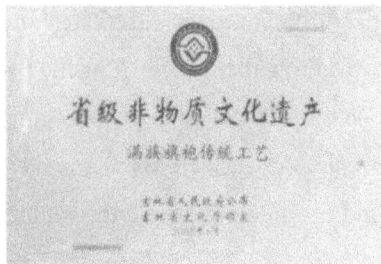

Figure 6-1 Certificate of Provincial Intangible Cultural Heritage Project in Jilin

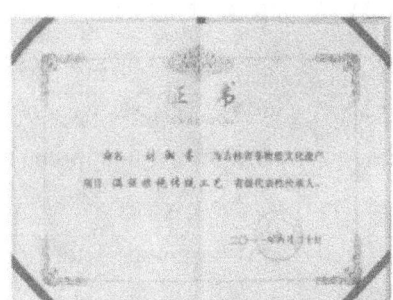

Figure 6-2 Certificate of Representative Inheritor of Provincial Intangible Cultural Heritage Project in Jilin Province

Section I Origin and Development

There is a definition of cheongsam in *Cihai* Dictionary (a comprehensive Chinese dictionary with a wide range of entries covering various fields) : "It doesn't have slits on both sides, with sleeves measuring eight inches to one foot in length, and the edges of the clothes are embroidered with colorful patterns. After the 1911 Revolution, due to cultural integration, the Han women also began to wear the improved cheongsam, which features a straight collar, a right - angled cross - front opening in the middle, a tight waist, a length reaching below the knees, slits on both sides, and narrow cuffs."

I. Origin of Traditional Craft of Manchu Cheongsam

The cheongsam originated in the Qing Dynasty. In 1616, Nurhaci unified the tribes and established the Later Jin regime, implementing the Eight Banners system. In 1635, Huang Taiji abolished the old ethnic name "Zhushen" (Jurchen) and renamed it "Manzhou". From then on, the Manchu people's religious beliefs, language, writing, etiquette, and clothing gradually spread into the Central Plains. The Manchu people were called Bannermen, and since the Manchu cheongsam was the traditional clothing of the Manchu people, the name "cheongsam" came into being.

II. Development of Traditional Craft of Manchu Cheongsam

During the reign of Nurhaci, there were no set rules for clothing, and there was a situation of "the upper and lower classes wearing the same clothes". In the era of Huang Taiji, requirements for clothing production began to emerge. After the Manchus entered the pass, there were specific production requirements for the clothes of everyone from the emperor to the officers and soldiers throughout the year, from spring to winter, and no one was allowed to violate the rules. As for Manchu Bannermen without official positions, men wore gowns made of silk or cloth, with a mandarin jacket over them, and this style persisted until the 1911 Revolution.

After the Manchus entered Beijing in 1644, the original Manchu hunting culture merged with the Han farming culture, and the characteristics of the Manchu-style clothing also changed in the late Qing Dynasty: A standing collar over an inch high replaced the original round collar. This arc-shaped collar was the forerunner of what is commonly known as the cheongsam collar later. The four-sided slits changed to two-sided slits or no slits at all. Narrow sleeves were replaced by flared sleeves, and several bright lace or colored edgings, commonly known as "painted lines" or "dog-tooth edgings", were added to the cuffs and side flaps. The workmanship became more and more exquisite, and cotton fabrics began to be the main material, while silk also gradually became popular.

As the clothing for women of the Eight Banners, the Manchu-style gown not only provided warmth but also symbolized social status. At that time, it was the formal dress in the palace and was exclusive to those in high positions. Only the empress dowager, concubines, princesses, and personal maids in the palace were allowed to wear the Manchu-style gown, while ordinary maids and servants in the palace could only wear short jackets and long trousers. Among the common people in the society, although there was no strict class division, there were differences between the rich and the poor. Families of the upper-middle class paid great attention to the fabric even though the style was simple.

In the 1930s, both Manchu men and women wore straight-tube gowns with wide collars and large sleeves. Women's cheongsams reached the calves and were embroidered with floral patterns. Men's cheongsams reached the ankles and had no patterns. After the 1940s, Manchu men's cheongsams were no longer in use, and women's cheongsams became narrow-sleeved, tight-fitting, hugging the waist, with a slightly larger hip area, a retracted hem, and reached the ankles.

"Grand ceremonies in the court, clothing is of great importance." The Manchu cheongsam has strong ethnic characteristics and is a cultural symbol, conveying a gentle, generous, elegant, and dignified temperament. The cheongsam has gone through nearly 400 years of development and evolution, and each evolution has carried the cultural characteristics of the era, with only the reserved oriental cultural characteristics remaining unchanged.

"In solemn court ceremonies, attire is of utmost significance.", the Manchu cheongsam has strong ethnic characteristics, and is a cultural symbol, conveying a gentle, elegant and dignified demeanour. Cheongsam has undergone development and evolution of nearly 400 years, each of which carries the cultural qualities of the times. What has remained unchanged is the reserved characteristic of Eastern culture.

At the end of the Qing Dynasty, Ms. Liu Shufen's grandfather made handmade cheongsams for the royal family in the palace. Later, Ms. Liu's father inherited this craftsmanship from his father. There are six siblings in Ms. Liu's family, and only Ms. Liu chose to inherit this ancient craftsmanship, for which she is very proud. Both Ms. Liu's grandfather and father made cheongsams with their left hands, and Ms. Liu also chose to use her left hand to make Manchu cheongsams. When Ms. Liu was a child, she often watched her father make Manchu cheongsams and gradually developed an interest, then began to learn from him. At the age of sixteen, Ms. Liu independently completed her first work. Over the years, Ms. Liu has always adhered to using the traditional craftsmanship of Manchu cheongsams to make them. Although Ms. Liu has not done any promotion, her craftsmanship in making cheongsams is well-known, and many people come to her out of admiration. Her apprentice, Ms. Chen Yuqiu, is one of them. Ms. Chen Yuqiu majored in fashion design. In 1992, Ms. Chen saw a well-made black cheongsam in a store counter, and from then on, she developed a strong interest in making cheongsams. After inquiring, Ms. Chen found Ms. Liu Shufen, the maker of the black cheongsam, and since then, she has been learning cheongsam- making from Ms. Liu. Later, Ms. Chen joined the Jilin City Intangible Cultural Heritage Protection and Research Center and continued to contribute to the protection and inheritance of the traditional craftsmanship of Manchu cheongsams.

Section II Customs and Interesting Anecdotes

I. Characteristic Sleeve Style: "Horsehoof Sleeves"

The characteristic sleeve style of Manchu banner costumes is known as "horseshoe sleeves". In the early Qing Dynasty, the cuffs of Manchu men's banner costumes were narrow, and there was a semi-circular piece of animal skin at the end of the sleeves that could expose the fingers. Its shape resembled a horseshoe, hence the name "horseshoe sleeves". The advantage of these sleeves was that they provided warmth and were convenient for battles and hunting.

After the middle of the Qing Dynasty, this style of clothing was no longer used as everyday wear but as formal attire. Most everyday clothes were made with flat sleeves, while formal clothes still had horseshoe sleeves. When performing the greeting ceremony, one had to first flick down the horseshoe sleeves before performing the ceremony. This etiquette was applicable in formal occasions and when visiting elders. Most of the formal dresses for Manchu women also had horseshoe sleeves.

II. Women's Banner shoes "Horsehoof-soled Shoes"

Manchu women's banner shoes are called "horseshoe-soled shoes", also known as "inch -high shoes" (Figure 6-3). Manchu women did not need to bind their feet. A piece of wood about 3 inches high was inlaid in the arch of the shoes. They got their name because the sole was in the shape of a horseshoe. Older women and those engaged in labor usually wore flat-soled embroidered shoes with a flat wooden sole, also known as "net-cloud shoes".

Walking in banner shoes showed a woman's upright posture and swaying gait. Noble women often decorated their shoes, such as adorning them with jewels and hanging tassels on the toe. Manchu girls started wearing horseshoe-soled shoes from the age of thirteen or fourteen.

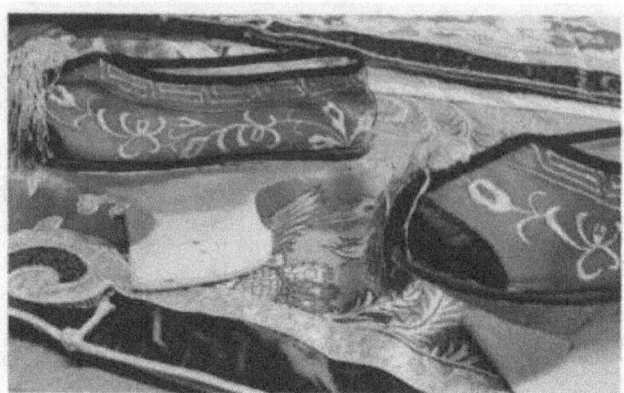

Figure 6-3 Horsehoof-soled Shoes

III. Various Manchu Women's Hairstyles

The hairstyles of Manchu women changed as they grew older. During their teenage years, they simply coiled their hair up at the back of their heads. When approaching marriage, they would comb their hair into a braid and then coil it into a single bun. After getting married, there were various hairstyles, such as the double-bun style and the single-bun style. The double-bun style involved parting the hair on the top of the head into a front and a back section. The front part was flat-topped, which made it convenient to wear a headdress, while the back part was in the shape of a swallow's tail, spreading out and requiring the wearer to keep her neck straight all the time. Obviously, such hairstyles made Manchu women look more noble.

During the reigns of Emperor Guangxu and Emperor Xuantong, the most popular and favored hairstyle among Manchu noblewomen was the "Da La Chi" (big spreading wings). The hair on the top was combed into a round bun, and the back part was in the shape of a swallow's tail. The headboard was made of black velvet, satin or silk in an inverted "T" shape. The base, made of wire in the shape of a button-bowl and called the headrest, was fastened onto the bun on the top of the head and fixed by winding hair around it. In the middle of the headboard, a large colored silk flower was placed, known as the "head center". Alternatively, long colored tassels could be inserted on the right side, or it could be decorated with jade hairpins, pearls, hair pendants and fresh flowers.

Section III Production Materials and Tools

In addition to the common materials and tools used in the traditional craftsmanship of Manchu cheongsam, there is another tool of historical significance: the sizing knife.

I. Fabrics

According to the various uses of the cheongsam, appropriate fabrics should be cut (Figure 6-4). For formal occasions such as banquets, solemn styles and high-end fabrics should be selected. For example, materials like silk and antique satin, which are soft in color, sophisticated, and elegant, can not only show a woman's curves but also highlight her intellectual charm. For daily-wear cheongsams, they should be simple, generous, and comfortable, so materials like cotton and linen are preferred. Elderly women can choose plain colors that are relatively dark. Young women should choose soft-textured fabrics that make them look fresh and charming, such as printed silk and spun silk, to show their youthfulness and vitality. Middle-aged women often prefer fabrics with elegant patterns and bright colors, like antique satin and brocade, to demonstrate their grace and luxury.

II. Embroidery Needles

The Embroidery needles are the most common tool in cheongsam making process and is used to sew fabric, as shown in Figure 6-5.

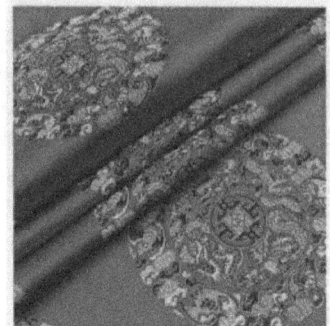

Figure 6-4 Fabrics　　　　　　　Figure 6-5 Embroidery Needles

III. Embroidery Threads

Embroidery threads are used for sewing cheongsam, and the choice of embroidery thread color should be determined according to the color of cheongsam, as shown in Figure 6-6.

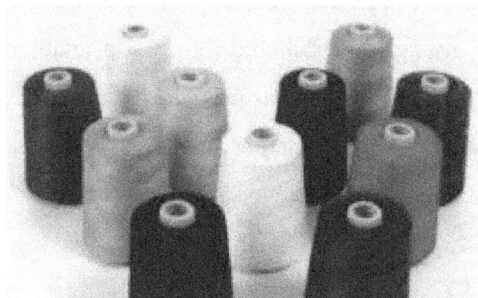

Figure 6-6 Embroidery Threads

IV. Sizing Knives

The sizing knife (Figure 6-7) is one of the essential tools for manual tailors. It is flexible, light, and non-rusty. It is not a knife in the traditional sense and has no cutting function. Fabrics such as silk and satin are prone to deformation and wrinkling. During the clothing- making process, in order to make the fabric flat and stiff, a thin layer of starch paste must be applied. It is reported that the raw material for making the sizing knife is "sonorous copper". Ms. Liu Shufen has a sizing knife with a history of over a hundred years.

V. Scissors

Scissors are used to cut fabric, as shown in Figure 6-8.

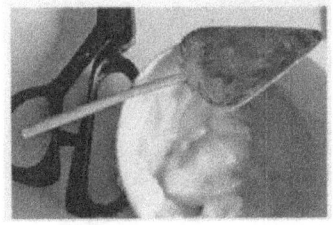   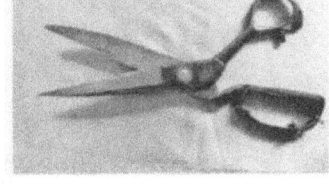

Figure 6-7 A Sizing Knife   Figure 6-8 Scissors

VI. Sewing Machines

Sewing machines are commonly used for stitching. The stitches they make are neat, beautiful, flat, and firm, and the sewing speed is fast. Most Manchu cheongsams involve stitching between garment pieces, and only with good craftsmanship can a perfect cheongsam be sewn.

Section IV Production Process and Techniques

The traditional craft of Manchu cheongsam is complicated, and the main process is shown in Figure 6-9.

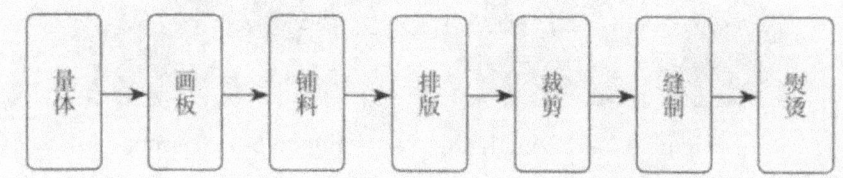

Figure 6-9 Traditional Process of Manchu Cheongsam

I. Measuring the Body

Measuring the body refers to using a tape measure to measure the dimensions of the human body and record the data. Nowadays, data at 16 points are generally measured. Body-measuring runs through the entire process of making Manchu cheongsams. It is necessary to put people first. To ensure the accuracy of the measurement, it is advisable to have a proper conversation with the customer to understand the customer's characteristics. In the Qing Dynasty, only the length of the garment and the length of the sleeves needed to be measured when making cheongsams because the bodies of the royal family could not be easily touched. Instead, the cheongsams were more customized according to the wearer's status. As shown in Figure 6-10.

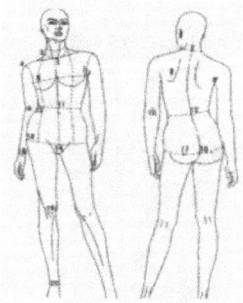

Figure 6-10 Measuring the Body

II. Drawing on the Board

Drawing on the board means transferring the body-measurement data onto the board. When drawing on the board, first determine the positions of each point, and then draw from top to bottom. You can use soap flakes or a pencil to draw, ensuring clear markings. As shown in Figure 6-11.

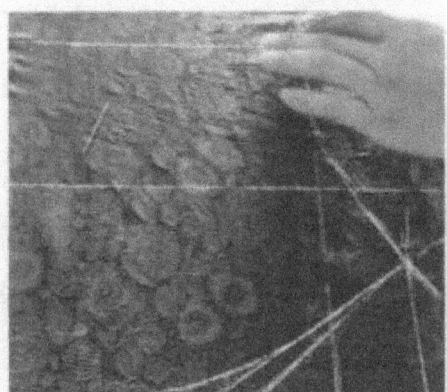

Figure 6-11 Drawing on the Board

III. Spreading the Fabric

Spreading the fabric refers to laying the fabric to be cut flat on the workbench. Pay attention to the front and back sides of the fabric, and make sure there is no overlapping. It is best to spread the fabric horizontally for easy layout.

IV. Layout

Layout means placing the pattern on the spread fabric. Align the front and back centerlines of the pattern with the warp direction of the fabric, and you can use nails to fix the points. When doing the layout, try to arrange the pattern along the edge of the fabric to save materials. As shown in Figure 6-12.

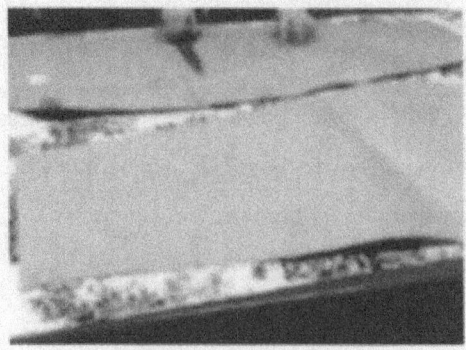

Figure 6-12 Layout

V. Cutting

Cutting refers to the process of trimming the fabric according to the pattern template, with different areas having specific cutting requirements, as shown in Figure 6-13.

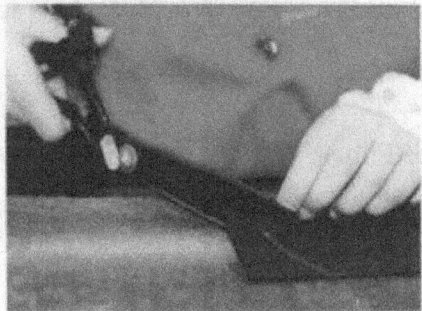

Figure 6-13 Cutting

VI. Sewing

Sewing means using different craftsmanship techniques to stitch and piece together the cheongsam. Prominent craftsmanship techniques include inlaying, binding, inserting, and coiling. After stitching and piecing are completed, some decorations can be added. The sewing process is very complicated and will not be elaborated here.

VII. Ironing

Ironing refers to the process of ironing the cheongsam to make it smooth and conform to the shape of the human body. Before ironing, it is necessary to trim the loose threads and clean any stains. When ironing, choose an appropriate temperature, and it is advisable to cover the fabric with a cloth to avoid direct contact with the iron.

Section V Process Characteristics and Patterns

I. Process Characteristics

The cheongsam is the traditional clothing of the Manchu people, which comes in four types: single-layer, fur-lined, cotton-padded, and lined. The traditional cheongsams for men and women of the Manchu people are called "qizhuang", which are the traditional costumes of the Manchu ethnic group in China. The common features of the cheongsam include: a round-neck opening, a right- side cross-over front, narrow sleeves, a waistband, slits on all four sides of the hem, and buckle loops. The fabric of the horse-hoof-shaped cuffs is mostly leather. When going out hunting, one can put dry rations and other items in the front flap.

There are two prominent features of the Manchu cheongsam. One is that it has no collar, and the other is the half-moon-shaped cuff. During the time of Nurhaci, the clothing system was unified and formulated. Only the court dress worn when entering the court could have a large collar, which looked like a shawl. The half-moon-shaped cuff is also called the horse-hoof cuff. Usually, it is rolled up. In winter, when fighting or hunting, it is put down to cover the back of the hand. It not only keeps warm but also does not affect archery, so it is also called the "arrow cuff", which is "waha" in the Manchu language. After the Manchus entered the Central Plains, when officials went to the court to pay homage to the emperor, they had to flick down the horse-hoof cuffs and then kneel on the ground with both hands, which was called "putting down the waha". This was a prescribed movement in the Qing Dynasty's etiquette.

Outside the cheongsam, there is a short jacket with a round collar. The sleeves reach the elbows, and the length of the jacket reaches the navel. The Manchus put it over the cheongsam for the convenience of horse-riding and archery and to protect against the cold, so it is called the "magua". Originally, the magua was the military uniform of the Eight Banners soldiers. Later, it became popular among the common people. There were also formal and casual versions, and the styles and fabrics became more complex. There are various styles of magua, such as the front-buttoned style, the front- cross-buttoned style, and the pipa-shaped front-buttoned style. What the Manchus like to wear is the front-cross-buttoned small cotton-padded jacket evolved from the magua.

The Manchu cheongsam in the Qing Dynasty had a straight and wide shape. The whole body was covered without revealing the body. It emphasized decoration rather than structure and followed the traditional Chinese flat cross-shaped structure. The ancient Chinese thoughts are perfectly reflected in such a structure. For example, the Taoist concept of the unity of heaven and man and the Confucian doctrine of the mean. The vertical, wide-fronted and large-sleeved long robe is loose and free, which is completely in line with Chinese aesthetics.

II. Patterns

In the Qing Dynasty, the production of Manchu cheongsams had to follow strict hierarchical orders. Different decorations symbolized different identities. Cheongsams demonstrated the wearer's status and wealth, and the quantity of decorations also had to adhere to strict hierarchical rules. The Qing-Dynasty court dresses (Figure 6-14) played a role in strictly classifying the ranks of court officials. In the ninth year of the Shunzhi reign, there was an imperial edict stating that any prohibited clothing, such as those with three-colored fox fur or embroidered patterns of three-clawed or five-clawed dragons, was not allowed to be kept at home. Clothing that exceeded one's rank could only be worn if bestowed by the emperor; otherwise, it was forbidden.

The court robes of princes were embroidered with five-clawed golden-yellow dragon patterns. Those of the heir apparent to a prince and the Junwang (second-level princes) featured five-clawed blue or cerulean dragon patterns (they were allowed to wear golden - yellow ones if bestowed by the emperor). For imperial clan members below the rank of Beile down to assistant state dukes and imperial consorts' husbands, as well as external ministers below the rank of duke down to civil and military officials of the fourth rank, their court robes were only permitted to use four-clawed python patterns in blue or cerulean (they could use five-clawed python brocade if bestowed). The court robes of civil and military officials from the fifth to the seventh rank were embroidered with square-shaped walking python patterns throughout the year, regardless of winter or summer. The court robes of civil and military officials of the eighth and ninth ranks and those without a specific rank only used cloud- patterned brocade without any other decorative patterns.

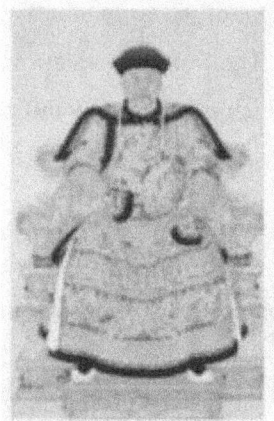 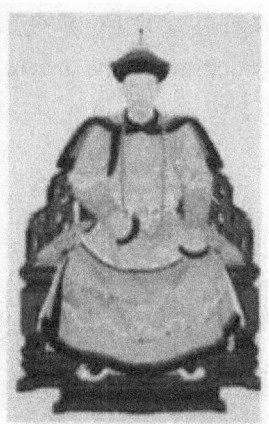

Portrait of the emperor in a bright-   Portrait of a prince in a golden-

yellow winter court dress (Yongzheng)   yellow winter court dress (Prince Yi)

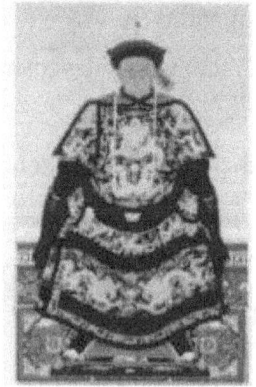 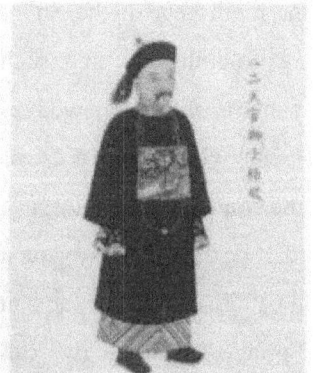

Portrait of an official in a blue winter court dress (Aobai)

Figure 6-14 The Styles of the Court Dress

De Ling, the chief imperial female official beside Empress Dowager Cixi, once described in her book that in the Qing Dynasty, there were strict requirements for everyone's clothing, which were written into laws. Everyone had to follow the regulations; otherwise, it was considered disobeying the imperial edict. For example, people should wear different clothes in different seasons, and each season had fixed color patterns and clothing styles. Figures 6-15 and 6-16 show the styles of the empress's winter and summer court dresses.

Apart from the strict clothing system, the patterns and decorations on cheongsams represented the identities of the Manchu people. In the Qing Dynasty, the society was male- dominated, and male chauvinism prevailed. In such an environment, women had to abide by various rules and could not express themselves freely. For example, the more noble a woman's status was, the more luxurious and magnificent the decorations on her cheongsam were. Figure 6-17 shows various patterns and decorations on cheongsams.

It can be said that the cheongsam is a precious heritage passed down from Manchu culture. It has very distinct style characteristics. After integration and a series of improvements based on modern women, in modern times, it became a symbol of Chinese women's clothing culture by integrating Chinese and Western cultures.

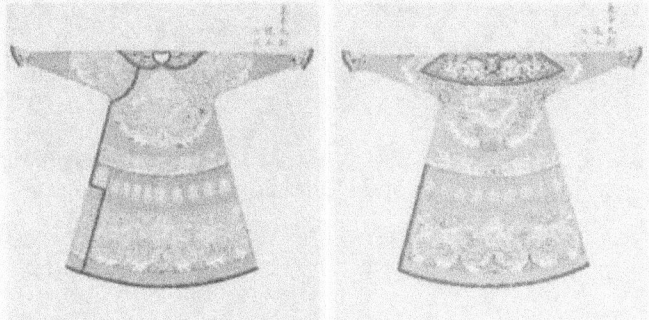

Figure 6-15 Style of the Empress' Winter Court Dress

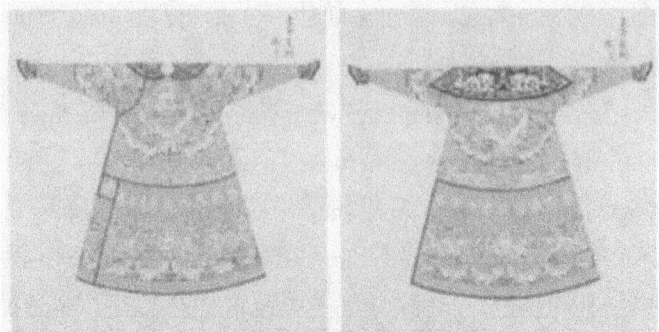

Figure 6-16 Style of the Empress' Summer Court Dress

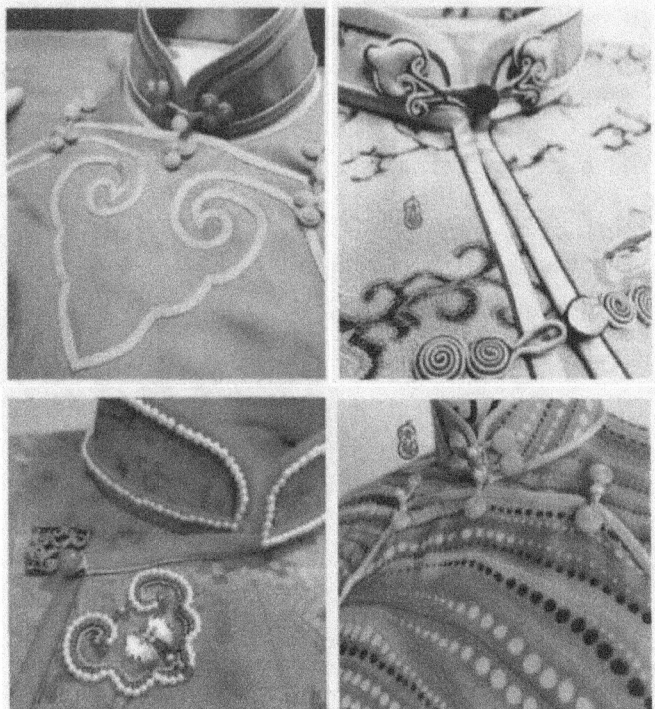

Figure 6-17 Patterns and Decorations on the Cheongsam

Section VI Appreciation of Works

There are two categories of Ms. Liu Shufen's works, one is Manchu court dresses for exhibition, and the other is improved cheongsam.

I. Traditional Court Dress

The red Manchu cheongsam with embroidered phoenix shown in Figure 6-18 is a Manchu cheongsam specially hand-sewn by Ms. Liu Shufen for the Shanghai World Expo. The process of this cheongsam is complicated and took Ms. Liu Shufen several months.

II. Improved Cheongsam

The cheongsam that Ms. Liu Shufen currently produces for her clients is mainly this type of improved cheongsam (Figures 6-19 to 6-22), which can be completed as a finished product in just a few days. The improved cheongsam is even better at outlining the beauty of the female figure's curves.

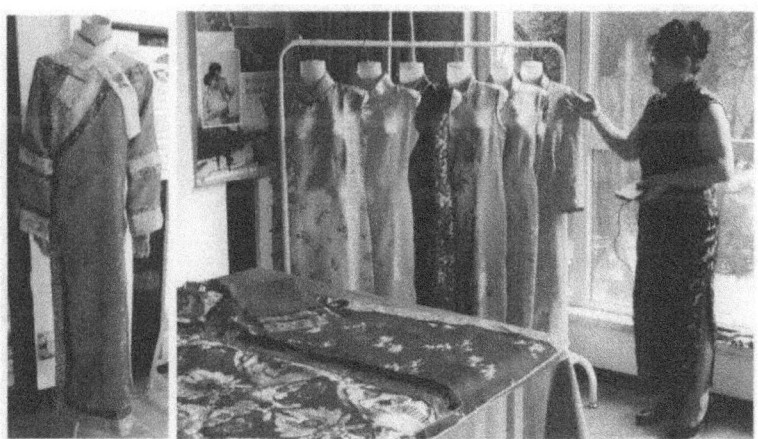

Figure 6-18 Manchu Cheongsam   Figure 6-19 Improved Cheongsam

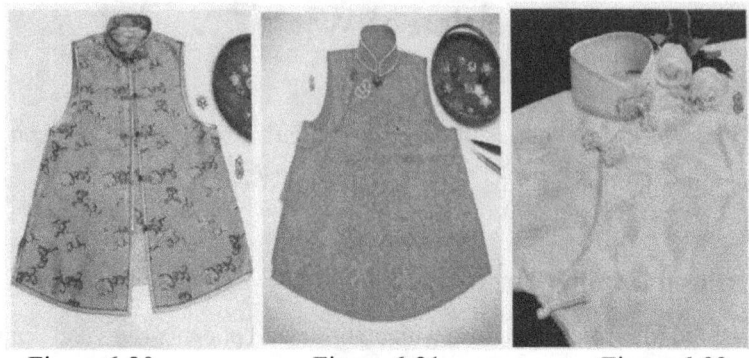

| Figure 6-20 | Figure 6-21 | Figure 6-22 |
| Cheongsam Style (I) | Cheongsam Style (II) | Cheongsam Style (III) |

Section VII Interviews with Inheritors

I. May I ask: How did you embark on the path of this inheritance of the traditional craft of Manchu cheongsam?

Ms. Liu Shufen: My grandfather was a cheongsam maker who used to tailor for the imperial court. Back then, everything was handmade. My grandfather passed this craft on to my father. From the age of three, I watched my father sew exquisite cheongsam by hand. As I grew older, I became increasingly interested in and even obsessed with making cheongsam, so my father passed this craft on to me. By the time I was in my teens, I was able to complete the production of court cheongsam independently. In my "cheongsam world", every piece is handmade. I have made more and more of them, improving with each piece, and becoming more and more fascinated by the craft. That's how I've been doing it all these years.

II. May I ask: What improvements and innovations have you made to the Manchu cheongsam?

Ms. Liu Shufen: After my father died in 1991, I inherited my father's crafts and dreams, and made some improvements and innovations in the craft of cheongsam. I not only adopted new fabrics, but also made different treatments on the waistline and chest of cheongsam. The improved Manchu cheongsam was loved by everyone, and there were an endless stream of people who came to me to make Manchu cheongsam.

III. May I ask: If you have any secret weapons for making these exquisite Manchu cheongsams?

Ms. Liu Shufen: For an authentic Qing - Dynasty style cheongsam, every process, from material selection and cutting to production, is highly particular.

In the production of each cheongsam, I use a copper sizing knife that is over a hundred years old. This is my "secret weapon". The traditional method is to use sizing paste to fix the edges of the cheongsam, which is rarely used nowadays. Colorful ivory trims or floral strips are inlaid at the edges. The most perfect cheongsam should have 18 layers of edging.

IV. May I ask: Do you have any particularly memorable customers?

Ms. Liu Shufen: The classically crafted Manchu cheongsam, stitched thread by thread, have attracted many foreigners who have come seeking to purchase them out of admiration. Once, two elderly American women specially sought me out and ordered over a hundred cheongsams at once. They had made cheongsams for their family members in the United States and specifically provided me with their family members' measurements, asking me to complete them as soon as possible. Normally, it takes me a few days to make one cheongsam, but in order to fulfill the wish of these two elderly American women, I worked day and night to finally complete over a hundred cheongsams, allowing the two women to return to the United States satisfied.

V. May I ask: Do you have any apprentices now? How are they learning?

Ms. Liu Shufen: I currently only have two apprentices. My eldest apprentice, Chen Yuqiu, is also nearly 40 years old. Fortunately, my granddaughter is also learning from me now. In 2007, the craftsmanship of Manchu cheongsam was listed as an intangible cultural heritage of Jilin Province, and I became the sole inheritor of this project. Over the years, I have always wanted to take on more apprentices. My only requirement is that they must love Manchu cheongsam. Learning to make Manchu court cheongsam requires excellent "eyesight", as the stitching involves a great deal of meticulous work that taxes one's vision.

VI. May I ask: What is your vision for the future development of the traditional craftsmanship of Manchu cheongsam?

Ms. Liu Shufen: There are very few people nationwide who still make this traditional type of Manchu cheongsam. I don't want this craft to be lost. I hope more clever and passionate young people can take it up and pass it on. The craftsmanship passed down by my grandfather will not be lost on my generation. I will ensure that this skill is passed down from generation to generation.

Section VIII Current Situation and Countermeasures of Inheritance

I. Current Situation of Inheritance

Manchu cheongsams are mostly handmade in the folk, with seasoned artists either taking in apprentices or continuing the trade passed down from their fathers, thereby preserving the unique traditional craftsmanship of Manchu cheongsam making. The craftsmanship handed down in Ms. Liu's family has always been unique, with each handmade Manchu cheongsam embodying the essence of China's ancient traditional culture. The exquisite details, such as embroidery, hemming and Chinese frog clasps, have amazed the fashion industry. Ms. Liu Shufen currently runs her own shop, but due to her advanced age, her two apprentices—the elder of whom has already completed his training and the younger who is still learning—are also on the older side. Fortunately, her granddaughter is following in her footsteps and learning from her.

1. Lack of Inheritance

One of the issues facing the traditional craftsmanship of Manchu cheongsam is the absence of a sustainably-developing inheritance team. This craftsmanship heavily relies on sewing skills, which, when done well, result in cheongsams that are comfortable and well-fitted when worn. Currently, the situation facing the traditional craftsmanship of Manchu cheongsam is that the existing inheritors are relatively old, and there is a shortage of successors, which urgently needs to be addressed. Furthermore, the inheritors have inadequate protection of the inherited products, lacking the habit of preserving photos of their works. The intangible cultural heritage learning center for the traditional craftsmanship of Manchu cheongsam is located in the home of Ms. Liu, the inheritor, which poses limitations on better disseminating intangible cultural heritage knowledge, enhancing public awareness and appreciation of intangible cultural heritage, and conducting large-scale training.

2. Lack of Effective Integration of Resources

The resources of Manchu culture are abundant, yet what is lacking is scientific planning and integrated development. Firstly, relevant materials have not been preserved in written form. It is nearly impossible to find information on the traditional craftsmanship of Manchu cheongsam online. Currently, this knowledge is passed down through families, and if there are no successors, this intangible cultural heritage is in danger of disappearance. In addition, there are few researchers in this field, and there is overlap with other intangible cultural heritages, which fails to highlight its unique characteristics. Secondly, the integration efforts are insufficient. Due to regional biases and ideological constraints, the intangible cultural heritage resources of various regions have not been integrated using modern means; instead, they remain isolated and independent. The traditional craftsmanship of Manchu cheongsam is a single skill, with its core being the cutting and sewing of cheongsam. Restricted by fabric, it fails to display the essence in its frozen artistry in terms of patterns and designs. As a result, it has not yet formed a Manchu cheongsam that is both tangible and spiritually alive.

3. Inaccurate Market Positioning

Manchu clothing products have gradually gained recognition and popularity among the general public due to the booming tourism and collection markets. Therefore, producers whose main products are Manchu clothing primarily target tourists and collectors. The tourism market is flooded with Manchu clothing, but the craftsmanship is relatively crude, and the designs and styles of the garments are simple and monotonous. What should have been handmade craftsmanship is often replaced by mechanized production, such as in the case of mixed borders. However, the traditional craftsmanship of Manchu cheongsam employs handcrafted techniques throughout, targeting a higher-end consumer group and carrying a higher price tag, which results in a low market share. This has led to two extreme phenomena: the Manchu cheongsam dominating the tourism market are overly inferior in quality, while the finely embroidered products are priced too high, failing to meet the consumer demands of the majority of customers.

II. Countermeasures of Inheritance

1. Improving Inheritance Protection Mechanisms

Firstly, it is recommended to seek diversified inheritance channels to form a stable inheritance entity. The traditional inheritance methods for intangible cultural heritage include individual inheritance and community inheritance. It is difficult to sustain inheritance by relying solely on ancient methods in modern society, so it is necessary to expand the channels. One approach is through social and school education to ensure that the inheritance of representative works of intangible cultural heritage continues. In this regard, we can learn from Ningguta Manchu Embroidery, which has set up a classroom in a school specifically for learning Ningguta Manchu Embroidery, with fixed teachers and class times to facilitate inheritance. Inheritors of Manchu cheongsam should seek local schools to collaborate with and regularly conduct courses on the traditional craftsmanship of Manchu cheongsam. For primary schools, middle schools and universities, as well as vocational and technical schools, different measures should be adopted. During the elementary school stage, which lays a comprehensive foundation for students, easily accessible intangible cultural heritage projects (such as the traditional craftsmanship of Manchu cheongsam) can be introduced into extracurricular activity curricula, with interest classes or experience courses held to bring students closer to traditional culture. In middle schools, textbooks featuring the traditional craftsmanship of Manchu cheongsam and other intangible cultural heritage with Jilin Province's characteristics can be compiled to enhance students' understanding of traditional culture. At the university level, public courses on intangible cultural heritage can be offered, student clubs can be established, and inheritors can be invited to regularly conduct related courses. In vocational colleges, talent cultivation emphasizes practicality, and through the teaching of practical skills, high-quality workers are trained. Vocational colleges have many advantages in terms of talent cultivation in vocational skills, educational experience, venues, and other aspects, providing new channels for the inheritance of intangible cultural heritage in schools. It is recommended to conduct inheritance and training in the traditional craftsmanship of Manchu cheongsam through the educational methods and approaches of vocational colleges. The second way to expand influence is through new media communication platforms. For the learning of the traditional craftsmanship of Manchu cheongsam, a dedicated exhibition platform can be established. Every day, inheritors share and display the process of making Manchu cheongsam, as well as showcase and explain their works on this platform. Interested learners can repeatedly study the materials and ask questions online. After learners have built a solid foundation, offline exchange activities can be organized to further immerse them in the charm of Manchu cheongsam and stimulate their interest in learning. The promotion on the online platform allows learners to access the content regardless of time and location, achieving the goal of dissemination and popularization, and attracting more people on a broader platform.

Second, improve the inheritor training mechanism. After conducting a survey, it was found that there are indeed issues of insufficient theoretical knowledge and limited opportunities for practical exchanges in the training of inheritors of Manchu cheongsam. Based on this situation, it is recommended to regularly organize general training courses to broaden the audience coverage. These courses should not only strengthen the analysis and interpretation of macro-principles but also delve into the cultural connotations of the specific project of traditional Manchu cheongsam craftsmanship. By improving the training mechanism, it is hoped that inheritors can deepen their understanding of intangible cultural heritage policies, related skills and cultural connotations, increase their comprehension of industry trends and social demands, and cultivate their cultural and artistic accomplishments and cognition.

2. Integrating and Utilizing Effective Resources

Historically, the transmission of intangible cultural heritage in China has largely relied on oral teaching from one generation of inheritors to the next, with a lack of written records. Ms. Liu Shufen, the inheritor of the traditional craftsmanship of Manchu cheongsam, is advanced in age, and her eldest apprentice is also over forty years old. Therefore, it is recommended to organize relevant content as soon as possible and carry out a digital preservation project. Currently, the oral history research of some intangible cultural heritage items has been included in the social science development plan, indicating that this is a major trend. It is suggested that the Jilin Municipal Government should consider incorporating the collection and compilation of the oral history of inheritors of the traditional craftsmanship of Manchu cheongsam into the local social science plan, supporting relevant scholars in interviewing them and conducting academic research to provide theoretical and technical support for the preservation and inheritance of this traditional craftsmanship. Leveraging the advantages of digital resources, relevant materials of the traditional craftsmanship of Manchu cheongsam should undergo digital recognition, organization, preservation, and exhibition. Through modern technological means, the content of this traditional craftsmanship can be dynamically or virtually displayed in three dimensions online. Additionally, Ms. Liu Shufen's interview videos and research materials can be placed in digital museums to expand social influence and dissemination.

It is recommended to effectively integrate social resources and establish comprehensive exhibition venues of inheritance to facilitate skill exchanges. For Jilin City, cultural facilities such as museums can be utilized to conduct related activities and attract the public. A dedicated exhibition hall or inheritance base for Manchu intangible cultural heritage can be established, where inheritors of related projects can display and teach their crafts within the planned exhibition areas of the inheritance base. This would allow interested individuals to learn about and experience Manchu-related intangible cultural heritage in one location, saving them the trouble of traveling around, and providing learners with a fixed venue for study and research. Meanwhile, inheritors of related projects can undergo training and exchanges at these venues, providing them with a fixed place for communication. Renowned scholars can also be invited to conduct training on history, culture, and other relevant topics for the inheritors, with the aim of enhancing their innovative capabilities. Furthermore, inheritors of projects from other regions can be invited periodically for exchanges and exhibitions, allowing them to learn from each other and improve their own inheritance projects.

3. Building Scientific Management of Brand

Conducting clear market positioning and segmentation is the prerequisite for building a brand. Firstly, it is necessary to segment the consumer groups for Manchu cheongsam, which can be divided into ordinary consumers, stage costume (film and television) consumers, tourist souvenir consumers, and collectors (museums or individuals). For ordinary consumers, Manchu cheongsam should integrate modern aesthetics in terms of style, patterns, and functionality, blending tradition with modernity and designing with a distinctive concept. At the same time, it is advisable to draw on the technology and sales strategies of experienced ready-to-wear brands, allowing both to learn from each other and improve together. For stage costume consumers, Manchu cheongsam should focus more on adhering to the historical attire of various social classes in the Manchu culture, emphasizing the diversity and tradition of colors and decorations. Contracts for costume production can be signed with relevant performance units, such as theaters and film studios, to create the Manchu cheongsam that meets their requirements. For tourist consumers, Manchu cheongsam should showcase their inheritance characteristics and satisfy their cultural pursuits. As for collectors, who belong to the high-end consumer group, the design and production of Manchu cheongsam must ensure a complete adherence to traditional styles, designs, and craftsmanship, presenting the essence of Manchu traditional culture.

Market segmentation is the prerequisite for Manchu cheongsam brands to occupy a broad market. At the same time, we must adopt effective marketing strategies and professional talent management to fully demonstrate the regional characteristics and ethnic flavor of Manchu cheongsam. It is recommended to invite NPC deputies and CPPCC members of the Manchu to wear Manchu cheongsams with distinctive features at major national conferences, positioning them as representatives of the Manchu image. Especially for female Manchu cheongsams, they should become the first choice for women attending banquets and gain international recognition. Furthermore, Manchu cheongsam brands should connect with inheritance practices, cultivate and enhance the professional competence of their personnel, and introduce creative and management talents. Innovation should be embodied not only in the design aspect of existing traditions but also in the orderly production process and modern operational methods in the sales aspect. While building the Manchu cheongsam brand, a scaled industrial chain should be formed to better develop and inherit the ethnic cultural industries.

References

[1] Hou Xia. "Research on the Changes of Cheongsam Shape and Its Aesthetics" [J]. *Textile Industry and Technology*. 2017.46 (2): 38-41.

[2] Xia Danqiong. Research on the Structure and Technology of Contemporary Cheongsam [D]. Beijing: Beijing Institute of Fashion Technology, 2018.

[3] Wang Xuemei. "Effective Protection of Inheritors of Intangible Cultural Heritage in Jilin City" [J]. *Journal of Beihua University (Social Science Edition)*, 2019, 20 (6): 43-49.

Chapter VII Fengcheng Manchu purse

Fengcheng Manchu purse technique originated in Dandong City, Liaoning Province. As the main settlement of the Manchu, the custom of making and wearing purses in Dandong City can be traced back to the before and after the Qing Dynasty's entry to Shanhai Pass. As a traditional Manchu embroidery folk crafts, Fengcheng Manchu purse carries the deep connotation of thousands of years of Manchu culture, rich in Manchu cultural genes, with important historical value, use value, artistic value and cultural value. In 2007 Fengcheng Manchu purse was listed as the second batch of provincial intangible cultural heritage in Liaoning Province and the list category was folk art. Huang Jiaxiang, the inheritor of the art, was awarded as the representative inheritor of the project for his outstanding contribution to the production and promotion of Fengcheng Manchu purse over the years (Table 7-1). Huang Jiaxiang' purse works not only inherited the style, method and pattern of the previous generation's purse production, but also innovatively added cultural elements, poems, aphorisms and lyrics into the purse production, which improved the cultural connotation of the purse and more profoundly expressed the deep feelings of the purse maker. Since the 1990s, after Mr. Huang Jiaxiang's discovery, collation, inheritance and further development, Fengcheng Manchu purse has been formed into more than 20 varieties of five categories of Manchu folk cloth, pendants, etc., and has been awarded the gold, silver and excellence prizes of national and provincial folk arts and crafts works for a number of times.

Table 7-1 Introduction to Fengcheng Manchu Purse

Directory Name	Fengcheng Manchu Purse
Directory Category	Folk Art
Directory Level	Provincial
Declaration Unit or Region	Dandong City, Liaoning Province
Inheritance Representative	Huang Jiaxiang

Section I Origin and Development

I. Origin of Fengcheng Manchu Purse

Fengcheng Manchu purse originated in the Spring and Autumn Period, and the earliest unearthed purse was found in the Han Tomb in Mawangdui, Changsha. Mrs. Xinzhui was holding the purse in her hand. A lot of literature on the purse have records. For example, *The Book of Rites* mentioned that "Grain is wrapped in purses and bags". Purses and bags are pockets carried around with the stuff. The bigger ones with a bottom are called bags, and the smaller ones without a bottom are called purses; Qu Yuan's *Li Sao* depicts that "Fill the dung and dirt with sachet and instead say that Shen pepper has no aroma."; *The Peacock Flies Southeast* describes that "Red silk fabric covers the bucket tent and scented pouches hang at the four corners". These are the descriptions of different kinds of purses. In the seventeenth "Couplets for Talent Examination in Grand View Garden" of *Dream of the Red Chambers*, Jia Baoyu was praised by his father for his quick thinking, happy to send the purse given by Lin Daiyu to the servants. Lin Daiyu was of the great annoyance after knowing about it, which led to an interesting story.

From here we can see that the purse has become an important link between people to convey emotions and express their feelings.

Purses in Manchu called "Fadu" was first sewn from animal skins to hold things. In *The Legacy of the Qing Palace*, it is described "Manchu ancestors, Sushen people, lived in the wild mountains and forests. When they made a living by fishing and hunting, they often hung leather bags sewn with leather around their waists to hold food to satisfy their hunger on the way". Later, it was gradually replaced by silk, and decoration became the main function of purses.

After the Qing Dynasty took over the reign, in 1644, the Manchus gained power and were in the upper echelon of society, but the custom of wearing purses did not disappear and instead became more refined in the process of continuous integration with the Han culture. Under the influence of the Han culture, the material, pattern and technique of the purse have changed a lot. The fabric of the purse was changed to cloth, silk, satin, brocade, and supplemented with embroidery patterns of flowers, birds, fish and insects. With the change in the form of purse, as a practical function of the food utensils gradually disappeared, which is no longer loaded with food, but spices, scattered silver ingots and some snacks and as an accessory, its aesthetic function gradually emerged. With its auspicious meaning, exquisite production technology and practicality, the purse has also become a gift for Manchu people in various festivals and happy events. The court also set up an organization specially responsible for purse making, and made a number of purses every year for the emperor's reward to show his favor, so Manchu purses flourished.

II. Development of Fengcheng Manchu Purse

Mr. Huang Jiaxiang, the representative inheritor of Manchu purses in Fengcheng, came into contact with this skill by chance. In 1993, Mr. Huang Jiaxiang, who had nearly retired, was hospitalized due to illness. During his illness, he read a lot of books about Manchu history and customs, and thus became interested in Manchu purses. After consulting a lot of literature and the elders in his family, he found that the purse has very high artistic and aesthetic value, and decided to devote himself to the research of the purse. Before that, he had never engaged in any work related to the purse, and he started from the most basic work-collecting and organizing literature. From Fengcheng Library to Dandong Library to Capital Library, he recorded all the information he could find about the purse. At the same time, Mr. Huang Jiaxiang also conducted field research in person, visiting various museums, antique markets, and colleges and universities, observing physical objects and consulting experts and scholars. In this process, he not only deepened his understanding of the Fengcheng Manchu purse and the determination to continue the inheritance, but also slowly began to carry out some of the purse collection and imitation work. Among the collections, the one that Mr. Wang is most proud of is the cigarette purse used to hold tobacco, which uses the process of gold coiling and silver pressing, but unfortunately, this process has been lost in the Qing Dynasty. After gaining an initial understanding of the purse, he began to learn how to make them. So he began to learn from his mother. Huang's mother was young, the purse embroidered by her mother was well-known in the countryside. Under this oral instruction, Huang Jiaxiang gradually mastered stitching, patterns, closing the opening of the purses and other skills.

For an old man in his sixties, learning to make purses from scratch is not a simple matter. After more than 20 years of continuous exploration, excavation and innovation, Mr. Huang and his wife, Ms. Ren Zhaolian, have reached a high level of purse-making skills. The beautiful shape, exquisite workmanship, elegance and popularity of their purses are so appealing that they have not only been highly recognized by the industry and praised by art lovers, but also won a number of awards and various honorary titles. For example, in April 2001, he participated in Dandong Tourism Commodity Design Grand Prix and won the first prize; In August of the same year, he participated in Liaoning Tourism Souvenir Design Competition and won the gold medal; In April 2002, he participated in the first China Tourism Souvenir Design Competition and won the silver medal; In June of the same year, Mr Huang's work was named as "Top Ten Tourist Souvenirs in Liaoning Province"; In 2007, the Fengcheng Manchu purse was included in Liaoning provincial intangible cultural heritage list; In August 2008, Mr Huang's work was awarded the title of "My Top Ten Favorite Tourism Commodities" by Dandong City. Mr. Huang Jiaxiang, the inheritor of Fengcheng Manchu purses was awarded the title of "Top Ten Folk Artists in Dandong City" in February 2007, and the title of "Excellent Folk Artists in Liaoning Province" by Liaoning Provincial Department of Culture in July of the same year. In October 2017, he was appointed as a distinguished expert of Dalian Art Institute. Table 7-2 shows the various awards and honors won by Huang Jiaxiang and Ren Zhaolian.

Table 7-2 Awards and Honors List won by Huang Jiaxiang, Ren Zhaolian

Date	Awarding Institution	Award Description	Certificate Display
June 2002	Liaoning Provincial Tourism Bureau Liaoning Province	Top Ten Tourist Souvenirs in Liaoning Province	
June 2007	Liaoning Provincial Department of Culture	Huang Jiaxiang was awarded the title of "Excellent Folk Artists in Liaoning Province (Manchu Purse)"	
August 2008	Dandong City Federation of Trade Unions, Dandong City Tourism Bureau , Dandong City Bureau of Commerce, Ri Lin Construction Group Dandong Radio and Television Newspaper , Municipal Tourism Commodity Development Association	Manchu Purse Series were awarded the title of "My Favorite Top Ten Tourism Commodities"	
January 2009	Dandong Municipal Bureau of Culture	Huang Jiaxiang was named as "The Representative Inheritor of The Municipal Intangible Cultural Heritage Project of Fengcheng Manchu Purses"	

Date	Awarding Institution	Award Description	Certificate Display
June 2013	Liaoning Provincial Economic and Information Technology Commission, Liaoning Provincial Women's Federation	Comrade Ren Zhaolian was awarded as the honorary title of "Liaoning Provincial Women's Excellent Arts and Crafts Worker"	
December 2015	Liaoning Provincial Department of Culture	Huang Jiaxiang was named as "The Representative Inheritor of Intangible Cultural Heritage Project of Fengcheng Manchu Purses in Liaoning Province"	
October 2017	Dalian Art Institute	Mr. Huang Jiaxiang was appointed as "Lecture Expert of 2017 National Art Fund Project of Cultivation of Manchu Folk Handicraft Innovative Talents"	
October 2017	Dalian Art Institute	Mr. Huang Jiaxiang was appointed as "Distinguished Expert of Dalian Art Institute"	

Section II Customs and Interesting Anecdotes

I. Two Stories, a Life-long Love Affair

Mr. Huang Jiaxiang joined the Chinese People's Liberation Army in 1947 and followed the army to fight in the north and south. In 1976, he transferred from the army to work in the government agency of Fengcheng County (now Fengcheng City). In 30 years of military career, he received a total of two purses. The first one was given to him by the local people during the liberation of the Great Southwest China when when they expressed their condolences to the People's Liberation Army; and the other one was sent by the common people during the War to Resist U.S. Aggression and Aid Korea, before they went to North Korea as a volunteer. These two purses are saved for a long time, but they were unfortunately lost in the end. However, it was these two experiences that convinced the old gentleman that he had a magical fate with the purses, which made the old gentleman start to study the purses in the year of destiny, and persisted for decades. Only then did he gather such achievements and let us see the beauty of Manchu purses again.

II. Combination of Ancient and Modern times to Innovate Purses

Although Mr. Huang Jiaxiang is 86 years old, he can still quote classics when introducing the origin of purses, from Ci Yuan (Dictionary of Chinese Etymology) to The Book of Songs, from The Book of Rites to A Dream of Red Mansions... When talking about the meaning of the purse, Yan Shu's words also came from his mouth: "A new word and a glass of wine, last year's weather and the old pavilion. When will the sun set in the west? There is nothing I can do to help the flowers fall. Familiar swallows come back, wandering alone in the small garden and fragrant path." Put words into the purse, and explain the meaning of words with embroidery on the purse.

This old gentleman believes that the introduction of literati's poetry culture has a great influence on the development of purse, which improves the aesthetic value of purse and affects the evolution of purse's aesthetic style. The combination of poetry, calligraphy and purses is not only the inheritance of ancient Chinese traditional culture, but also an innovation in the development of purses. At the same time, Mr. Huang did not stick to the same old rut, but followed the trend of the times and incorporated some fashionable elements into the production of purses. For example, during the exhibition, in response to the problem of obscure content of the purse raised by some visitors, Mr. Huang Jiaxiang embroidered some popular and familiar lyrics and Internet buzzwords onto the purse. At the same time, in some important festivals, such as National Day and Mid-Autumn Festival, he will embroider some purses to express his blessings to the country and the people.

III. Present Gifts to National Day and Seize the World Expo

In September, 1999, preparations for the celebration of the 50th anniversary of National Day were in full swing all over the country. Mr. Huang Jiaxiang learned from the newspaper that Liaoning Taiping Drum Dance Troupe was rehearsing in Beijing. The Manchu Taiping Drum Dance dashing in the photo was elegant, but the actors didn't wear the most important ornament in Manchu costumes—purses. He made an urgent call to Beijing, and after many twists and turns, he finally contacted the general director of the National Day Anniversary Gala, and expressed his willingness to give his purse to Liaoning Taiping Drum Dance Troupe for free. The next day, he personally rushed to Beijing with fragrant purses and related Manchu costumes to introduce them to the directors. The directors were impressed by his seriousness and enthusiasm, and decided to provide the troupe with more fragrant purses. After Mr. Huang Jiaxiang's unremitting efforts, the purse finally appeared in the scene of the evening show, making the traditional Manchu costumes more soft and gorgeous, and playing the effect of the finishing touch.

In 2010, Mr. Huang Jiaxiang received a notice to participate in the Shanghai World Expo, and was asked to bring the object to the site to show the production process. Considering the physical and age factors, the family originally didn't want the elderly to participate in the World Expo. However, the Manchu purse is the only folk handicraft in Dandong to participate in the Shanghai World Expo. Mr. Huang Jiaxiang wanted to take this opportunity to enter the international market. The main performances at the World Expo were colorful brocade purses and unique zodiac purses. The performance production process was mainly to make the final closure of the semi-finished purses, so that more people can intuitively understand the purse making process, and the small purses shine brilliantly at the World Expo.

Section III Production Materials and Tools

The materials and tools used to make Fengcheng Manchu purses mainly include: embroidery needles, scissors, embroidery hoops, colored silk threads (or wool yarns), silk fabrics (or other types of cloth), cotton wadding, spices (or Chinese herbal medicines), and accessories.

I. Embroidery Hoops

The embroidery hoop is a small tool used to tighten the embroidered cloth, which is convenient for later embroidery to produce a flat and beautiful picture. Usually, in the process of making purses, the corresponding embroidery hoop will be selected according to the size of the format. Putting the cloth on the embroidery hoop is an important step in the process of making purses. No matter how advanced the purse-making skills are, if the cloth is not properly placed on the hoop, the quality of the finished purse will not be high. Figure 7 - 1 shows embroidery hoops.

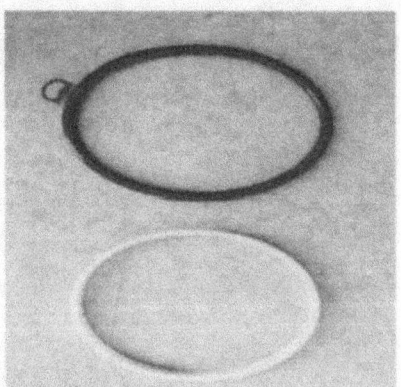

Figure 7-1 Embroidery Hoops

II. Colored Silk Threads (or Wool Yarns)

Colored silk threads (or wool yarns) are generally used to sew purses, and the silk thread of the corresponding color should be selected according to the pattern painted on the fabric. Figure 7-2 shows the silk threads of various colors.

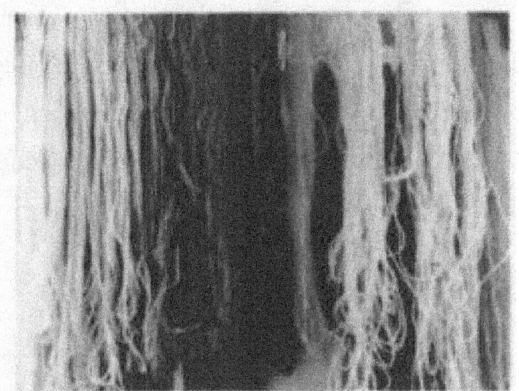

Figure 7-2 Colored Silk Thread (or Wool Yarns)

III. Cotton Wadding

Cotton wadding is mainly used to wrap crushed spices or Chinese herbal medicines. Figure 7-3 shows the cotton wadding.

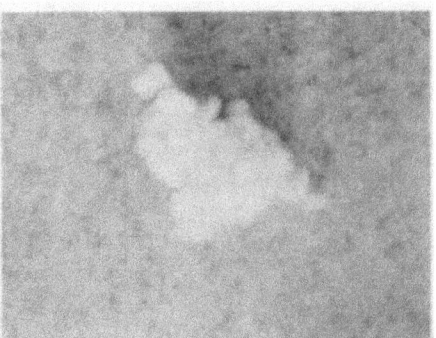

Figure 7-3 Cotton Wadding

IV. Spices or Chinese Herbal Medicines

The purse is filled with spices or Chinese herbal medicines, which not only takes its fragrance, but also can achieve the effects of repelling mosquitoes, flies and pests, preventing diseases and keeping fit. After trials and errors, a precious vanilla from the mountainous area of the Yao ethnic minority-Lingxiangcao (Lysimachia foenum-graecum) - is finally chosen. As shown in Figure 7-4, this herb is borer-proof when placed in a box; It can also be used for medicinal purposes. It has the effects of dispersing wind and cold and removing filth. It can be used to treat colds, headaches, chest tightness and abdominal distension. It is a valuable aromatic plant.

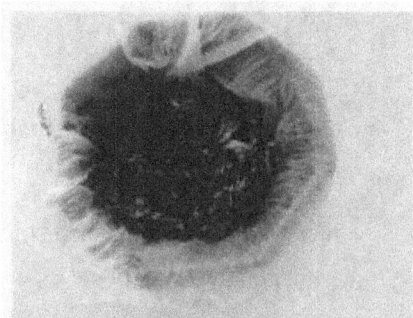

Figure 7-4 Lingxiangcao (Lysimachia foenum-graecum)

V. Accessories

Folk purse accessories are generally colored beads or Chinese knots, as shown in Figure 7-5 and Figure 7-6.

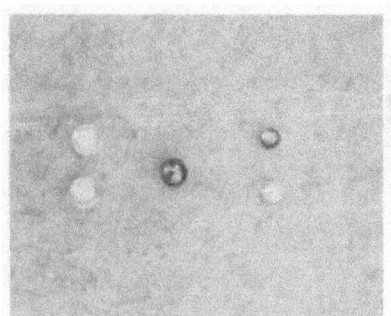 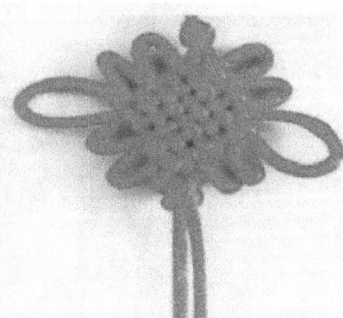

Figure 7-5 Colored Beads   Figure 7-6 Chinese Knot

Section IV Production Process and Techniques

The process of Fengcheng Manchu purses is not complicated, and it is mainly made by hand. The main process is shown in Figure 7-7.

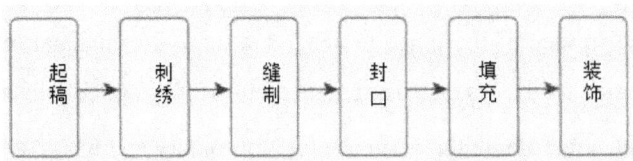

起稿 → 刺绣 → 缝制 → 封口 → 填充 → 装饰

Figure 7-7 Main Process of Fengcheng Manchu Purses

I. Drafting

Drafting means that before cutting, you need to first make a pattern of the style and shape of the purse to be made, and then cut the silk fabric according to the length of the cardboard. More than 60 heart-shaped purses with a diameter of 6 cm can be cut from 1 meter of silk fabric, and more than 20 small purses with a diameter of 3 cm can be cut from the remaining scraps. If you want to embroider patterns on the fabric, after measuring with a pattern template, you don't have to cut it out immediately. Instead, you can draw it according to the size of the template first, and then stretch it on an embroidery hoop for manual embroidery. As shown in Figure 7-8.

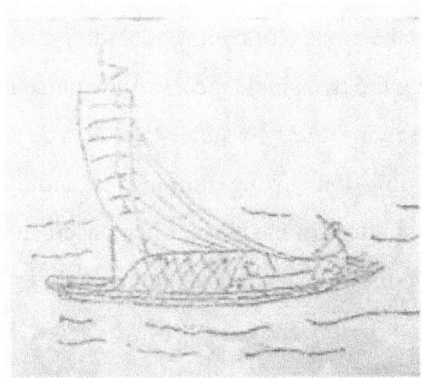

Figure 7-8 Drafting the Pattern

II. Embroidering

Embroidery refers to the process of using needles and threads to embroider on the surface of the purse according to the designed patterns. As shown in Figure 7-9. Specifically, fix the fabric on the embroidery hoop, and then use colored silk threads or wool yarns for embroidery. Some people also cut colored silk fabrics into patterns such as peaches, pomegranates, and bergamots and sew them on the surface of the purse to achieve a three-dimensional relief effect. This production method is called appliqué embroidery or piled-silk embroidery.

As for which color of silk thread to use for embroidery and where to embroider each color of silk thread, it needs to be selected according to the colored pattern drawn on the paper.

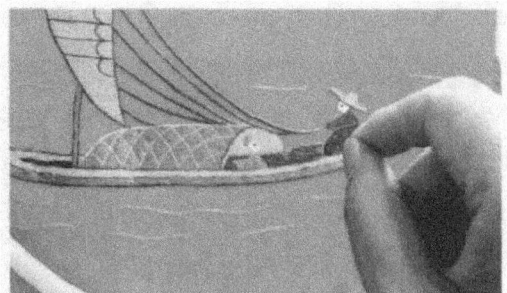

Figure 7-9 Purse Embroidery

III. Sewing

Sewing refers to the process of cutting according to the pre-designed purse shape and then sewing the two single pieces of the purse together. As shown in Figure 7-10. When sewing the two single pieces, you must sew the coiled-intestine tail pendant in. After sewing, turn it over, and the coiled-intestine tail pendant will be at the bottom of the purse. Then, insert shoulder tassels into the two shoulders of the purse to make them symmetrical.

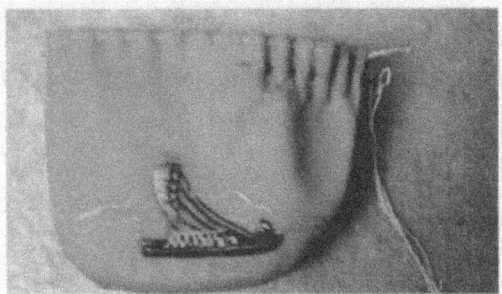

Figure 7-10 Purse Sewing

IV. Sealing

Sealing means using a needle and thread to stitch through the evenly folded purse mouth. As shown in Figure 7-11. Sealing is the most important process in making a purse. There is a saying among the folk that "the beauty or ugliness of a purse depends entirely on the sealing". Since the purse is made by folding the front and back pieces of fabric respectively, the number of folds must be equal to make it neat and good - looking. Tie the two strands of thread together at the starting and ending points of the stitching, and the sealing is completed. In order to make the purse mouth stiff when sealing, easy to fold, and not collapse due to the soft fabric during folding, you also need to paste a lining or padding on the inner layer of the purse mouth to increase its thickness.

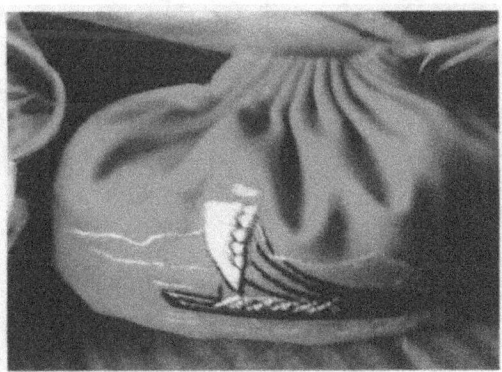

Figure 7-11 Purse Sealing

V. Filling

Filling means wrapping the crushed spices or Chinese herbal medicines with cotton wadding and putting them into the purse. Since the smell of spices or Chinese herbal medicines will volatilize, the finished purses must be packaged in plastic bags.

VI. Decoration

Decoration means adding some ornaments for beauty after the main part of the purse is completed. Court purses are generally decorated with pearls, agates, amber, jade, tassels and other decorative objects to make the purses look more gorgeous and noble. While the ornaments of folk purses are mainly Chinese knots and colored beads. As shown in Figure 7-12 and Figure 7-13.

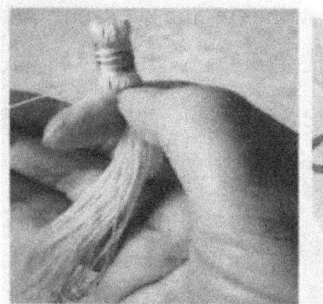 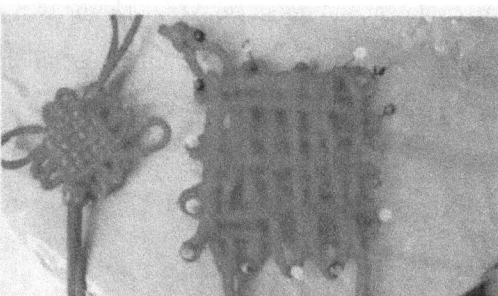

Figure 7-12 Braiding Tassels   Figure 7-13 Braiding Chinese Knots

Section V Process Characteristics and Patterns

I. Process Characteristics

1. Integration and Coexistence of Pictures and Texts, Art and Practicality

Fengcheng Manchu purses can be classified into tobacco purses, perfume purses, money purses, sewing purses, and yulian purses (Yulian is often regarded as a kind of folk art, symbolizing good luck and blessings) according to their functions. Tobacco purses are used to hold tobacco, perfume purses are for storing spices, money purses are for keeping banknotes and some loose silver, sewing purses are for placing needles and threads, and yulian purses can be put on horsebacks or slung over the shoulders. From the classification of purses, it can be seen that purses were initially used as practical items in people's daily lives. Therefore, the primary function of purses lies in their practicality.

At the same time, after the Qing Dynasty entered the Pass, influenced by the Han culture, poems, paintings, and calligraphy with profound artistic conceptions and elegant styles gradually appeared on the surfaces of purses, enhancing the cultural connotations of purses. The front side of a purse is used for embroidering patterns, while the back side is for embroidering words, achieving an artistic effect of combining pictures and texts. Figure 7-14 shows a purse designed by an inheritor. On the front side of the purse, a cicada is embroidered on a branch, and on the back side, the poem "Ode to the Cicada" by Yu Shinan, a poet of the Tang Dynasty, is embroidered. The entire purse combines the vivid and colorful concrete scenery on the front with the profound - meaning Tang poem, complementing each other and enhancing the artistic value of the purse.

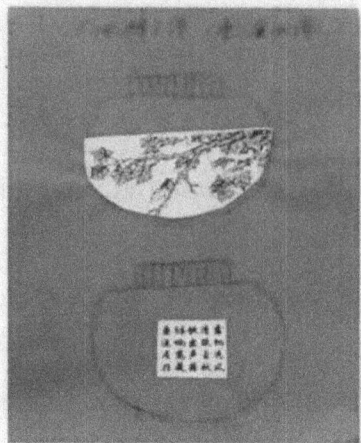

Figure 7-14 "Ode to the Cicada"

2. Profound Implications: Works and Sentiments in Harmonious Synergy

On the basis of inheriting the traditional techniques and patterns, Mr. Huang Jiaxiang has innovated in purse-making. This innovation is not only reflected in the selection of materials such as fabrics, spices, and accessories, but more importantly, in the innovation of concepts. He doesn't follow the beaten path and keeps up with the trend of the times, creating a series of excellent works that promote positive social energy and express the feelings of patriotism and family.

The purse specially designed to celebrate the 70th anniversary of the founding of the People's Republic of China uses bright red fabric to create a lively and festive atmosphere. Meanwhile, the purse has the same color as the national flag, symbolizing bravery, sincerity, enthusiasm, and the prosperity of the country (Figure 7-15). The main part of the purse features an embroidery of Tian'anmen Rostrum. Above it, there are the numbers "70", with a five-star embroidered inside the "0", signifying the 70th anniversary of the founding of New China. Below, the numbers "1949 - 2019" are embroidered. In this way, the inheritor pays tribute to New China and expresses his deep love for the great motherland.

In addition to expressing patriotism, the inheritor has also designed a series of purses that convey a positive attitude towards life. For example, "The setting sun is infinitely beautiful" (Figure 7-16) and "The old ox knows the twilight is approaching and spurs itself on without a whip" (Figure 7-17) express an attitude of not being afraid of old age and continuing to strive hard. Some purses combine popular lyrics with purses (Figure 7-18), which not only praise love but also cater to the preferences of young people, making them suitable for all ages.

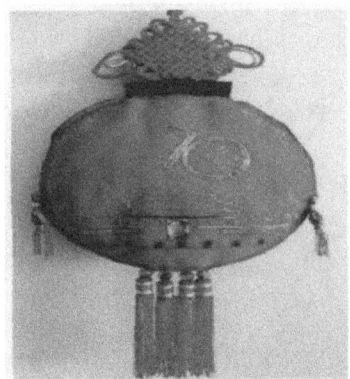

Figure 7-15 "The 70th Anniversary of the Founding of New China"

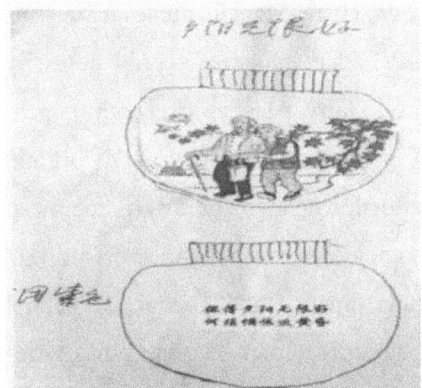

Figure 7-16 "The setting sun is infinitely beautiful"

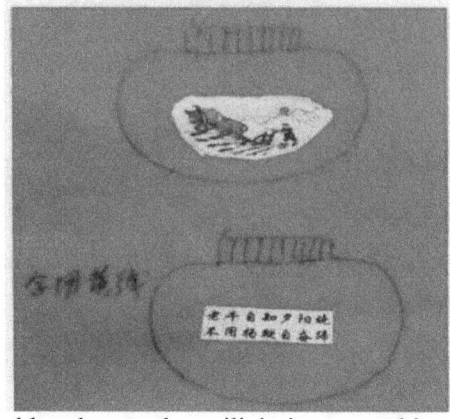

Figure 7-17 "The old ox knows the twilight is approaching and spurs itself on without a whip"

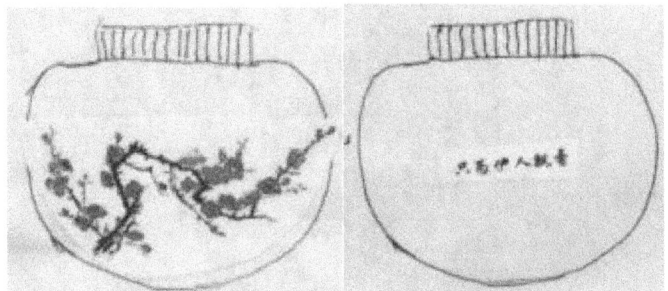

Figure 7-18 "Plucking a Plum Blossom"

II. Pattern

The patterns on Fengcheng Manchu purses mainly include plants, animals, and auspicious phrases. Plant patterns mainly consist of pine and cypress (symbolizing longevity), fairy peaches (longevity), persimmons (everything goes as one wishes), peonies (wealth and good fortune), twin lotus flowers (husband and wife's affectionate love), gourds (numerous descendants and long-lasting blessings), pomegranates (numerous offspring) and so on. Animal patterns mainly include dragons and phoenixes (good luck and jubilation), cranes (longevity), paired swallows (husband and wife's affectionate love), carps (a wealthy life and promising descendants), horses and deer (longevity, good fortune and emolument), butterflies (longevity and numerous descendants), magpies (good luck and jubilation) and so on. Auspicious phrases mainly include "living a hundred years", "having wealth and abundance", "a happy and harmonious marriage for a hundred years", "growing old together in conjugal bliss", "peace throughout the four seasons" and so on.

These plants and animals often appear in fixed combinations, highlighting the theme through such expressive techniques as homophony, pun, metaphor, and symbolism. For example, "lian (lotus) sheng gui zi" (giving birth to a noble son), "lian (lotus) nian you yu (carp)" (abundance year after year), "wan shi (persimmon) ru yi" (everything goes as one wishes), "xi (magpie) shang mei (plum) shao" (good news at hand), "san yang (sheep) kai tai" (auspicious beginning), "ma (horse) shang feng hou (monkey)" (getting promoted soon), "fish playing among lotuses" and "butterflies in love with flowers" (metaphor for the love between a man and a woman). These combinations have become conventional through generations of inheritance in the folk, evolving into a unique set of auspicious expressions in folk culture. The following introduces several commonly-used patterns.

1. Mandarin Ducks

Mandarin ducks are always together, flying and swimming side by side, and sleeping with their necks intertwined. Since ancient times, they have been regarded as mascots, symbolizing the harmony and loyalty between husband and wife. Embroideries themed on mandarin ducks often appear on items related to love and marriage. They are often used as love tokens or items that wives give to their husbands to wear, expressing the wish for a happy marriage and a long-lasting relationship. The pattern of mandarin ducks combined with lotuses is called "Mandarin Ducks and Noble Sons". When mandarin ducks are paired with ever-blooming flowers, it is called "Mandarin Ducks and Ever-lasting Happiness" or "Mandarin Ducks and Ever-lasting Peace". Mandarin ducks frolicking in a lotus pond are known as "Mandarin Ducks Playing among

Lotuses". Figures 7-19 and 7-20 show works with various mandarin duck patterns.

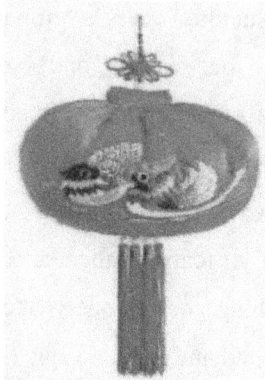

Figure 7-19 "Mandarin ducks frolicking in the pond"

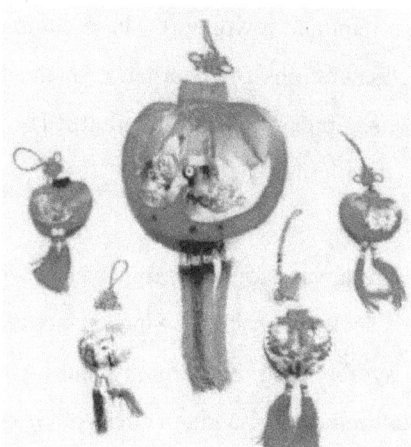

Figure 7-20 "Mandarin Ducks and Ever - lasting Peace"

2. Peonies

The ancients said, "Peonies are the flowers of prosperity." Peonies are also known as the "King of Flowers". As the poem goes, "Only peonies possess true imperial splendor; when they bloom, the whole capital is in a frenzy." Peonies not only have high ornamental value but also carry profound auspicious meanings. They are synonymous with wealth, good fortune, beauty, and honor.

Mr. Huang Jiaxiang created a set of purses themed on peonies (Figures 7-21 to 7-24). The embroidery of peonies and hibiscus on them represents "eternal prosperity and longevity"; the combination with crabapple flowers means "bringing glory to the family"; the combination with narcissus implies "immortal wealth". The pattern of "Phoenix Playing with Peonies", where the king of flowers (peonies) is combined with the king of birds (phoenix), is the ultimate expression of wealth and good fortune.

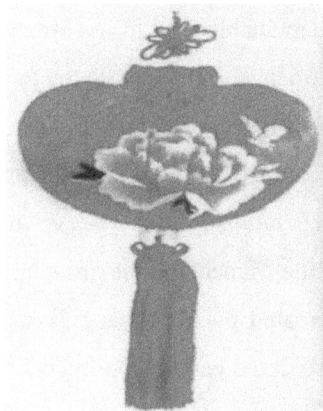

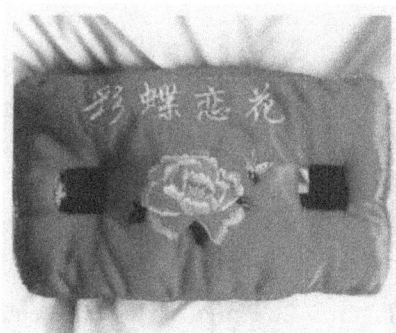

Figure 7-21 Peonies

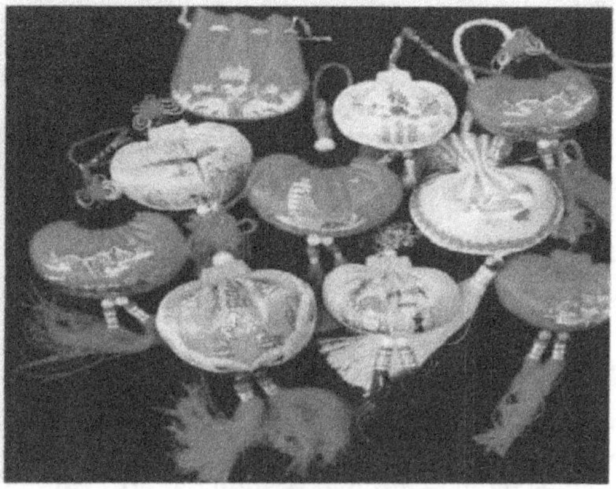

Figure 7-22 Blooming Peonies, Auspicious Prosperity

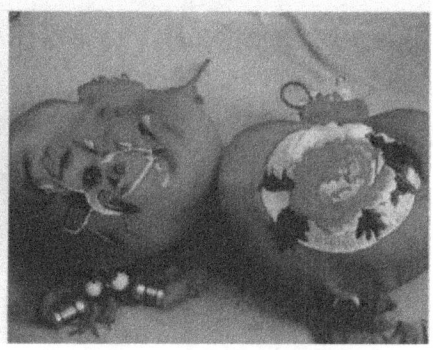

Figure 7-23 Colorful Butterflies Chasing Flowers

Figure 7-24 Mandarin Ducks and Peonies

3. Chinese Dragons

In China, the dragon, with its supreme and all-powerful image, has become the exclusive totem of the highest rulers in the feudal society. In Chinese folk art, dragon images are generally similar. Classified by their styling features, a dragon surrounded by clouds and mist is called a cloud dragon; one running with all four limbs is a walking dragon; a dragon soaring into the sky is a flying dragon; one coiled into a circle is a circular dragon; and one with its head up and tail down is an ascending dragon. Since the available area for embroidery on a small pouch is limited, the dragon image is often simplified, with the focus on the head and tail. The patterns on the pouches usually draw inspiration from the dragon patterns on ancient bronze mirrors and the "Dragon and Phoenix Bringing Auspiciousness" design in architectural paintings, and they are circular in shape. The emblems of the Eight Banners of the Manchu ethnic group are a set of patterns themed on the Eight Banners created by Mr. Huang Jiaxiang (Figure 7-25 to Figure 7-27). The dragon- embroidered patterns on large-sized pouches include circular dragon patterns, flying dragon patterns, double-dragon competing for the pearl patterns, dragon and phoenix patterns, and double-dragon and double-phoenix circular flower patterns.

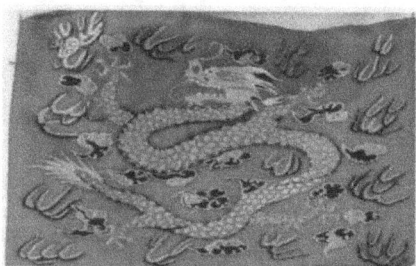 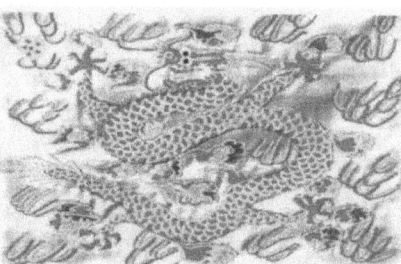

Figure 7-25 Manchu Eight Banners Emblems　　Figure 7-26 Partial View of Manchu Eight Banners Emblems

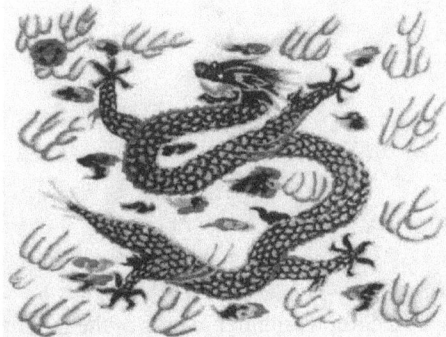

Figure 7-27 Partial View of Manchu Eight Banners Emblems

In short, the dragon is a sacred, auspicious and festive thing, and the embroidered dragon on the purse symbolizes fearlessness, vigor, and always full of vitality and energy.

4. Gourd

Mr. Huang Jiaxiang also often designs purses with the theme of gourds (Figure 7-28 to Figure 7-31). Gourds are regarded as auspicious symbols for praying for numerous descendants because of their long-winding vines, abundant fruits, and numerous seeds. The Chinese character for "vine" (蔓) is a homophone for the character meaning "ten thousand" (万), implying that descendants will multiply for generations. Gourds not only carry auspicious meanings but also have beautiful shapes and lines. Therefore, the gourd shape itself is one of the designs for Manchu purses. Embroidery of gourds with vines and flowers on purses makes them more suitable for the elderly and children to wear.

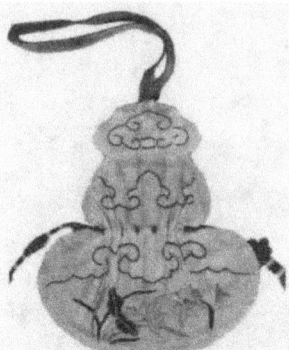

Figure 7-28 One of the Representative Works of the Inheritor: "Gourd" (I)

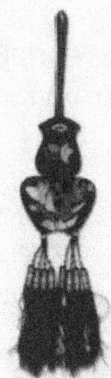

Figure 7-29 One of the Representative Works of the Inheritor: "Gourd" (II)

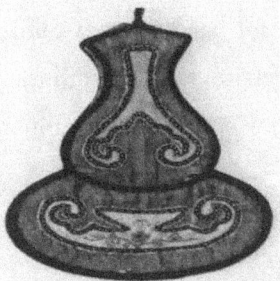

Figure 7-30 One of the Representative Works of the Inheritor: "Gourd" (III)

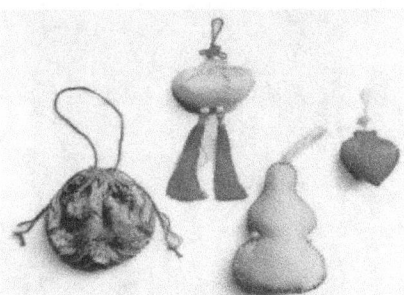

Figure 7-31 One of the Representative Works of the Inheritor: "Gourd" (IV)

5. Bat

Bats are creatures that are active at night and rest during the day. According to folk legends, bats can recognize the hiding places of evil spirits, so they have become symbols of driving away evil and bringing good fortune, and are regarded as symbols of longevity. The Chinese character for "bat" ("蝠") is a homophone for "good fortune" ("福") and "wealth" ("富"), and "bats" ("蝙蝠") is a homophone for "widespread wealth" ("遍富"), implying happiness, contentment, and boundless longevity and good fortune. Common patterns include the embroidery of five bats surrounding a character for "longevity" on a purse, which means "Five-Blessings Adoring Longevity"; the combination of bats and peaches of immortality embroidered together implies a long and prosperous life. Other common patterns include "Good Fortune, Salary, Longevity, and Happiness" and "Double Happiness of Longevity and Good Fortune", as shown in Figures 7-32 and 7-33.

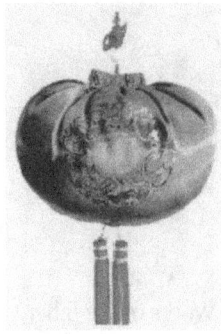 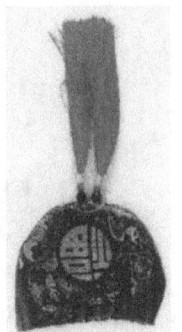

Figure 7-32 Bat-pattern Purse　　Figure 7-33 Double Happiness of

Longevity and Good Fortune

6. Auspicious Words

In the process of embroidering Fengcheng Manchu purses, in addition to the selection of patterns and design of motifs, sometimes words are also used to directly express the yearning and pursuit of happiness by the working people. As shown in Figure 7-34 to Figure 7-37.

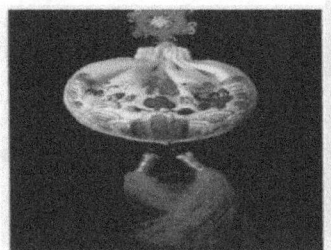 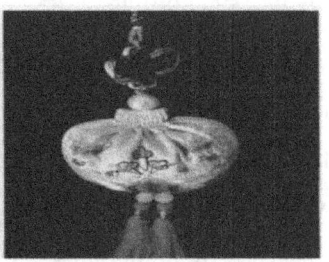

Figure. 7-34 Good Fortune　　Figure. 7-35 Elegant and Noble

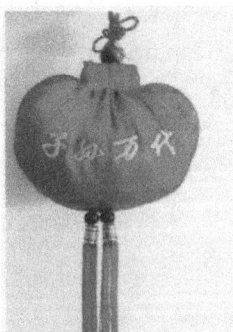 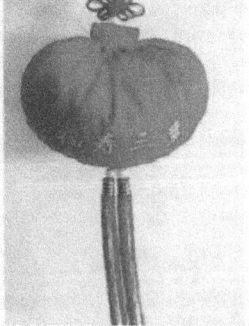

Figure. 7-36 Descendants for　　Figure. 7-37 Three Auspicious

Generations　　Treasures of Longevity

III. Pattern Characteristics

Through consideration of the above-mentioned patterns, it can be found that the cultural character reflected in the production process of Fengcheng Manchu purses is optimistic. People yearn for happiness in hardship, pursue prosperity in poverty, long for well-being in adversity, and pray for many children and grandchildren in the face of life's vicissitudes.

1. Yearning for Happiness and Well-being

China was in a long-stagnant feudal society, where the vast majority of working people lived a difficult life with extremely scarce material resources and spiritual life. Under such circumstances, people hoped to lead a stable and peaceful life, with good weather throughout the year, enough food and clothing at the end of the year, healthy and long-lived elders, successful children, and many descendants.

For example, embroidering a carp on a purse implies "the carp leaping over the dragon gate", expressing the hope that children will stand out and achieve success. Embroidering patterns of plants and animals such as peaches of immortality, deer, and ganoderma, as well as characters like "wan" (万), "fu" (福), "shou" (寿), and some auspicious phrases such as "live a hundred years", "grow old together in happiness", "peace throughout the four seasons" directly on the back of the purse all express people's longing for longevity and well-being.

There are also birthday-congratulatory purses praying for a long and prosperous life. The patterns on these purses are mostly plants and animals symbolizing longevity, such as pine trees, cypress trees, and cranes. These purses often have a complete structure, bright colors, are full of interest, and have strong decorative value.

2. The Pursuit of Life and Reproduction

In the past, China was in a closed and backward agricultural civilization era. With frequent natural disasters and a low level of medical care, the mortality rate remained high. More descendants meant more labor force and a more prosperous life. Therefore, the concept of reproduction has been deeply rooted in people's minds.

Common patterns in embroidered purses such as pomegranates, gourds, and lotuses all imply having many children and grandchildren. The gourd-shaped design of Manchu purses contains a profound connotation of the worship of life and reproduction. The gourd-shaped purse itself implies the union of men and women. In addition, gourds have many seeds, and their vines grow very long, which contains the meaning of having many descendants, a long and prosperous life, and the continuation of the family for generations.

3. Yearning for Health and Happiness

The yearning for health and happiness is first reflected in the painstaking efforts made for the well-being of children. For example, embroidering "Five Poison" purses is used to drive away evil and avoid disasters; embroidering purses with pomegranates and Buddha's hands also implies protecting future generations to live a long life. In addition, filling purses with various spices and Chinese herbal medicines not only makes them fragrant but also can drive away mosquitoes and pests.

Section VI Appreciation of Works

I. Tobacco Purses

This is the purse of the highest grade and best quality among the collections gathered by the inheritor (Figure 7-38). It is a tobacco purse used to hold tobacco. At that time, those who could wear such a tobacco pouch had extraordinary status. The fabric used to make this tobacco purse is indigo cloth, and the technique applied is gold-coiling and silver-pressing. This technique involves making metal into extremely thin gold foils and then cutting them into very fine metal wires. This technique was lost by the Qing Dynasty, so this purse is at least three hundred years old. Two small squirrel patterns are embroidered on the surface of the purse with gold and silver threads. In Buddhism, this pattern is called "endless knot" and is one of the eight auspicious symbols. It is a very delicate pattern.

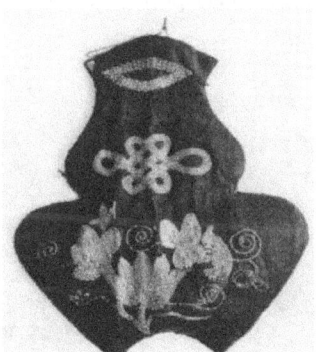

Figure 7-38 Imperial Court Purse

II. Fragrant Purses

Fragrant purses, also known as sachets or perfume bags, are often used as love tokens between men and women. They are exquisitely made and come in various forms. They are embroidered with auspicious patterns, flowers, animals, and characters. Inside the purses are various spices and Chinese herbal medicines such as realgar, Chinese arborvitae, asarum, cloves, and sandalwood, which have the effects of cleaning, removing odors, and preventing insects and sterilizing. A woman would give a purse she embroidered herself to a man to express her intention to spend the rest of her life with him, and the man would reciprocate with an archer's ring.

The opening of a traditional fragrant purse is usually of a folding type, threaded with colored silk cords. Pulling the cords tight closes the pouch opening, and pushing the opening with a hand opens it. Since the traditional Chinese herbal medicines and spices in the purses had overly pungent and unpleasant odors, the inheritor conducted on-site investigations and finally discovered a spice called Lingxiangcao (Lysimachia foenum-graecum) in the Yao ethnic minority mountain areas. This spice has a mild fragrance that lasts for years. As the preferences of young people change, the inheritor also keeps updating the types of spices. Jasmine, sandalwood, osmanthus, roses, and various international-style scents have replaced the traditional Chinese herbal medicines, making the pouches very popular among young people, as shown in Figure 7-39 and Figure 7-40.

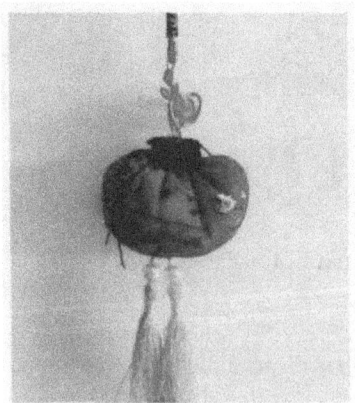 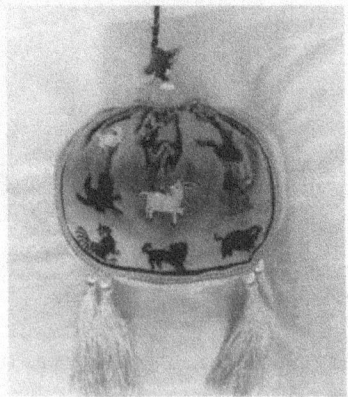

Figure 7-39 Fragrant Purse (I)   Figure 7-40 Fragrant Purse (II)

Section VII Interviews with Inheritors

I. May I ask: How did you come to the non-genetic inheritance road of Fengcheng Manchu purses?

Mr. Huang Jiaxiang: I came into contact with the purse when I was very young, my mother and aunt are good at making purse, and the purses they made are very famous in all the villages. When I was a child, I often wore my mother's purses. I really started studying purses in 1994. At that time, I was hospitalized for a period of time because of poor health, and I saw a book introducing purses. Then I felt that such a delicate purse and such a splendid culture could not be passed down without anyone, so I began to grope for it myself, look for materials and documents, collect purses myself, and finally start designing and making purses myself. In this way, trying step by step and exploring step by step, we have come to this day, and it has been 26 years this year.

II. May I ask: What do you think are the characteristics of Fengcheng Manchu purses compared with other purses?

Mr. Huang Jiaxiang: Manchu purses are similar to those of other ethnic groups in practicality, such as gifts given to each other by men and women as tokens of love, birthday purses given to the elderly, and purses for eliminating disasters and avoiding evil spirits. But Manchu purses have their own unique characteristics. The first is that Manchu purses are aristocratic purses, and the nobles in the Qing Dynasty had a special preference for purses. From the emperor to the nobles and high-ranking officials, they all had the habit of wearing purses. During festivals, the emperor gave purses as rewards, which shows that the nobles attached great importance to purses. This kind of royal favor makes Manchu purses particularly exquisite in material selection, embroidery, production technology and accessories. It is no exaggeration to say that the purses in the late Qing Dynasty are the culmination of purse making technology for thousands of years. The second is that Manchu women are ingenious and good at needlework. They have absorbed the strengths of other ethnic groups' pockets for lessons and integrated them into the creation of Manchu purses, which makes Manchu purses, a traditional folk handicraft production process, increasingly perfect and is called "Pearl of the Oriental Art" by foreigners.

The biggest feature of Manchu purses lies in the combination of cultural elements and purse making. Elegant calligraphy and poetry on the surface of the purse not only improve the cultural connotation of the purse, but also express the feelings of the purse maker. You see, a small purse, with its beautiful and round shape, rich patterns and constantly emitting fragrance, can naturally become a small object that people love to hand.

Another characteristic of Manchu purses lies in their simple designs. Manchu purses can generally be classified into four types according to their shapes: heart-shaped, kidney-shaped, round, and gourd-shaped. When designing, they draw on the concept of "blank space" in traditional Chinese paintings, leaving enough space on the surface of the purse for embroidery. This not only makes the purses more aesthetically pleasing in style but also simplifies the production process, saving time and materials. In terms of fabric selection, bright red, blue, and yellow are commonly used, and different-colored silk threads are added to form a strong contrast, enhancing the artistic effect.

III. May I ask: What innovations have you made in the inheritance process of Fengcheng Manchu purses?

Mr. Huang Jiaxiang: To talk about innovation, the first thing should be the innovation of embroidery stitches. There are many schools of embroidery stitches, such as the famous Suzhou embroidery, Hunan embroidery, Shu embroidery and Guangdong embroidery, which are called the four famous embroideries. Liao embroidery should belong to a kind of Lu embroidery. At first, people had their own embroidery methods. Later, Shandong people came to the northeast more, so they brought Lu embroidery to Liaoning. After long-term integration and reference, Liao embroidery was formed. But the real embroidery is still the four famous embroideries. My innovation may be to introduce the embroidery methods of Suzhou embroidery and Shu embroidery into the production process of Manchu purses. Embroidering traditional Chinese embroidery techniques and patterns on purses has improved the overall production level of purses. Moreover, Manchu embroidery often uses appliqué embroidery and plain stitch embroidery. During my continuous learning process, I discovered many more advanced embroidery techniques, such as counted-thread embroidery, couching stitch embroidery, seed stitch embroidery, and buttonhole stitch embroidery. I tried to apply these stitches to purse-making, hoping to create purses that can rival ancient treasures in terms of patterns, quality, and forms.

In addition to introducing new embroidery stitches, I also made innovations in the selection of spices. Traditional purses usually use Chinese herbal medicines as spices. Although Chinese herbal medicines are beneficial to people's health, their odors are often unpleasant, which many young people today cannot accept. I encountered this situation when I participated in the Shanghai World Expo, and many young consumers gave me feedback. So I thought about finding an unused plant that could be widely accepted by the public. After much searching, I finally found Lingxiangcao (Lysimachia foenum-graecum) in the Yao ethnic minority mountainous area. Lingxiangcao (Lysimachia foenum-graecum) not only has a pleasant aroma but also retains its fragrance for a long time, and it is very popular among consumers.

IV. May I ask: Are you still training the inheritors? What is the training method?

Mr. Huang Jiaxiang: I have an apprentice now, who is also my son-in-law. He also has his own job. When he is not busy, he usually comes to learn how to make a purse, but his energy is limited after all. Therefore, every time someone comes to my house for an interview or attends a public event, I will leave my contact information, hoping that more people will pay attention to Fengcheng Manchu purses, pass on my skills and Manchu culture. Besides these, I also give lectures in school. Two years ago, Dalian Art Institute hired me as a distinguished expert to give lectures. I have also held a purse exhibition in the community. Besides promoting Manchu purses, I also hope to find like-minded people to study together.

V. May I ask: What difficulties have you encountered in the process of inheritance? Is there any further plan for the future?

Mr. Huang Jiaxiang: I think the biggest difficulty is collecting data. The purses belongs to the small objects, and they are not valued by people, so the records about the purse in the historical materials are often scarce and fragmentary. Many times, collecting information about purses is like looking for a needle in a haystack. After flipping through a thick whole book, you can only find a few words. I have a notebook full of information that I have cut out or recorded when I read newspapers, magazines, ancient books and articles about purses. For myself, my future plan is to take the written and pictorial materials I have collected and organized over the years, and add them to my own practice over the past 20 years, and publish a booklet on the stories and meanings of the purse. I can systematically sort out the origin and development of Manchu purses, as well as my own understanding and innovation. At the same time, I also hope to do more publicity to attract more and more people to pay attention to Manchu purses, and I also hope that more well-cultivated and educated young people can join the process of inheriting Manchu purses and truly make Fengcheng Manchu purses a brand.

Section VIII Current Situation and Countermeasures of Inheritance

I. Current Situation of Inheritance

With the strong support of Fengcheng People's Government and the hard exploration of inheritors for more than 20 years, Fengcheng Manchu purses have been fully developed. However, due to various reasons, Fengcheng Manchu purses still face many challenges. The main reason is that the impact of globalization and urbanization makes people more adapt to the communication mode of modern popular culture, while Chinese traditional clothing culture is gradually neglected. The production cycle of Manchu purses is long, and almost all processes can only be completed by hand embroidery, which can't meet the requirements of modern assembly lines and large industries, so it is difficult to realize its industrialization development. Moreover, the current inheritors are old, and no more young people are willing to join the inheritance team of Manchu purses, which makes their future development prospects worrying.

1. Problems in the Training of the Inheritors

As a kind of folk handicraft, Fengcheng Manchu purses have always been passed down from mouth to mouth by master with apprentice. Learning to make a purse takes a lot of time to learn every step from the initial design of patterns to sewing to the final finished product. The long study period and meager income discourage many young people who are interested in Manchu purse making. At present, the inheritance of Fengcheng Manchu purses is in a state of lack of connection. The inheritor, Mr. Huang Jiaxiang, is over 80 years old, so it is difficult to engage in large-scale and high-intensity purse embroidery. Although his apprentice, also his son-in-law, is also learning purse making skills with him, it is only a hobby. Other than that, the inheritor had no other followers. There is an extreme shortage of young inheritors, and the existing inheritors are too old. The lack of continuity in the inheritors of Fengcheng Manchu purses has become an urgent problem to be solved in the future.

2. Disappearance of Traditional Crafts

The earliest time the inheritor began to contact and study the purse, has been sixty years old and close to retirement. His mother and aunt who taught him the skills of making purses were also over 90 years old. It can be said that the inheritor has not been systematically trained in purse knowledge and skills. When it comes to purses, many elderly people only remember that they used to embroider a lot of things, but the specific patterns and stitches are all blurred. At the same time, the traditional purse process is complicated and the production cycle is long, so the price is high, while modern mechanization shortens the process production time and improves the production efficiency, so it has a price advantage over the traditional purse.Today, with the high development of commercialization, machine embroidered purses have gradually become a substitute for handmade purses. The lack of systematic inheritance and two-way extrusion of assembly line production technology makes the traditional Manchu purse technology disappear faster.

3. Problems in the Scale of Fengcheng Manchu Purses

As early as 1996, when Mr. Huang Jiaxiang imitated the first purse, he had the intention to put his purse into the market. Then after three years of preparation, he finally opened a factory that can produce products, but the scale was very small. After more than 20 years of painstaking management and continuous development, although the scale of the factory has expanded, it has not formed a complete industrial chain, and there is no large-scale embroidery factory. The production is mainly carried out in the form of small family workshops. Therefore, Fengcheng Manchu purses can only be maintained in the hands of inheritors, and cannot form scale effect and brand effect.

II. Countermeasures of Inheritance

The protection and inheritance of Fengcheng Manchu purses requires not only the efforts of inheritors, but also the support and help of the society. Efforts should be made in the following aspects:

1. Establishing a Diversified Inheritance Training Mechanism

An important feature of the inheritance of intangible cultural heritage is the mouth-mouth mode of master and apprentice. In some aspects, the core of protecting intangible cultural heritage is to protect the inheritors of these intangible cultural heritages. Therefore, in view of the lack of continuity in Fengcheng Manchu purse talents, it is necessary to increase the support for inheritors. It is advisable to give financial subsidies to old artists to participate in various purse exhibitions and sales activities, encourage them to actively participate in social and public activities, promote Manchu purses, and enhance the influence of Manchu purses. At the same time, it is necessary to retain young people who have just engaged in purse making with appropriate treatment. While retaining talents, we should also attract new talents. We can use public media for publicity and inheritance, and we can carry out social education activities of appreciating, learning and making purses in the form of Intangible Cultural Heritage Days and Intangible Cultural Heritage Days. Through social publicity and education activities, on the one hand, more and more people are interested in Manchu purses, thus becoming potential reserve troops; On the other hand, strengthening the public's awareness of the protection of Fengcheng Manchu purses can effectively solve the problem of people's insufficient understanding of the protection and inheritance of purses.

At the same time, we can also cooperate with colleges and universities that train specialized upstream talents to set up general courses about Fengcheng Manchu purses, and set up a teaching base for the inheritance of Fengcheng Manchu purses. On the one hand, it enriches the curriculum of the school; on the other hand, it attracts students with both professional knowledge and practical experience to continue to study and develop Fengcheng Manchu purses.

2. Strengthening the Product Design

For the traditional purse craft, on the one hand, we should find and protect the treasures of the folk purse, on the other hand, we should also use the new technology to drive the development of the purse. It can take the road of diversified development by absorbing modern fashion design concepts. The continuous research and development of new materials and the influx of foreign design concepts provide more possibilities for the redesign of Fengcheng Manchu purses. With the progress of society, Fengcheng Manchu purses must also adapt to the trend of social development, combining traditional craftsmanship with popular concepts. Fengcheng Manchu purses need not only to maintain the characteristics of the traditional Manchu purses in the design style, but also boldly to use new materials, new technologies, to achieve the combination of practicality and art.

3. Promoting the Formation of Large-scale Production of Fengcheng Manchu Purses

First of all, we can integrate scattered small family workshops that make Manchu purses, expand the production scale, develop new products with local characteristics, and form a word of mouth to expand popularity. Secondly, we can consider dividing the domestic and foreign markets of purses to meet the needs of consumers at different levels.

References

[1] Lu Yao. Personal, Emotion and Thing [D]. Beijing: Minzu University of China, 2013.

[2] Zhu Hua, Zhang Yanping. "Study on bat patterns in Manchu purses" [J]. *Liaoning Silk*, 2016 (3): 11-13.

[3] Hu Ma. "Manchu purse" [J]. *Manchu Literature*, 2007 (5): 51-52.

[4] "Intangible inheritance" Fengcheng Manchu purse [OL]. [2018-05-17]. http://www.nfc.gov.cn/a/fengchengshiweng uangju/20180517/13669. html.

[5] Zhang Yichang, Chen Xin, Liu Jinfeng. "A small purse sends deep affection" [J]. *Guangcai,* 2001 (11): 22-23.

[6] Chen Qingju. "On the emotional expression of folk embroidery purse theme" [J]. *Art Education*, 2011 (4): 40-41.

[7] Sun Yingqing. "A purse that witnessed the fashion of accessories in Qing Dynasty" [J]. *Oriental Collection*, 2012 (10): 49-51.

www.ingramcontent.com/pod-product-compliance
Lightning Source LLC
Chambersburg PA
CBHW051304220526
45468CB00004B/1207